Bringing History Home

Local and Family History Projects for Grades K–6

M. Gail Hickey

Indiana University–Purdue University Fort Wayne

Allyn and Bacon

Boston   London   Toronto   Sydney   Tokyo   Singapore

Series editor: Frances Helland
Series editorial assistant: Bridget Keane
Manufacturing buyer: Suzanne Lareau

Library of Congress Cataloging-in-Publication Data

Hickey, M. Gail
    Bringing history home : local and family history projects for
grades K-6 / M. Gail Hickey.
        p.   cm.
    Includes bibliographical references (p.   ) and index.
    ISBN 0-205-28169-9
    1. United States--History, Local--Study and teaching (Elementary)-
-Activity programs.   2. United States--Genealogy--Study and teaching
(Elementary)--Activity programs.   I. Title.
    E180.H5   1999
    929'.1'071273--dc21   98-39352
                                                                 CIP

Printed in the United States of America
10 9 8 7 6 5 4 3 2 1   02 01 00 99 98

Dedicated to my parents,
Alvena and Earl Hickey,
for sharing that first family memory
and inspiring me to dig deeper;

to the memory of my grandparents,
Edith and Clyde Sullivan and
Emma and Will Hickey;

and to my husband Robert,
with whom I share new family memories

Contents

v

PART II   Community and Local History   71

Suggested Activities and Recommended Grade Levels

P = primary (prekindergarten through grade 2); I = intermediate (grades 3–5); M = middle (grades 6–8)

Preface

This book grew out of my work with elementary and middle school teachers in the Fort Wayne, Indiana, area as they searched for, planned, and implemented strategies for celebrating the city's bicentennial in the mid-1990s. As the "social studies person" at the local university, I was called on by the bicentennial planning commission to create classroom-ready materials and resources for teachers to use. Soon, students in my graduate courses (and later, undergraduate courses) expressed interest in the usefulness of these resources beyond the bicentennial celebration. A few teachers even shared my vision of these activities as opportunities to "bring history to life." Together, we embarked on a journey that began with classroom testing of specific activities and culminated with the publication of this book.

For more than two years, I visited classrooms, consulted with teachers and students, disseminated activities with requests for feedback, and taught demonstration lessons using the materials in this book. Many of the teachers who field-tested materials employed a reflective teaching procedure I designed to help them learn more about the teaching/learning process while at the same time improving their instructional techniques. All in all, we learned a great deal together. One of the most intriguing patterns to come out of our collaboration was the realization that family and local history projects do more to foster community among students with diverse backgrounds than anything else any of us has tried. At the same time, many of us were having our own worldviews challenged as we learned about the home lives and family/ethnic values experienced by our students.

This, then, is the premise behind *Bringing History Home:* Teachers who use family and local history projects in the classroom find that classroom community is fostered as learners discover similarities as well as differences in their backgrounds. Take these activities and resources, use them, and see for yourself. Adapt, adjust, update, personalize the ideas presented here to better fit the experiences of the students in your class. But above all, show your students that history is not just about dead people and interminable dates—it's about *them!*

Acknowledgments

I am indebted to many people for their assistance and encouragement during the process of writing this book, and to others for the inspiration provided by their teaching and their work with children. This list is by no means exhaustive; help was provided by librarians, colleagues, family, and friends over a period of more than two years. Some people, though, must be mentioned by name.

I want to thank my editor at Allyn and Bacon, Frances Helland, for believing in the concept of the book and making me aware of its timeliness, and for her expert guidance in the final stages of the manuscript. Lynda Griffiths's expert copyediting helped bring shape and structure to the final draft. Thanks are due also to my mentor and friend Tom Turner, at The University of Tennessee, who often acted as a sounding board, and whose creative scholarship served as a model and an inspiration.

Thanks are offered to the teachers and former students who permitted me to showcase their lessons, ideas, or students' work in the Trying It Out sections for each chapter: Leanne Bailey, Nancy Bergstedt, Beth Bixby, Jann Braumberger, Karen Charters, Stacia Czartoski, Scott Fudge, Julie Funk-Kurtz, Mindy Gawthrop, Linda Gibson, Tita Gordon, Dawn Hamlin, Sandra Herman, Wenoma Hoham, Deborah Hudson, Vicki Lindsay, Susan Livensparger, Linda Lucenta, Tracey Malcolm-Myers, Lisa Miller, Tammy Morey, Pandora Ott, Terry Snyder, Cindy Stiver, Virginia Thorpe, Toni Whitney, and Michelle Yantz. Without these from-the-classroom examples, *Bringing History Home* would be just another activities book.

My appreciation goes to the following reviewers for their comments on the manuscript: Janice K. Davis, Ladue School District; Dr. Jacqueline Collier, Centerville City Schools and Miami University; John Cowens, Three Rivers School District, Fort Vannoy School; and Cynthia Wisdom, Hoover City Schools, Trace Crossings Elementary.

Finally, I owe a huge debt of gratitude to my husband Robert for his patience during those times when my entire attention was devoted to writing, and for his supportive encouragement throughout the manuscript development process.

Introduction: Doing Family and Local History in Diverse Settings

A Review of the Research

In the search for ways to celebrate and honor the diverse cultures present in U.S. classrooms, time is often spent revisiting one's own perspectives of the world. Perhaps you have had the opportunity to examine, through graduate work or staff development workshops, Giroux's (1983) belief that good teachers in contemporary classrooms "provide the conditions that give students the opportunity to speak with their own voices, to authenticate their own experiences," and have wondered how to implement this vision of transformative teaching in your own classroom. Maybe you have bemoaned your lack of knowledge or expertise as you struggle to help make the school experience meaningful for students who speak English as a second language (ESL). And perhaps there were times that you wondered how to reach out to the child whose family had recently emigrated to the United States, especially when that child's cultural background and behavioral styles seem so very different from your own.

If you can identify with any of these scenarios, this book is for you. "Doing" family and local history projects can help your classroom become a place where, as Giroux says, children speak with their own voices and authenticate their own experiences. These projects and activities can help you organize your classroom and your teaching in such a way that all students' school experiences will build on their home and ethnic community resources as well as their native-language abilities (Diaz, Moll, & Mehan, 1986). You can become the kind of teacher who aims to bring out the voice of each student in your class, who values and honors the backgrounds of all ethnicities represented in the school and community (Poplin, 1991).

Campbell (1996) believes that "to be a guide to culture, the teacher must be able to communicate with students." Good teachers know that the effective use of prior knowledge is the most appropriate means of guiding children to learn and appreciate new information. Campbell confirms that "effective teachers use the concepts and strategies the children have acquired at home to teach them new concepts and strategies . . . [since] students from microcultures are more successful in learning and adapting to the school culture when their own home culture is recognized and used as a basis for instruction." When teachers use strategies and plan lessons that build on prior knowledge by incorporating the child's own cultural learning and experiences, the child is empowered as a learner. Students in classes such as these have been found to demonstrate improved skills, abilities, and sense of self-worth (Campbell, 1996, p. 28). McAdoo (1993) adds that when "the student's cultural life becomes an important aspect of classroom learning . . . the possibility for academic success is enhanced."

Levstik and Barton's (1997) research on children's historical thinking shows that although all children "know something about how life was different in the past," not very many children have a clear understanding of what "history" means: "Because students usually don't encounter [history] at school before fourth grade, they sometimes don't even know what the word means; those who have heard it may link it with the past generally...or may associate it with famous people or events. But rarely do they recognize that *they* are part of history, or that they have a history of their *own*" (p. 26, emphasis added).

Current research on children's historical thinking also shows that teachers should begin children's study of the subject by focusing on students' own lives and the lives of their family members (Barton, 1994; Levstik & Barton, 1997). For example, creating a personal time line or developing a simple family tree—and engaging in thinking, conversing, and writing activities connected to these graphic organizers—gives students an opportunity to examine their own lives from historical perspective. This enhanced perspective, then, sets the stage for increased understanding of historical concepts and increased appreciation for the connections between personal histories and a more global perspective.

Children usually do not know how people go about learning about the past. In fact, collecting data can be very difficult for students in elementary school, especially those in the early grades. The activities and suggestions in this book will help you, the teacher, provide the sense of structure necessary to begin historical inquiry.

When we teachers incorporate children's personal and family history into the curriculum, and children become participants in the history-gathering process, we can expect their thinking and reasoning skills to improve, their academic achievement to increase, their sense of self-worth to be enhanced, and their curiosity to be piqued. And if in the process we portray history itself as *experiences* instead of *facts*, we help children learn to value the *personal* aspects of history—an attitude that may help increase their abilities to make sense of the world around them.

To explore this theory a little further, consider what a difficult concept historical time is for young children. Children in the early grades often are unable to comprehend distinctions between decades and centuries. By the intermediate and middle grades, students have begun to make sense of historical time, but find the study of history itself remote and irrelevant to their own lives. Because children have such trouble understanding and developing appreciations for historical events, teachers must make every effort to portray these events as *experiences* rather than just facts. The portrayal of history as experience *brings history to life*, creating a learning environment where students find the study of history meaningful and fascinating at the same time.

"Starting with what they know" is an effective way to introduce new topics in the classroom. Children's concepts of historical time are usually limited to days, weeks, and months, as they attempt to relate their own lives to a past, present, and future. Children of all ages are interested in things that happened "long ago," but they may be confused about when and how these events occurred, particularly about if and how events relate to students' own lives. Using students' own experiences serves as a springboard to new and/or difficult subjects. Starting with what is already familiar to them ensures their psychological and intellectual involvement in the new topic.

Elkind's research (1981) reminds us of children's intuitive sense of the past, a sense that tends to be of a very personal nature. Things from the past that children are most interested in include themselves and their families. Thus, to personalize the field of history as a whole, we must begin with what is familiar to students—their families. We may then proceed to the study of the local community. With this foundation, students begin to view history as *relevant* and *alive* and, with continued good planning on your part, as knowledge and skills they will want to add to their repertoire for lifelong learning.

NATIONAL SOCIAL STANDARDS AND THEMES

In 1994, the Task Force on Teaching and Learning for the National Council for the Social Studies (NCSS) published *Expectations of Excellence: Curriculum Standards for Social Studies*. This document identifies 10 thematic strands that build on the NCSS (1994) definition of social studies as the "integrated study of the social sciences and humanities to promote civic competence [with the primary purpose] to help young people develop the ability to make informed and reasoned decisions for the public good as citizens of a culturally diverse, democratic society in an independent world." A brief explanation of each of these 10 thematic strands is helpful to teachers who plan to incorporate them into their classroom instruction.

1. Culture
The study of culture prepares students to answer such questions as: What are the common characteristics of different cultures? How do belief systems, such as religion or political ideals, influence other parts of the culture? How does the culture change to accommodate different ideas and beliefs? What does language reveal about the culture? In schools, this theme typically appears in units and courses dealing with geography, history, sociology, and anthropology, as well as multicultural topics across the curriculum.

2. Time, Continuity, and Change
Human beings seek to understand their historical roots and to locate themselves in time. Knowing how to read and reconstruct the past allows students to develop a historical perspective and to answer questions such as: Who am I? What happened in the past? How am I connected to those in the future? Why does our personal sense of relatedness to the past change? This theme typically appears in courses in history and others that draw on historical knowledge and habits.

3. People, Places, and Environments
The study of people, places, and human/environment interactions assists students as they create their spatial views and geographic perspectives of the world beyond their personal locations. Students need the knowledge, skills, and understanding to answer questions such as: Where are things located? Why are they located where they are? What does *region* mean? How do landforms change? What implications do these changes have for people? In schools, this theme typically appears in units and courses dealing with area studies and geography.

4. Individual Development and Identity
Personal identity is shaped by one's culture, by groups, and by institutional influences. Students should consider such questions as: How do people learn? Why do people behave as they do? What influences how people learn, perceive, and grow? How do people meet their basic needs in a variety of contexts? How do individuals develop from youth to adulthood? In schools, this theme typically appears in units and courses dealing with psychology and anthropology.

5. Individuals, Groups, and Institutions
Institutions such as schools, churches, families, government agencies, and the courts play an integral role in people's lives. It is important that students learn how institutions are formed, what controls and influences them, how they influence individuals and culture, and how they are maintained or changed. Students may address questions such as: What is the role of institutions in this and other societies? How am I influenced by institutions? How do institutions change? What is my role in institutional change? In schools, this theme typically appears in units and courses dealing with sociology, anthropology, psychology, political science, and history.

6. Power, Authority, and Governance
Understanding the historical development of structures of power, authority, and governance, and their evolving functions in contemporary U.S. society and other parts of the world, is essential for developing civic competence. In exploring this theme, students confront questions such as: What is power? What forms does it take? Who holds it? How is it gained, used, and justified? What is legitimate authority? How are governments created, structured, maintained, and changed? How can individual rights be protected within the context of majority rule? In schools, this theme typi-

cally appears in units and courses dealing with government, politics, political science, history, law, and other social sciences.

7. Production, Distribution, and Consumption

Because people have wants that often exceed the resources available to them, a variety of ways have evolved to answer such questions as: What is to be produced? How is production to be organized? How are goods and services to be distributed? What is the most effective allocation of the factors of production (land, labor, capital, and management)? In schools, this theme typically appears in units and courses dealing with economic concepts and issues.

8. Science, Technology, and Society

Modern life would be impossible without technology and science. But technology brings with it many questions: Is new technology better than old? What can be learned from the past about how new technologies result in broader social change, some of which is unanticipated? How can people cope with the ever-increasing pace of change? How can technology be managed so that the greatest number of people benefit from it? How can fundamental values and beliefs be preserved in the midst of technological change? This theme draws on the natural and physical sciences, social sciences, and the humanities, and appears in a variety of social studies courses, including history, geography, economics, civics, and government.

9. Global Connections

The realities of global interdependence require understanding the increasingly important and diverse global connections among world societies and the frequent tension between national interests and global priorities. Students will need to address such international issues as health care, the environment, human rights, economic competition and interdependence, age-old ethnic enmities, and political and military alliances. This theme typically appears in units or courses dealing with geography, culture, and economics, but may also draw on the natural and physical sciences and the humanities.

10. Civic Ideals and Practices

An understanding of civic ideals and practices of citizenship is critical to full participation in society and is a central purpose of the social studies. Students confront such questions as: What is civic participation and how can I be involved? How has the meaning of citizenship evolved? What is the balance between rights and responsibilities? What is the role of the citizen in community? How can I make a positive difference? In schools, this theme typically appears in units or courses dealing with history, political science, cultural anthropology, and fields such as global studies, law-related education, and the humanities.

Activities and suggested uses of resources within this book deal with many of the thematic strands identified by the National Council for the Social Studies curriculum document, especially Culture; Time, Continuity, and Change; People, Places, and Environments, Individual Development and Identity, Individuals, Groups, and Institutions; Power, Authority, and Governance; and Civic Ideals and Practices. Teachers and schools that employ a thematic approach to instruction can easily make connections between the activities and teaching ideas included in this book and the broad curricular themes such as those just listed.

Oral History Technique and the Interview Process

Remember those stories Grandpa told about his childhood? Remember how, as the family left the table after Thanksgiving dinner and settled in the living room, he and Grandma could be coaxed into talking about "the good old days"? How we loved to listen to those stories of times gone by!

To teachers, these stories have more than reminiscent value. Grandpa's tales and Aunt Rose's stories of her work in a defense plant during World War II are the stuff of which oral history is made. We teachers are constantly challenged to find fresh, active alternatives to textbook learning, particularly for social studies. An oral history project can help you bring history to life for your students. Oral history is a authentic technique used by historians to gather firsthand information about recent events from persons who have experienced them. Particular emphasis is placed on oral history projects and interviews in this book, because these activities allow students to learn to think and behave as historians.

History literally comes alive for students who participate in oral history interviews. Students act as junior historians, investigating and recording *real events* from the past through the memories of *real people* who experienced those events. As an added bonus, the process often results in opportunities for students to examine the same event from a variety of perspectives, perhaps even through conflicting reports—enhancing development of critical thinking skills.

Oral history projects can stand alone or be incorporated as an essential part of family history projects and/or local history study. Historians have long used oral history procedures to collect and preserve the memories of the living and their knowledge about the past. As a teaching technique, it helps to remove the remoteness of many historical concepts, bringing them to life by helping students see them as integral parts of other people's lives.

Good teachers are always on the lookout for ways to stimulate students' interest beyond the textbook itself. An oral history approach differs from a textbook approach to the study of the past in three major ways. First, oral history is active, whereas textbook learning is passive. Second, an oral history project takes students beyond the walls of the classroom to collect research by interviewing local residents and compiling information. "The purpose of oral history is the creation of primary resources. Through oral history, students gain a sense of the past that transcends what they can get from books" (Hennings, Hennings, & Banich, 1989). Third, textbooks generally present only one side of an historical event, whereas the oral history approach encourages examination of multiple perspectives of the same event. When students share what they learn through their interviews with other students in a large group format, multiple perspectives are presented for examination and consideration.

Classroom oral history projects often focus on historical events in the memories of local citizens, or events in the local community that were considered newsworthy or memorable. Elliott Wigginton's students in rural Georgia published their oral history projects in the well-known *Foxfire* series, which concentrated on the cultural heritage and folklife of their Appalachian community. Oral history projects motivate students to learn about family, community, and ethnic heritage. Students gain respect for and learn to appreciate the experiences of others with whom they live. They acquire an enhanced understanding of self, as well as a strong sense of community.

HOW DO I CONDUCT AN ORAL HISTORY PROJECT?

Having a formula or recipe for conducing an oral history project can help offset problems or disorganization that can easily occur when students embark on activities involving family and/or community members. Use the following checklist as a guide:

CHECKLIST FOR CONDUCTING A CLASSROOM ORAL HISTORY PROJECT

1. *Determine a focus for the project.* This may be an event, a special topic, or an era in local history. Local resources that may serve as a focus include cornerstones and plaques, monuments or other historical markers, museums, and local newspaper columns such as those titled "Fifty Years Ago Today."

2. *Begin background research.* Once you and your students have agreed on a topic, students should begin background research to provide a basis for later interviews. Textbooks and reference books can provide a general overview of the topic, but students' research should not stop there. Letters, diaries, ledgers, newspaper articles, and courthouse and church records help enlarge the perspective on the subject. When students have compiled and shared background research within the classroom setting, they should begin to develop questions to use in interviews.

3. *Identify potential informants and make appointments for interviews.* The next step in the oral history process involves identifying local residents who may be able to contribute firsthand information and memories about the identified topic. Have students make appointments with these people to conduct interviews.

4. *Develop interview questionnaires.* Help students develop interview questions. These questions should be used as a guide rather than a strict script, since the stories that emerge from this process may be far more fascinating than simple answers to interview questions.

5. *Practice interviewing techniques.* In the safe environment of the classroom, help students get accustomed to the interview process. Use tape recorders during the practice sessions to help students develop ease of use. (Additional helpful hints are discussed later in this chapter.)

6. *Conduct the actual interviews.*

7. *Provide class time for students to exchange their experiences and information.*

8. *Copy and distribute oral history booklets.* Have the interview tapes transcribed (or ask the students do this, if they are capable), compile collected data, and create a booklet to commemorate the project. These booklets may be duplicated to send home with students at the end of the year, and a copy should certainly be donated to the school library.

WHAT RESOURCES ARE AVAILABLE FOR GATHERING INFORMATION?

How can students find specific information about events in local history? Olsen and Gee (1989) suggest they consult the following:

- *Private memorabilia:* Letters, photographs, newspaper clippings, diaries, scrapbooks, and other "attic trunk" type items
- *Public memorabilia:* Political party headquarters, broadcasting organizations, and local, state, and world fair organizations
- *Interviews with community members:* Elderly residents, older family members, residents of retirement homes, public figures, professionals in particular fields, local artists, and representatives from religious and ethnic groups
- *Historical and conservation societies:* Relics, correspondence, and records
- *Historical sites and museums:* Visits to these locations can provide students with documentation and primary sources that will enhance the study of the local past.
- *Public, private, and military records:* Government offices, census bureaus, embassy offices, and miliary data of historical, demographic, and statistical interest

WHAT ELSE DO I NEED TO KNOW?

Oral history projects are particularly well-suited to the study of family and local history because of the wealth of resources available in students' hometowns. To ensure a broader coverage, break down the local history topics into subcategories, such as urban history, agricultural history, immigration/settler history, ethnic history, women's history, children's history, and so on.

The actual planning and structuring of an interview technique is extremely important to the success of the project. Without a set of planned questions and in-class practice before actual interviewing, students are likely to end up with a hodge-podge of conversation that defies analysis. If students understand what objectives they are to achieve by interviewing a local resident or family member, interview quality will be higher.

As an additional aid to teachers who are new to the oral history process, Welton and Mallen (1992) offer suggestions from teachers who have experience with class oral history projects:

ORAL HISTORY PROJECTS: HELPFUL HINTS BY EXPERIENCED TEACHERS

1. The focus should be on one topic, especially in K–3.

2. Prepare carefully for the interview, including helping students to "bone up" on the topic by using other sources, such as wills, diaries, and other accounts. On the other hand, do not do so much preparation that your students lose interest.

3. Equipment for the interview may include props like an old photograph or picture, but a tape recorder is essential. Tape recorders with built-in microphones are the least obtrusive, but those with external microphones usually provide better sound quality.

4. Appointments for interviews should be made through official sources, so students do not face the burden of explaining the entire project. Interviews should be restricted to one hour or less.

5. The interviewee should be asked to sign a release form describing the extent to which the taped material may be used. Early in an oral history activity, you may wish to interview a lawyer about the legal implications of interviewing (libel, slander, etc.), then play this tape for your class as a model.

6. Send students in interview teams of two or three.

7. Contact a high school typing teacher (well in advance) for possible assistance in typing the transcripts.

For those teachers who have tried oral history projects and are looking for something new and different, these suggestions on preparing multimedia presentations with data collected during oral history research may prove an inspiration:

ORAL HISTORY MULTIMEDIA PRESENTATIONS

1. Develop an edited audiotape on a topic of local concern. Have several informants describe related details and/or experiences, then edit the tape in a fashion that allows the listener to make sense of the topic and local citizens' experiences with and contributions to the topic. Collect or make photographs and displays to commemorate the topic, highlighting people, places, and materials/equipment from the local area.

2. Create a synchronized slide presentation from old photographs about the community or a local event. Dub the presentation with comments made by eyewitnesses and people with firsthand information. (Small grants often are available from state historical societies to fund such projects, especially if the project results in a program where the entire community is invited to view/hear the students' work.)

3. Identify one or several local crafts or "artifacts" made in the community by individual residents or groups (e.g., quilts, baskets, handmade soap, etc.) Using interviews conducted with people directly involved, edit a tape describing how the artifact was made. Invite these individuals to visit your school and bring examples of their work. Pass relevant items around the classroom as the tape is being played, or have visitors create a display where students can look and touch.

4. Make a video documentary about the history of the school. Try to identify the oldest living graduates or former students, and ask them to do the narration. Involve selected former students and teachers throughout the development of the documentary—the memories of other persons sometimes trigger memories of more events and aid in turning up additional primary sources, such as old photographs, textbooks, and report cards.

5. Create a Hypercard stack or HyperStudio program from data gathered during oral history interviews on the classroom computer, or ask for assistance from your school's computer lab. If students have interviewed residents at a local home for the elderly, for example, they might create one "stack" for each person interviewed, beginning with a photographic display of that person along with simple biographic information (e.g., date and place of birth, marital history, number of children). Short excerpts from oral history tape recordings and videos can be added to the stacks.

MORE ABOUT INTERVIEWING

Many of the lessons or activities contained in this book recommend that students be involved in an interview process of some sort. The preceding section recommends involving students in oral history projects, but on some occasions a simple interview will do. If your students have little or no experience conducting interviews, you may appreciate some helpful suggestions for getting started. *History Spoken Here* (Spinner Publications, various dates) contains a wealth of hints for training students to conduct interviews; a few are shared here.

As students engage in practice interview activities, and later in authentic interviews with identified informants, they develop greater interest in and motivation for learning about local and community history. In addition to historical understanding, students develop literary and verbal skills, practice grammar and punctuation as they transcribe taped interviews or write reports from notes, learn editing skills, and begin to learn how to ask good questions. When interviews involve a person who speaks a different language, students may even have the opportunity to hone foreign language skills. And seeing their works in print—whether it takes the form of a bound collection of transcripts for the school library or a formally published contribution to the local historical museum—infuses students with a sense of pride in both their accomplishments and in their local community.

Students can start sharpening their interviewing skills by interviewing a classmate. This initial interviewing experience helps them appreciate the subtleties of responsive listening, and perhaps discover that poorly written questions result in short answers or a lack of relevant information. Next, students practice their interviewing technique on a teacher or school staffperson, an adult with whom they are familiar or who seems less threatening than a stranger might. In this second interview, students try out what they have learned from the first interview and exercise a bit more confidence in the interviewing process. Then, students try out their new skills on a classroom guest, who usually is not someone known to them. Finally, students use what they know about good interviewing skills with an identified community informant for the purpose of gathering first-person data to be used in classroom research. These steps in the interviewing process are described in more detail here.

Interviewing Peers
As a result of students interviewing each other, they will develop an understanding of the difficulties associated with obtaining information through personal interaction, learn to listen carefully for information on identified topics, and figure out how to follow leads that develop outside identified topics without losing focus.

Interviewing Teacher/Staff
After practicing interviewing techniques with their peers, two or three students should individually interview a staff member (e.g., a secretary, a janitor, or cafeteria worker) or another teacher at the school—in front of the whole class. Afterwards, students should discuss the strong and weak points of the interview and how this experience can help them become better interviewers. (All students in the class

should take notes as well as listen during these sessions, and write their own accounts/reports of the interview after it takes place.)

Interviewing a Classroom Guest

Interviewing an adult who works at the school is practice for interviewing a relative stranger. The teacher invites one or more special guests to the classroom to be interviewed in much the same way as the children interviewed a teacher or staffperson. In the interest of furthering students' motivation for learning about community history, the guest should have some special skill or background related to the community; students compose questions ahead of time to find out more about the guest's expertise and/or experiences, thus preparing them to plan and conduct interviews on their own.

These practice interviews should be followed by some sort of student assessment. A class discussion when students recall the highlights of the interview and critique the strategies used can be very helpful, as can a writing assignment where students respond to questions such as:

- Which part of the interview did you enjoy most? Why? Tell about parts of the story or description in your answer.
- Which interview question, in your opinion, resulted in the best response? What do you think made this a good question? Rewrite or rephrase another interview question to make it better.
- What questions did you have that were not answered in the interview? What are some ideas or events you would like to explore further? What question or questions could you ask that would help you learn more about this topic?
- Think of something about this interview that could be improved. What might have been done differently?

Using This Book

The chart at the front of this book (pages xi–xii) shows which activities are recommended for particular grade levels. Primary-level (prekindergarten to grade 2) activities are designated with a *P*, intermediate-level (grades 3–5) activities with an *I*, and middle-level (grades 6–8) activities with an *M*. Certainly, teachers need not feel bound by these designations, but the chart serves as a quick reference for instructional planning.

Read on to find out more about bringing history to life for your students. Part I, Family History invites students to research their own and their family's history through the use of student biographies, family trees and genealogy, rituals and traditions, storytelling, and making family scrapbooks. Part I contains ideas, activities, and resources for involving your students in learning more about their family's history, ancestors, ethnic backgrounds, traditions, stories, and themselves as members of that family. You will find ways to incorporate students' own cultural learning and experiences in the curriculum. In the sections called Trying It Out, descriptions of classroom teachers' recent experiences with these and similar activities provide authentic examples to draw from, duplicate, or alter to fit your own classroom situation.

Part II, Community and Local History, contains ideas, activities, and resources for stimulating interest in and motivation for learning about their local area. Students can investigate the local history by developing historical time lines, investigating local geography and landmarks, using primary and secondary source materials (e.g., old radio tapes, historical photographs, post cards, etc.), finding out about local folklore (e.g., old sayings, toys and pastimes of long ago, etc.), and researching how local women contributed to the settlement and subsequent development of the town or community. They can research and document the history of their own school, and/

or the histories of schools in the local area used and no longer used. Again, Trying It Out provides examples to draw from as you consider how best to tailor a particular lesson to your own students' needs.

Teachers who want to incorporate the use of children's trade books in their curriculum will find valuable suggestions in Part III, Using Books to Teach about Family and Local History. In Chapter 12, selected books are accompanied by suggestions for introducing, sharing, and concluding or extending the story. Chapter 13 is an annotated bibliography of children's books on family history, recommended by teachers or in the recent literature. Chapter 14 is an annotated bibliography of children's books on local or community history topics, also recommended by teachers or in recent literature. Chapter 15 details cooperative learning experiences suggested by the content of several family- or community-related topics.

Additional resources and contacts for researching personal, family, and local history not mentioned elsewhere in the text can be found in the Appendix. Professional organizations with publications and/or curriculum materials related to topics and issues inherent in family or local history are listed, as are additional sources for instructional materials.

Part

I

Family History

Learning is an ongoing construction of meaning. When children learn history, they need scaffolding similar to that used when they learn to read and write. Children make sense of text by setting up and confirming predictions; they make sense of history by setting up meaningful context for events and ideas, and by predicting and confirming historical understandings through interaction with others.

Teachers help their students construct historical meaning by anchoring instruction within meaningful contexts. The study of self and family represents one of the most meaningful of all contexts. Students already know quite a lot about the subject and are likely to exhibit interest in studying the topic further—both characteristics that facilitate learner motivation.

In this section, students will write about their own lives, consider similarities and differences through sharing their writings with one another and reading and hearing about family issues and problems, depict important events in their lives with time lines, and compare and contrast events or circumstances in the present with similar events or circumstances from the past. Eventually, students will learn to move beyond a focus on their own lives and interests toward a focus on collective experiences of the class, family, or community as a group.

Chapter 1

Our Families, Ourselves

One of the challenges we teachers face on a daily basis is how to link new knowledge and skills to what our students already know. In the area of history or social studies, you can invite your students to connect personal experiences with relevant current events or historical happenings. First, however, you must provide a structure that allows children to share comfortably what they know about their own experiences. Such activities (see descriptions of "Student Biographies" or "Time Lines") lead naturally to a desire to explore one's experiences and that of one's family during a time when the child was too young to recall personal events. This, in turn, leads naturally to a desire to know more about "the time before I was born."

Family and personal history activities can be very motivational. In fact, experience shows that it is a good idea to inform parents and administrators of the planned study and to invite parents' participation before introducing the topic to students, since students have been known to get so excited they telephone relatives from school because they cannot wait to get home to discover more about their histories! Structure with flexibility is key here, though—some families may be reluctant at first to share information they consider personal when that information may be shared aloud in class. These personal and/or family history assignments should require that students share significant events of their lives, not *everything* about themselves and their families. With enough flexibility, many alternatives are possible. As Levstik and Barton (1997) suggest, teachers could give students the option of collecting information on someone's life other than their own, since the objective of the activity is "to find out how the past affects the present, not to force students into putting themselves on display" (p. 32). Ease students into the idea of thinking about the connections between their lives and the passage of time with a group activity such as a "Class Time Line" (discussed in the next major section).

Student Biographies

Young children have trouble distinguishing last *week* from last *year*, so creating personal biographies can be especially difficult unless you give them a workable structure. Try beginning with a time line. Introduce the concept of time lines with a Class Time Line of the past week, such as that shown in Figure 1.1.

After discussion, create a Class Time Line together, recalling significant or memorable events of the past week and illustrating them on the chalkboard, overhead projector, computer enlargement, or even butcher paper, using the format shown in Figure 1.1. When students understand the idea behind the time-line format, spend a few days or a week helping them make a Personal Time Line, using these directions:

1. Get a long piece of bulletin board or butcher paper, or tape some sheets of notebook paper together to form a long strip. Use a big marker to draw a horizontal line in the middle across the whole strip of paper, end to end.

2. Draw a vertical line through the horizontal line to represent each year of your life. The first line at the left will represent the year you were born. The next line will represent your first birthday; the next line, your second birthday; and so on. Number each line with a year, and think of all that you know or can remember about what happened to you during each year. (See Figure 1.2 for an example of a student-created Personal Time Line.) Here are some events you might want to include:

A birthday party
A favorite toy
The very first thing you remember happening
Your first day of school
Taking a special trip, with your family or by yourself
Learning to ride a tricycle, bike, skateboard
Learning to swim, ice skate, sail
The first book you ever read
Doing something with a best friend
The time you broke your arm or leg
Losing a tooth
Learning to play the piano or other musical instrument

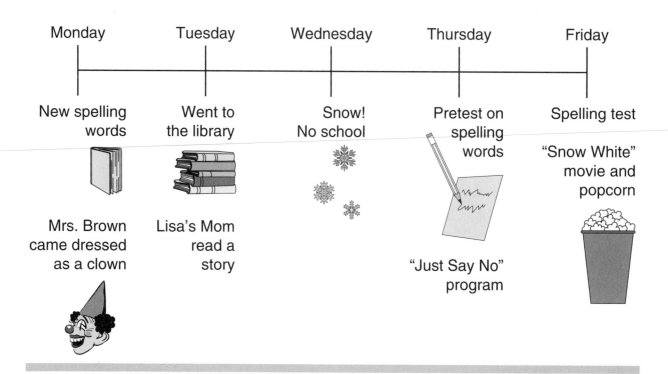

Figure 1.1 Example of Class Time Line

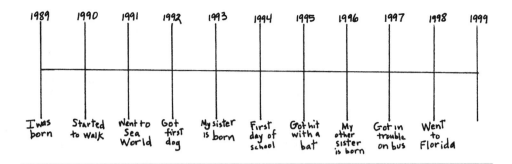

Figure 1.2 Example of a Student-Created Personal Time Line

3. Ask your parents or other family members to help you remember more times in your life, and add these to your Personal Time Line. (You may need to add more paper to the strip to make it longer!)

Make certain each student's name is on his or her Personal Time Line. Make a display of Personal Time Lines to hang on a bulletin board or in the hallway. Encourage students to talk about the events and people they remember.

▌ Trying It Out

A Memory Web

Lisa Miller and her first-graders explored the making of memories by using Mem Fox's (1985) *Wilfrid Gordon McDonald Partridge.* "What is a memory?" asks Wilfrid Gordon McDonald Partridge. "Something that makes you laugh, my darling, something that makes you laugh," replies Miss Mitchell in the book. Lisa's students discovered that the memories they made of their experiences in first grade at least made them smile....

When Lisa introduced the book to her students, they predicted from its cover that the book would be about a little boy and his grandma. As Lisa read the story, however, the children began to understand that the book has a very different meaning. Lisa displayed a story elements poster to facilitate discussion about the book. (The students were familiar with the concept of story elements.) "Where was the setting of this story?" she asked. "In a nursing home," one boy responded. This helped Lisa to know the student must have personal experience with a relative or family friend in such an institution, since the book refers to the setting as "an old folks' home" rather than "a nursing home." They talked briefly about what is meant by an "old folks' home," then moved on to the element of characters, which the children readily recalled. "What is the problem in the story?" Lisa wondered. This, too, the children answered readily: Miss Nancy had lost her memory. Lisa proceeded to discuss the story element of events with the children, reminding them that events are things that happened in the story.

After creating their story elements web together, Lisa's students began to develop another kind of web. "I want you to create a web explaining what a memory is," she instructed them. In the center of their web, one of the children wrote "What is a memory?" Attached to this were all of the responses of the elderly people in the story: something that makes me laugh, something that makes me cry, something from long ago, something warm, something precious as gold. "Think hard about some memories that we have from first grade," Lisa told the children as they drew their webs.

Since this project was taking place within the final two weeks of the academic year, the children had ample material from which to draw. To help prod their thinking, Lisa brought in several items related to the current school year: pictures, objects, and crafts. When she showed them a paper bear, one boy said, "I remember that! We made one the first day of school!" Immediately, all the other children began to talk about this experience. Another thing Lisa showed them was an apple. "I remember when we made applesauce," one child said, and others recalled the field trip to a nearby apple orchard. She showed the children a photo of the class dressed up in angel costumes, which encouraged them to talk about their memories of the Christmas play.

"Where will we put these memories on our web?" Lisa asked. Most agreed that the photo should be placed under "something that makes me laugh," although one student insisted they put it under "something precious as gold." The apple should be placed under something warm if it reminded them of making applesauce, or under "something from long ago" if it reminded them of the trip to the orchard and the ride in a hay wagon.

Lisa acknowledged that beginning this lesson so close to the end of the school year handicapped her from extending it as she would have wished. "I would have the children, with the help of their parents, create their own family trees," she suggested. "The children could then create an oral history project, by talking with their grandparents about some of their memories after we read the book. In this way, children are not only spending time with their grandparents but they are also learning a lot about their family histories." In any event, Lisa explained that the children were "very enthusiastic and confident in sharing the special events that they remembered from the beginning of school. The children learned to work together to accomplish the goal of creating a web of memories. I also feel that the children began to realize how important friends are in our lives. They learned that a memory is more than just remembering something. A memory is a precious gift we can share with someone else."

As a beginning teacher, Lisa felt that this activity influenced her thinking about her relationship with her students. "I saw children excited about learning because they were able to share many of their own experiences.... [This sharing] enabled them to encourage each other and to become more confident in voicing their contributions."

Time Lines

A second-grade teacher wanted her students to have an idea of what a time line is all about, and to realize that they themselves have become a part of a sequence of history by living their lives from birth to the present moment. She began this project by discussing time lines as she drew one on the board. The teacher demonstrated sequence and order while stressing that time lines have a beginning and an end. "When the kids gave me that glazed-over look," she said, "I decided to try something else that was more fun." She drew another time line and made up some "facts and dates" about the students in her room: "Tom got his first haircut" and "Brian was potty trained" were memorable examples. At this point, the children's interest was piqued, and they began to consider creating their own time lines.

The teacher and her assistant traced each student's body on white paper, then the students colored these outlines. (This process took two days, since available floor space had to be shared.) A homework page was assigned, inviting parents to help students recall and list important life events on a form created by the teacher. As the forms were returned, information from each student's form was copied onto small strips of paper. "These were too small for our students to handle," the teacher admitted, which led to their changing to 3" × 5" index cards. The cards were placed in sequential order. In class, students cut out the body outlines that had been traced and colored earlier. Each student glued the cards listing events from his or her life onto his or her body outline, starting at the feet and working toward the head, which represented the "most current end" of their human time line.

"I decided to do this project because time lines were a part of reading and social studies lessons...this lesson seemed to liven up an otherwise dull topic," this teacher recalled. As far as suggestions for other teachers, she noted that "the project could be sized down. The students could just draw pictures of themselves on construction paper and label their pictures using life events." Other recommendations include giving parents and students at least three days to complete the homework assignment, and asking them to print the life events/dates neatly on 3" × 5" cards the teacher provides.

Divorce and Separation

Beth Bixby teaches preschoolers in a day-care setting in her own home. Being sensitive to the fact that one of her students was experiencing the difficulties of her parents' divorce, Beth decided to use Brown and Brown's (1986) book, *Dinosaurs Divorce: A Guide for Changing Families* (Boston: Atlantic Monthly Press) to explore this topic with the children in her care. "Being a full-time day care provider . . . affords me many opportunities to have informal discussions about those things that are most important to children," she says. "They chatter on endlessly with their own special ideas about birthdays, illnesses, life and death . . . and what goes on in their own families. One of the children . . . has recently faced the trauma of her parents' divorce." The father's remarriage and the experience of acquiring a stepmother and dealing with the loss of her father from their home had become the focus of this little girl's daily conversations at the center. When "another family experienced a separation . . . there were many quivering chins and questions" from Beth's charges. "I hope that by reading this book, [I'll help] the children see that other families do have conflicts and that there are a variety of ways to solve them. I also want this story to be a comfortable springboard to any more unanswered questions," Beth explains.

The children giggled and wriggled as they sat on the floor while Beth read *Dinosaurs Divorce*. Storytime is their favorite activity of the day, and the children were quickly attracted to the book's cover. They began to ask questions and speculated on what the story may be about. Some of the children laughed at the picture of two dinosaurs arguing, and all of them thought the idea of dinosaurs being angry with each other was funny. The picture spurred one child's imitation of his dad's expression when he complains to the boy's mother about dinner. When Beth got to the page illustrating different emotions, all of the children were up on their knees, trying to get close to the book and imitating their favorite emotional facial expression. At this point, the children's involvement with the book was so great that Beth decided to paraphrase the story in order to keep the book and its pictures facing the children at all times.

The section about living with one parent brought shrieks and shouts from the boy whose parents had recently separated. There were several simultaneous and elaborate conversations going on at once as the children speculated how this boy's experience was similar to the dinosaur's. Everybody wanted to give explanations of their feelings, their parents' arguments, living arrangements (who lives where and for how long). Beth patiently allowed each child to contribute to the discussion.

After the book had been read, Beth asked the children to draw pictures of their own family or, if they wish, what a dinosaur's family might look like. Beth had, of course, hoped the experience of reading and discussing the book would relieve the anxiety of the girl whose parents had recently divorced, and would enable the child whose parents had separated for several days to talk about worries associated with this event. Instead, she says, "I received the most questions from the three children who recently have witnessed an apparently troubling (although brief) separation of their parents."

As Beth discovered, the children who had felt free to talk about their anxieties were not the ones who most responded to *Dinosaurs Divorce*. It was the children who had never mentioned their parents' troubles who seemed to most need to discuss them after the reading of the book. As for advice she would give to teachers who plan to replicate her activity, Beth says, "The only change I would make would be in my expectations. I would not limit my thinking to one specific learner, but would try to encompass the experiences of every child." She smiled when she recalled that, hours after the reading of the book, as the children were playing in the house center, she overheard one of them say, "Who wants to be my stephusband?"

Death and Dying

Tita Gordon also used a book to help preschoolers in a day-care setting deal with family problems—in this case, death and dying. Tita used Lucille Clifton's (1983) *Everett Anderson's Goodbye* with 4- and 5-year-olds. She began by gathering the children around her on the floor for storytime. She showed them the book and told them, "This is the story of a little boy named Everett Anderson. The title of the book is *Everett Anderson's Goodbye.*" Tita showed the children the first picture in the book. "How does Everett look?" she asked. "Sad," "Lonely," "Unhappy," "Like he has no friends," the children responded. She asked the children if they had ever had to tell anyone goodbye. "Yes," they answered quickly, and began to shout out, "Miss Nancy," "My mommy," "My friend—she moved," and "My grandma." Tita and the children proceeded with the sharing of the book until she came to the page where Everett says to his mommy, "I will do everything you say if Daddy can be alive today." At this point, the children knew Everett's daddy had died. Immediately, the children responded to this realization with announcements that someone close to them had died: "My grandpa died," "My stepdad died," "My dog died."

As the story progressed, the children became very quiet, sensing that Everett is very sad and depressed. The book ends with Everett saying, "I knew my daddy loved me through and through, and whatever happens when people die, my daddy loves me. . . . I love my daddy. . . . Love doesn't stop, and neither will I."

"Does Everett still love his daddy?" Tita asked. "Yes," they chorused, and "Sure he does!" Tita completed this experience by asking the boys and girls to draw a picture of what their faces might look like if, like Everett, they lost their father.

"It was truly amazing to me that each and every one of them had had some type of experience with death in their little short lives," Tita later told me. "I expect this from older people, but was totally unprepared for this from children of this age." Tita feels that exploring sensitive topics like death and dying in this way helps young children begin to understand that their own experiences with the death of a pet or family member are actually universal experiences, shared by everyone at some time.

Then and Now

For children in elementary grades, the years they already have lived are history. One way to make the past more relevant is to have students compare their *own* past with the present. A first-grade teacher, for example, divided long strips of paper into sections headed "When I was a baby . . . ," "When I was a little kid . . . ," and "Now . . ." before giving them to her students. Then the children drew pictures and/or dictated sentences to the teacher and aide related to the time frames depicted by the headings.

Older students might use rolls of adding machine tape to represent the different phases of their lives ("When I was a baby . . . ," "When I was a toddler . . . ," "When I started school . . . ," etc.). (Use topics mentioned earlier in this chapter in the section titled Student Biographies to help them remember even more events, and encourage them to write and/or draw pictures about important occasions in their lives.) Personal time lines such as these are a good starting point for motivating students' interest in history.

▪ Trying It Out

Connections: Our Stories

Teachers in an urban midwestern school district needed a high-motivation project to encourage summer school students at risk of being retained to attend classes. They worked together to plan a brief but personal oral history project that would be taught as a thematic unit incorporating social studies and literacy skills. Students were asked to research and write autobiographies, or "The Story of My Life." They then were told to interview one or more family members to obtain greater detail and background family history to include in a formal paper. After these papers were revised and edited in class, students obtained recent photographs of themselves, and a childhood photograph (if possible) of the family member featured in the interview portion. The final drafts were collected, organized, and bound with a colorful and informative cover, and copies were presented to each student and to the school libraries within the district. Much enthusiasm was evident throughout the summer, from both students and family members, and several teachers repeat the project each summer.

Following are three examples from the project:

LATISHA

On a sunny, beautiful spring day, May 21, a wonderful thing happened . . . I was born. A beautiful baby girl was born at St. Agnes Hospital at exactly 3:15 A.M. I am the oldest child of six children. After growing for a couple of years, I can recall going to Brighton School for pre-school at the age of two. I attended pre-school for two years. I also attended Brighton School for my kindergarten through my fifth grade years. I moved on to Barker Middle School for my sixth through eighth grade years.

I have four brothers and one sister. I was born to my mother, Pauline, when she was very young. My mom was only fifteen years old at the time that she had me. Since my mom had me at a very young age, my father really didn't know what to do. Don't get me wrong! My father did try to help my mom out, but my grandfather had a strong dislike for him. He didn't like my father from the very first time my mom started going out with him. . . .

In elementary school, I was a very active person. I began modern dance in the first grade. I began playing in the band when I was in fourth grade, I played the clarinet. In middle school I am in band, but I am on the cheerleading team also. I was in Girl Scouts for a while, until our troop leader stole our dues money and my mom made me quit.

My future goal, after I graduate from high school, is to hopefully go to college at one of the black universities. I don't know what I want to major in, probably some form of medicine.

We have a lot of family stories and sayings in our family. There is one family story that someone seems to tell each time the family gathers together on special occasions. It is the story about when my Uncle Leon was at home in the kitchen boiling some water on the stove. Uncle Leon had apparently fallen asleep and while he was sleeping, the water on the stove boiled out and the pan started to burn. The next thing we knew, the kitchen was full of smoke. Then the pan handle caught fire and fell on the floor, catching it on fire. Through all of this, my Uncle Leon was in such a deep sleep that he didn't even notice the smoke. Luckily my Aunt Cindy walked into the house and noticed that the house was full of smoke and that the kitchen floor was on fire. When she saw this, she screamed out, "Leon, wake your --- up! The house is on fire!" My uncle woke up, and my aunt and uncle ran to the kitchen and put the fire out.

GREG

February is the shortest month of the year, but destined to be something special. Leap Year, the celebration of Black History, the celebration of famed Civil Rights leader Martin Luther King, Jr., and last but definitely far from being least, February 4. Gregory A. was born. A moment among many others to be celebrated as one of February's famed holidays. The parents of this child, Michael C., Jr., and Eileen, viewed him probably as a second son, another to continue the legacy, to steer toward success. He was their second child, both children having a great number of years between them. My older brother Frederick J. was the first to be born in 1978.

My father was a main benefactor in a small, but successful construction company in southern Los Angeles, California. Six years after my birth he retired from this profession. My mother worked as a maid. My old neighborhood in the Projects of Los Angeles is far off in years, but still the most memorable to my recollection. Above all things, I loved to play football with my brother and my friends. I was mainly a receiver due to my great speed and receptions. I recall one catch when I caught the ball falling backwards into garbage cans for a touchdown.

My mother and my cousin Erykah ruled me with their iron fists. Family stories aren't in great abundance in my memory. However, my mother managed to recall amusing anecdotes, just bits and pieces of my history. One story she told me of is about one day in my childhood. The day started with my incredible ability to just cause trouble. From the moment I awoke, I managed to maneuver myself in total silence to a hiding area in a room, where I scouted for my brother's toys. Of course, I had toys of my own, but I wanted my brother's toys, too.

When I was younger, I trained myself to be a professional football player. Of course, this goal is far from my mind now. My present options are: psychiatrist, professional writer, lawyer, computer engineer, or even plumber. Whichever profession I chose, I plan to attend Howard University to steer me in the right direction.

MARIA

Still eating leftovers from the hearty Thanksgiving, people's stomachs were getting fat. My mother Juanita was one of them. She [gave] thanks for a new child soon to be born, her last, but not her least. My father Raphael Christos would soon have another child.

Being already in her middle age, and having five other children, this one seemed common to my mother. However, this child was separated by her good looks and joyful smile. Everybody adored her, and she was loved by her whole family.

Born on November 28, I am a Sagittarius. I consider myself able to gallop into people's hearts and raise myself to new heights. My mother gave me four names: Maria Concepcion Juanita Christos. For a while, I didn't even know how to spell it. But, being a young scholar, I learned my ABC's at the age of 3.

I consider myself an above average student. I have friends in school to play with, but some of my best friends were my teachers. I wasn't too much of an athlete in my younger years, so I concentrated on my schooling. School was probably so much fun because it was so boring at home.

My mother told me a story about how one day she was in the country hearing stories told by a blazing fire. She was told she wasn't supposed to go out at night because of the bears and snakes that came around the house. There was a story of a large snake her family tried to catch, a cat who beat up a man by diving off walls, and a woman who had puppies instead of babies. She tried to convince me these stories were true. Compared to all the violence this generation faces today, these stories mean very little and would have little effect. I think with all the technology we have today we miss out on storytelling, and don't use our imagination.

I want to go to Michigan State University and earn my Masters Degree in engineering. I plan to face new experiences: meeting new friends, hanging out, and the work would be a challenge. Knowing that, I would take all the classes I can get. I will learn to be responsible and independent. I would never forget my family; I would help other people in need because I am deep into religion and want to follow in Jesus' footsteps.

All about Me Books: Intermediate

Stacia Czartoski developed a personal history project to use with her fifth-graders, and found to her surprise that even older children can learn a great deal about themselves and the diverse backgrounds present in the classroom. "I wanted each student to explore their historical roots, and compare them to each other's [roots] in the classroom and other children's [roots] throughout the world," she says.

The impetus for the "All about Me" book came after Stacia shared a book entitled *People* (Spier, 1988) with her students. The book shows photographs of people from all around the world, and tells about their belief structures and everyday living practices. The students were "very curious about other people's culture and beliefs," Stacia notes, since "many students had never seen or experienced other types of cultures." She realized that her students were critical of appearances, skin colors, clothing, beliefs, and customs different from their own. As a way of counteracting these pervasive criticisms and stereotypes in her preadolescent students, Stacia decided to provide a way for them to learn that there is diversity in every classroom and every community, no matter how monocultural the population may be. She told the students that their next assignment was to make an "All about Me" book. The completed book would contain the student's autobiography from birth to fifth grade, information about family and cultural heritage, and photos.

Over the next two weeks, students brought in photographs of themselves and family members, baby books or memory books about themselves borrowed from their parents or grandparents, and copies of personal documents such as birth certificates and letters. In class, each student designed a cover for his or her book, put the book together using materials supplied by the teacher, pasted photographs or copies of photos into the book, and worked on his or her autobiographical writing. The children asked questions and researched at home to discover what their likes and dislikes had been since babyhood (and how these had changed over time), and found out many things about their families' histories they had not known before.

To make sure all students had a recent snapshot of themselves to include in the "All about Me" book, Stacia brought her camera to school and made photographs of individual students as they stood near a display in the classroom. When these were developed, all students in the class had similar snapshots; Stacia decided to have them use the snapshot she had made to represent themselves on the cover of their books (see Figure 1.3). Other snapshots, school pictures, and baby pictures, if available, were placed inside the book with accompanying labels or descriptions of activities.

Students were asked to draw a picture of themselves with their family, including all family members. Stacia notes that at this time, some students asked her what a family is: "We had an interesting [class] discussion, and basically it came down to who you think is in your family. I had a student who had three stepdads and numerous stepsisters!" she says. This drawing was to accompany the individual student's Family Tree, which also was researched and included in the "All about Me" book.

Each student also drew a picture of his or her house. In an effort to simplify things, Stacia agreed that students could either draw the exterior, or show the interior of their homes in blueprint style. "This seemed to be more successful [than each student's drawing the outside of his or her "house"] because there weren't any [teasing comments] on what their house looked like," she later reflects.

After students finished the first draft of their autobiographies, Stacia had them pair up to proofread each other's writing as they had learned as part of their process writing skill training. This was the first chance students had had to compare and con-

Figure 1.3 Sample Cover of "All about Me"

trast their own life story with that of their classmates. "Students were amazed at what they did or said when they were a certain age," Stacia says. "They compared what they did to what their friends did, and could see some similarities as well as some differences." When the "All about Me" books had been completed, students spent an entire morning sharing highlights of their lives and favorite parts of their books. This gave Stacia an opportunity to lead them in discussion of likenesses and differences in terms of family units, homes, experiences, beliefs and values, and long-term goals. Students began to understand that diversity is all around them, and Stacia noticed a slowly changing attitude about other cultures and ethnic groups among her students after this assignment.

Following are two examples of what students included in their "All about Me" books:

LINDSAY

Lindsay's "All about Me" book cover shows her in a favorite tie-dyed shirt and denim shorts. The photo is surrounded by neat geometric shapes, and the entire page is captioned "All about Miuo." The family drawing shows Lindsay, her parents, an older brother, and sister. Lindsay drew herself in a shirt displaying a colorful geometric color block pattern. Other family members' shirts communicate something about each one individually: Lindsay's older brother's shirt displays an athletic label, her older sister's shirt identifies her as a student at a local college, her mother's shirt is a souvenir from a family trip, and her father's shirt displays the name of his place of business.

Lindsay took great care to represent her home accurately in the house drawing. She chose to draw the house's exterior: a two-story, four-bedroom, single-family dwelling with siding; colorfully patterned curtains and shades of different lengths (even the shade pulls were depicted); a storm door completed with the lower mesh panel and tension chain, as well as an attractive wood-panel front door with a window and Welcome sign; carefully drawn individual roof shingles; and a lawn chair on the patio, green grass, and decorative stone walkways.

Lindsay's family tree chart depicts four generations. Her own name is at the base of the family tree's trunk, her parents' names are in the lowest branches, and her grandparents' names take up space in the middle of the "tree." Great-grandparents are represented for only two of four grandparents. While Lindsay chose to represent her own birthdate, she did not include those of other family members. Her siblings' name do not appear in the family tree record.

Two pages of photos follow Lindsay's family tree: a snapshot of four children dressed convincingly as members of a wedding party, with Lindsay as the flower girl and older sister Shanna as the "June bride"; a formal photograph of Lindsay with her two siblings; a school picture of Lindsay; and a recent outdoor snapshot of her entire family gathered around a tree, dressed in summer clothing.

Lindsay's autobiography confirms her love of collecting, especially Beanie Babies and handmade pillows. She says:

> I collect all sorts of Beanie Babies, like Bean Sprouts, Bean Bag Friends, and of course the original TY Beanie Babies. So far, all together I have seven Beanie Babies. Two Bean Sprouts, Honey and Pudgey a keychain, one Bean Bag Friend, Mama and her two babies with her, and four original Beanie Babies. Two from McDonald's, Snort and Seamore, and two big and real Beanie Babies from the Orthodontist (Dr. Whately) their names are Mystic and Bongo.

Lindsay's plans for the future include marriage "to someone nice and cute," three children ("a girl, a boy, and a girl"), and to live in a "brand new big country house."

KURT

Kurt's "All about Me" book cover shows him in denim shorts, basketball shoes, and a white shirt with the name of a local basketball team and the slogan "Expect to Win!" He decorated the area surrounding his cover photo with vivid red marker scribbles and the title "All about Me!" in black marker. Kurt's drawings are somewhat simpler in nature than Lindsay's. His family drawing shows himself, a younger brother and sister, an older sister, and his mother.

Like Lindsay, Kurt elected to portray his home from the outside: a two-story, single-family dwelling with three windows and a door surrounded by a pickett fence. All windows were depicted with Dutch-style cross-beams.

Kurt's family tree records himself, his parents, and his grandparents. Kurt includes his own birthdate, but not those of other family members. No siblings are included on the family tree.

Two pages of photographs from Kurt's early childhood are included in his "All about Me" book. In the first photo, a very young Kurt rides a rocking horse while his father looks on from a nearby recliner. The next photo shows Kurt and two other small boys standing in a garage, each boy proudly holding a rat by its tail. Another photo shows Kurt's older sister dramatically gesturing toward a riding lawn mover while their mother holds Kurt on her lap. The most recent photo is one of Kurt with a teacher inside the classroom.

Kurt's autobiography confirms his love of sports, especially basketball, as well as other outdoor activities such as fishing and hunting for mushrooms. He remembers falling down when he was very little, resulting in an injury requiring stitches to the head. Kurt has played on summer sports teams and has won trophies. His future plans include becoming a professional basketball player. He says:

> In fourth grade I got straight A's the whole year. I was in summer baseball one year and we came in second place. Once I was in the YMCA 3 on 3 contest. We won a first place trophy. My favorite field trip was in fourth grade we went to Science Central. My favorite vacation was when I went to Seaworld. In the future I want to be an NBA player.

All about Me Books: Primary

Jean Schroeder (1996) wanted the students in her mixed-age first- and second-grade classroom to begin to develop a concept of the past. She felt that time lines would help increase students' understanding of the passing of time, and of the then and now, but many of her students were too inexperienced to build concepts with time lines without some sort of lead-in introduction. "I began reading stories that focused on self and self-concept, such as *I Like Me!* [Carlson, 1988]," she states. "The class decided to make an "All about Me" book." Jean made a few suggestions about what they might include, and students discussed what the structure of their books would be. "They chose to include a self-portrait, a family picture, and pages on pets, best friends, feelings, likes and dislikes, and what they would do when they were adults," she recalls. This is where students learned to use time lines.

As they collaborated with parents and other family members to create their "All about Me" books, students found that they were able to make and use personal time lines. "They recorded personal events in their lives . . . such as when they had begun to walk or talk. Many of the students seemed to recognize that adults saw these [events] as important milestones," Jean adds. Even those students who decided not to include beginning to walk or talk as important personal events in their books thought these were worthy of inclusion on their time lines. Comparing their own time lines to those of other students helped the children discuss personally important events in ways that allowed them to comprehend that events serve as markers for segments of time.

"By expanding the focus on self to include the immediate family and then even further to include grandparents," Jean reflects, "children found themselves strolling into the past in a concrete context." Students collected stories about themselves and about their parents' childhoods, as well as family anecdotes and stories for inclusion in their books. They were excited about sharing pieces of their past with other students and with the teacher; after reading the stories aloud, the children typed them on a computer and drew pictures to illustrate the stories. Then Jean and the students worked together to make a class Family Stories Book.

"Through literature discussion, children stepped further into the past with grandparent stories," Jean says. They talked with their grandparents, or with older family friends or neighbors when grandparents were not available, and followed the same process as with the family stories—except this time the stories were published as a newspaper. "Typically, when history is taught in schools," Jean muses, "teachers begin at the earliest period in time pertaining to the period of study and move toward the present. . . . By beginning with the present and themselves and then moving back through time, children were better able to think about and understand the past."

Just Me and My Family

Jann Braumberger, a kindergarten teacher, wanted her students to explore their own and family members' roles in the family, and to improve their writing and thinking skills. She created a booklet for each student entitled "Just Me and My Family." On the cover of the booklet, Jann made a place for students to show authorship, and used computer graphics to illustrate a large, half-opened, gift box with question marks all around it to suggest students' many questions about their place in their families. Inside the booklet, five pages were included, each with the following sentence to be completed (and blank lines to complete the sentence as well as lots of space to illustrate the sentence): "Just me and my mom . . . ; Just me and my dad . . . ; Just me and my grandpa . . . ; Just me and my grandma . . . ; Just me and my [student's choice]."

Marla's "Just Me and My Family" booklet (see Figure 1.4) included these things:

My mom, and Darin, and I went to Chokee Chese. [drawing of pizza restaurant]

I like to eat fish. [drawing of Marla and her dad fishing]

Me and my grandpa went and play basketball. [drawing of Marla and her grandpa shooting hoops]

Figure 1.4   Example of "Just Me and My Family" Booklet

We sleep together. [drawing of Marla and her grandma sharing a big bed]

Just me and my grandpa . . . Me an my grampa whent fishing and I caught a catfish. [drawing of Marla and her grandpa fishing off a pier on a large lake]

MORE IDEAS

Here are a few more suggestions to help make your students' past more relevant.

TIME LINES

■ Have students talk to one of their parents and make a time line of the period when the parent was growing up. The parent may want to include major world events on his or her time line, to add perspective to personal events.

■ Have students talk to one of their grandparents (or other senior citizen) and make a time line of the period when that person grew up. As with the parent time line, important world events and happenings should be included.

■ Ask parents to supply a family photograph taken before their child was born, with a request that the parent not reveal any details about the photograph. When students bring their photographs to school, organize the children into small "detecting" groups whose assignment is to predict who is in the photo, what it is about, approximately when it was taken, and where—all based on visible evidence from the photos. Have each student write down the groups' prediction about its photo. Later, after they have interviewed family members at home that night, each child should then write down the "correct" information. The next day, detecting groups compare their predictions with the facts, and report their findings to the large group.

Grandparents' Day

Many schools set aside a special day or week during the year to bring grandparents and their grandchildren together in the school setting. If your school has not established a Grandparents' Day, please consider the joint benefits for seniors and children alike when all come together to celebrate and share their lives and learning. If your school does have a formal Grandparents' Day or Week, this section may bring a fresh perspective to the activities and festivities you have planned. Whatever you plan for visiting grandparents, make certain they have opportunities to get involved in classroom instruction. A limited list of things visiting grandparents might do includes:

Listen to child read

Tell stories to class

Share arts and crafts with class

Demonstrate arts and crafts within small groups

Help with cooking projects

Share slide presentations and/or photos from trips

Talk about their careers or special skills

Help students at learning centers

Participate in interview with individual students, pairs of students, or the whole class

■ Trying It Out

Celebrating Grandparents' Week

A brief survey demonstrates the variety of approaches different schools or classes bring to the celebration of Grandparents' Day (Indiana Department of Education, no date). Some highlights from the survey may serve to inspire or motivate fresh approaches to your school's Grandparents' Day or Week:

■ A grandfather brought his equipment for "raising bees" to the class. Students listened as he told about bees and showed them a part of the bee hive. Then, each child received a tiny container of honey to sample, as well as a cookie made with honey (contributed by the grandmother). Students later wrote stories about what they like to do with their grandparents, and these were "published" by being posted in the hallway for others to read.

■ Students participated in grandparents' demonstration of crocheting and ceramics, discussion of and slides about life and schools in Romania, talks about different occupations (a grandparent who had been a secretary taught students to write their names in shorthand, for example), and discussions of life on a farm and fishing in Canada.

■ Groups of students brought either cans of soup (same type/flavor) or a cold finger-food dish for Grandparents' Day. The soup was warmed in a big pot, and soup and finger-foods were shared with grandparents at lunch time.

■ Grandparents' Day was held in late October at one school. A teacher says, "In the past, our students decorated [without carving] pumpkins within each classroom and displayed their fine work," during the week preceding Halloween. This year, however, the school "invited grandparents to help their grandchildren do actual [jack-o-lantern] decorating." Pumpkin carving and decorating were done inside each classroom, and the finished products were displayed in the hallway near the classroom. Grandparents were invited to select the three "top pumpkins" from each class; these were entered in a schoolwide contest in the gymnasium, where grandparents were invited to vote on the "Greatest Pumpkin" of them all.

■ Students brought in grandparent memorabilia one week before grandparents were scheduled to visit. They created displays with the grandparent's name, and wrote descriptions or slogans for each item. For example, a display of small handpainted china plates included the description, "My Grandmother Patterson painted these China Plates," with the grandchild's name and grade. One teacher says, "Not only were the children proud to see [these displays], our grandparents felt very special that day, too!"

■ Students put on a "Grandparents' Tea" in the afternoon of Grandparents' Day. Invitations to the tea and program were designed and created by students, then mailed out beforehand. Students introduced their grandparents and told something special about them, refreshments were served, and grandparents were taken on a tour of the school building. After the tour, the visiting grandparents shared information about their hobbies and talents, or told the class about their own early school experiences.

■ Students' original poems about grandparents were read over the intercom each day during Grandparents' Week as part of the morning announcements. Students in all classes wrote poems; the best five were selected by committee to be read aloud each morning. Other poems ("Honorable Mention") were mounted and hung in the hallways. Individual students wrote their original poems on scroll paper (rolled up and tied with colorful ribbon) and presented these to their grandparents on Friday of Grandparents' Week.

■ Students and grandparents were paired for pre-Grandparents' Day writing activities. Experiences were shared and questions posed and answered. Finally, each student ended his or her joint correspondence with "Why My Grandparent Is Special." Copies of all correspondence were placed on a large wall chart for visiting grandparents to read.

■ Students in primary grades drew pictures of their grandparents and finished open-ended sentences (such as "A grandmother/grandfather is someone who..." or "If I were a grandmother/grandfather, I'd..."). Students also created a "name poem" with the word *grandparent,* starting each line of the poem (rhymed or not) with *G, R, A, N,* and so on. Sentence-completion pictures were mounted on construction paper and displayed for grandparents to read. Before grandparents left the classroom, these stories were folded in half to make them into a greeting card. Students decorated the outside and presented them to grandparents as a parting gift or mailed the story-cards to grandparents who were unable to visit the classroom.

■ A third-grade teacher received a collection of books about grandparents (provided by the local Retired Teachers Association). After reading and sharing these books, the class decided to host a Grandparents' Book Day. Children invited a grandparent or older friend to come to school to share the day with them. Refreshments were served, and grandparents or guests were invited to tell stories from their own lives. Students took notes in the form of a story web, since they were preparing to "write a book" about the grandparent's or guest's story. The visitors took part in every aspect of the book making, including developing story ideas, sentence structure, spelling, illustrations, and final editing. The art instructor joined the class to demonstrate simple portrait-drawing techniques. Grandparents drew children, and children drew grandparents. These portraits became the cover illustrations for the books students and grandparents had written together.

■ Grandparents from other countries shared stories from their childhoods.

■ Visiting grandparents were presented with a booklet containing quotations about grandparents taken from every student in the classroom, along with a sugar cookie in the shape of the school mascot.

■ Students wrote stories entitled "What Is a Grandparent?" These were placed on the hallway bulletin board for grandparents and others to see, and grandparents were invited to eat lunch with their grandchild on Friday of Grandparents' Week.

■ Students made drawings of their grandparents, and completed the sentence: "Grandparents are . . . ." These drawings and the accompanying sentences were displayed on the bulletin board. Each student introduced his or her own grandparent to the rest of the class and shared something special about the grandparent.

■ Students made stick puppets of themselves and their grandparents. They used these stick puppets to talk about their grandparents in a program prepared for Grandparents' Day.

■ A "Welcome Grandparents" banner was placed in the entryway of one school. Students made posters with statements about grandparents, such as "Grandparents: A Wonderful Image of Our Future" and "Grandparents Are Special People." There posters were illustrated and hung in hallways.

■ Students made original bookmarks for their grandparents and presented them on Grandparents' Day.

■ One school collected favorite recipes from each grandparent prior to Grandparents' Day. These were made into a "Grandparent Cookbook," featuring the grandparent's and child's name below each contributed recipe.

■ A school provided a continental breakfast for visiting grandparents and their grandchildren on Grandparents' Day.

■ Grandparents helped their grandchildren write about a school day or an activity they remembered from when they were their grandchildren's age. These essays were collected into a journal, which was placed in the school library.

■ Each student made and decorated a "Grandparent Coupon Booklet," which entitles the bearer to an afternoon visit, a hug, a read-aloud session, and so on. The coupon booklets were presented to visiting grandparents on Grandparents' Day.

■ Students brought photos of their grandparents and wrote short biographies to accompany these. Pictures and biographies were copied, printed, and bound into a Grandparents' Book for gift giving.

■ A class planned their field trip when grandparents could accompany them to share in the learning experience. Special Grandparent/Grandchild sack lunches were provided.

■ Fourth-graders (who were studying state history) held a State History Trivia Tournament between students and grandparents' during Grandparents' Week. Many students were surprised—not only at how much state and local history their grandparents knew but also at how much of it they had experienced firsthand.

■ In one class, each student and grandparent completed a Life Time Line. The Life Time Line included the dates the student and the grandparent were born, with a line marked in 10-year increments. On the Time Line, each listed important personal events (graduation, marriage, birth of child, etc.), as well as important historical events (presidential elections, wars, inventions, etc.). Students and their grandparents shared their Life Time Lines with the rest of the class.

Chapter 2

Family Trees

Once students have begun to consider themselves part of the history of a group—in this case, the family—many of them may be helped to conceptualize information collected if they can see the information displayed graphically. Graphic organizers are a means of visually organizing information so that students can think about it, make use of it, reorganize it, break it down into its component parts, and have a structure for adding more information as it is discovered. When students develop family trees, they are developing graphic organizers.

Not all family-tree formats require students to include information about both the mother's and the father's biological relatives. Alternate formats can be especially useful in classrooms where students or their families have concerns about sharing or revealing the kinds of facts usually listed on traditional family trees. Levstik and Barton (1997), for example, describe a family tree that requires students to depict facts only about three *generations* of family members, not about biological parents' family members. In this format, students may elect to depict information about a family other than their own, about only their mother's family or only their father's family, or about selected persons from both parents' families who represent various generations. Rather than requiring students to supply traditional information about family lineage, in which each student has two (and only two) parents, the chart allows students considerable choice yet still adheres to the graphic organizer structure for displaying information.

Class Family Tree

To start your students thinking about and visualizing family trees, make a Class Family Tree to decorate the bulletin board. On a lightly colored background, staple a large brown cut-out or torn-paper tree with multiple branches extending to the top of the bulletin board. Have the students bring photos from home showing their families. Place each photo in a zip-type sandwich bag to protect it and to provide a safe area to attach it to the Class Family Tree (staple, pin, or thumbtack the sandwich bag to the bulletin board, not the photo). Each student's photo should occupy a separate branch or limb of the tree.

In the blank bulletin board space around the tree, develop a graph or pictorial illustration showing the number of people in each student's family. For instance, use a broad-tipped marker to write the child's name. Then, draw figures or have the individual child sketch figures on a 3" × 5" or 4" × 6" notecard to represent the number of people in his or her immediate family or household.

Use the newly created bulletin board as a springboard for discussion and activities. Who has the largest family? Who has the smallest? How many students have fewer than three in their family? How many have more than four? What percentage of the boys have families larger than four? What percentage of the girls do? Have students practice interviewing skills by asking one another prepared questions about the family photos.

Counting Ancestors

Are you interested in thematic units or multidisciplinary teaching? Here is an activity that teaches about family history while building and reinforcing math skills. Ask the students, "How many parents do human beings have?" (The biological answer to this question is *two*. Young students who have always lived with only one parent may not comprehend this fact immediately.) Then ask, "So, how many parents did your mother have? Your father? How many grandparents in all is that?" Have students represent this information visually by making a chart on a large sheet of paper (such as that shown in Figure 2.1). Then have the students think of the figures on the chart mathematically, as in 1 + 1 = 2; 2 + 2 = 4; 4 + 4 = 8; 8 + 8 = 16. Ask, "Using this pattern, what is the number of great-great-great-great-grandparents you have?" Let them add the correct number of dots to their charts, then extend this activity with the one that follows.

Find a photograph (check the Sunday newspapers) depicting several generations, as in a baby, a young mother, a grandmother, and great-grandmother. It is preferable to use a photograph with an accompanying reference to each person's age. Enlarge the photo if needed and introduce the word *generation* to your students. Engage the class in a discussion about the memories each person in the photo is likely to have about their own lives. Consider using these activities to help your students visualize the lifespans of successive generations:

■ Students can estimate how old their great-grandparents (or great-great-grandparents) would be if they were alive today. Tell them, "If 25 years represents one generation, how old would your grandparents' parents be? Are your great-grandparents alive? If they are, figure out how old your great-great-grandparents would be if they were alive today."

ME

Father. . Mother

Father's parents   Mother's parents
(My grandparents) . . . . (My grandparents)

Father's parents'   Mother's parents'
parents   parents
(My great-grandparents) . . . . (My great-grandparents)

Father's parents'   Mother's parents'
parent's parents   parent's parents
(My great-great-grandparents) . . . . (My great-great-grandparents)

Figure 2.1 "Counting Grandparents" Chart

■ Discuss the topic of generations: "You represent one generation, your parents represent a second generation, and your grandparents represent a third generation. How many generations do you think can be living at one time? Why?"

■ Ask the children about inviting some older generations to share their experiences with the class: "Do you think older people may have some interesting memories to share with people your age? Shall we ask them to share their memories with us? What topic would you be interested in knowing about that happened 50 years ago?"

■ Trying It Out

Family Tree Fractions

Virginia Thorpe wanted to integrate social studies and math with her school's reading curriculum. She used the story "The Care and Feeding of Your Family Tree" (Eberly, 1986, in Heath Reading's [1989] reading series *Rare as Hen's Teeth*). "The objectives were for learners to apply knowledge of fractions to 'create' fractions representing their personal family trees, and to create visual representations comparing information through lowest common denominators about girls' grandparents versus boys' grandparents," she states.

Several days before introducing the lesson, Virginia asked her students to research their family's data, including the ages of all family members now living, and the ages of deceased family members at the time of their death. On the day of the lesson, Virginia provided a simple circle chart (see Figure 2.2) and asked class members to use the completed chart to create fractions by following these directions:

1. Create a fraction representing your living parents (2/2, 1/2, or 0/2).
2. Create a fraction representing your living grandparents (4/4, 3/4, etc.).
3. Create fractions representing the proportion of girls and boys in the class who have experienced the death of a grandparent.
4. Compare the fractions created above by finding the lowest common denominator (LCD) and making like fractions.

"The students seemed eager to create their fractions and share their findings with classmates," Virginia noted during the activity. "We quickly filled the board with their responses. The fraction representing the number of girls who had lost at least one grandparent was 4/12. The boys' fraction was 6/10. Then, after music class, I asked the class how we would go about comparing our two pieces of information. Had more girls or more boys lost grandparents? The students reviewed the process for

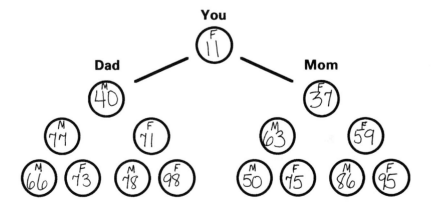

Figure 2.2 Family Tree Circle Chart

comparing unlike fractions. We found the LCD (60) and renamed the fractions: 4/12 = 20/60; 6/10 = 36/60. Therefore, more boys have had a grandparent die."

To end the lesson, Virginia explained that the purpose of the lesson was to give students some practice with fractions in a fun, meaningful way. "Next time I use this activity," Virginia notes, "I will be more clear with directions and thought-provoking questions as we integrate math into the curriculum. Hopefully, we can create some additional relevant fractions. I want to work on rephrasing my questions, such as instead of asking 'How many have had a grandparent die?' I could ask, 'What fraction of students has all four grandparents still living?'"

Grandpa and Me: Charting Family Facts

Michelle Yantz and her third-graders read the book *When I Was Nine* (Stevenson) as they began to talk about generations and grandparents. Michelle wanted her students to compare and contrast their own everyday and leisure activities with those of their grandparents. "I hope" she said, "they will conclude that their grandparents are more like them than they thought." Michelle shared the book by reading it aloud as her students listened for things that are like their own lives and things that are different.

"Then I gave them a paper on which we compared and contrasted the boy in the book with kids today. We started doing the first couple together on the board. The first comparison the students came up with was that they both ride bikes. The first contrast was that we have TV and [the boy in the book] had radio."

The students had 10 minutes to work with a partner and come up with as many comparisons and contrasts as they could, while listing them on the paper as a chart. After this buddy time, they formed groups of four (two buddy groups combined) to share ideas. Then students shared with the large group and discussed what they could learn from this activity. According to Michelle, "The first thing the students said was that grandpa did a lot of the same things they do!" Here are some of the "compare" activities students wrote:

JEREMY

We both do homework.

We both are nine.

We both like to play.

We both have ponds.

We are both boys.

We both have ducks.

We both go to school.

TODD

We both have toys.

We both have math.

We both go on vacations.

We both climb trees.

We both have telephones.

We both have friends.

CHELSEA

We have dogs.

We have hats.

We play baseball.

We have recess.

We both climb trees.

Items from students' "contrast" lists include:

TODD

He rode a horse and I don't.

Our phones are different.

JEREMY

We got skateboards, and he's got a scooter.

We got TV and he's got radio.

This activity was a lead-in to a more extensive family storytelling project.

Michelle suggests that teachers who replicate this activity plan for a large block of time. "We had to go to music right after the story, so when we started to do the [chart] activity, some of them had a hard time remembering the story," she states.

Looking for Your Family Tree

The previous activities are intended to spark students' interest in their own ancestry, so you will want to use that enlivened interest to the best advantage by beginning these activities based on development of family trees or family tree charts.

If your students are unfamiliar with the term *family tree,* you will want to plan some time to teach them about the terminology and its meaning. Also, you may wish to create a class handout to assist students as they begin their research (leave plenty of space for answers!). Start with questions such as these:

■ What is your full legal name (first name, middle name, last name)?

■ What is the date of your birth? Where were you born (city, state, and country)?

■ Who decided what to name you, and why? Are you named after a relative? How are you related to that person? Is he or she still alive?

■ Your last name is your "family name," or surname. What do you know about the origin of your family name? Does it come from some other country? Which one?

■ Long ago, people's family names described what they did, or who their parents were (*Johnson* = John's son; *Brewer* might mean someone in the family was known for his ability to brew good ale). Does your family name have any special meaning? If so, what is it? Does anyone know which ancestor was the first to be known by that name?

■ When people immigrated to the United States from another country, they sometimes changed their names to an easier spelling, or "Anglicized" (made them more English-sounding) their names for business reasons. Has your family name ever been changed? If you do not know, try to find out by asking older family members.

■ What are your parents' full legal names? What is your mother's family name (the one she was born with)? If your mother is married, does she still use her family name? (Many women use their own family name as their middle name after they marry.)

■ If either of your parents have been married more than once, list the names of other husbands/wives.

■ What are the full legal names of each of your parent's parents? Where were they born, and where did they live as they were growing up? If they are alive now, where do they live? If they have remarried, list the name(s) of all husbands/wives that you can.

■ What are the names of your parents' brothers and/or sisters (and their husbands and/or wives)? Where do they live?

■ What are the names of your grandparents' brothers and/or sisters? Do you know the names of their husbands and/or wives? Where do/did they live?

▪ What do you know about the origins of your mother's family name?

▪ Do you have any brothers and/or sisters? What are their full legal names (first, middle, last)? When and where were they born?

▪ Where have you lived during your lifetime? If you have lived in more than one city or state, list all the places you have lived. What schools have you attended? Do you have any special interests? What are they? What do you feel is the most memorable moment of your life so far?

▪ Where did your parents live when they were growing up? If they lived in more than one place, list all of the places where each of them lived.

▪ Where did your parents meet? Find out other important information, such as the date and place of their marriage and their first home.

After they have answered these questions, students are ready to develop their own family tree, using the chart in Figure 2.3. Make two copies of the chart for each student—they will want to do the first in pencil, since "new" information may be forthcoming from various family members. (This activity seems to stimulate response from even the most reticent of family members!)

Extend the search for ancestors by sharing with students resources and methods for uncovering family history facts and documents, as described next in Mystery of the Missing Clue.

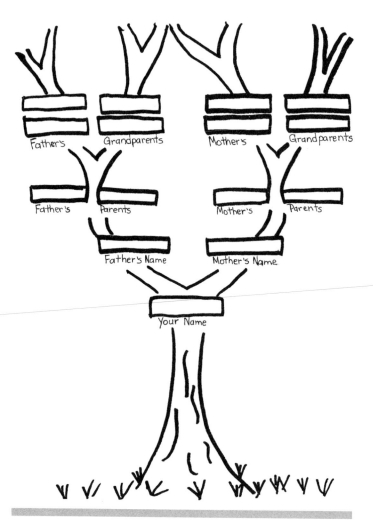

Figure 2.3 Family Tree Chart

Mystery of the Missing Clue

Doing family trees is only the beginning point for students' investigations into their ancestry. By now, the children must have many questions, because the more they find out about their past, the more mysterious it seems!

Digging into one's past is like searching for buried treasure: You can be sure there is something there—you just don't know where to find it! There are many, many people, places, and records of the past that can help, however. It is all in knowing where to start. As the students researched their family's past, they probably noticed that it was easier to find out information from or about one branch of the family than the other. *That* is where to begin the hunt for ancestors.

Genealogy is the study of one's family's roots. Some people spend years, or even lifetimes, researching their roots. Your students are about to learn some of the fundamentals of what can become a fun and exciting hobby. They already have a good start by doing their own family tree and finding out which branch of the family is easier to research. Now you can help them take it a bit further. First, help the children set an achievable goal. "Look at your family tree," You might say. "Is there *one* piece of information you still don't know? Choose just one name, date, or place blank that you'd like to complete."

INTERNET SEARCHES

Discuss with the students how, if just one of their relatives has set up a family tree website on the Internet, the answers to the student's questions may be found there. Even if they cannot find their family names in a website search, they may be able to access information on the web that will shorten their search. Students with Spanish or Puerto Rican surnames, for example, can try one of the websites listed in the Appendix of this book. Even an Appalachian mountain family website exists. Stress to your students that they may ask a librarian, parent, or any adult for help in the web search.

PUBLIC LIBRARIES

If the main public library in your town has genealogy records, that is the best place to begin. Suggest to the students that they take the information they have to the library, but that they think about their questions before they ask the librarian for assistance. Many public libraries have collections of books, documents (such as the church record shown in Figure 2.4), and newspaper clippings about people who lived in the town long ago. Of course, this suggestion primarily benefits the child whose ancestor lived in the same town as the child. Regardless, patience is essential—not every ancestor hunt is this easy!

Maybe a newspaper or book of records from another city or state will help some with their search. The local librarian may be able to borrow such materials from another library in another state. Or, students could write to the public library near where their ancestors lived and request information. (Look for the addresses of other libraries in the Reference Section of your own public library, in the *American Library Directory,* published by R. R. Bowker.)

If a student needs to write a letter to another library, it might look something like this:

> I am researching my family's history, and I need to find out where my great-grandfather, William Edward Kendall, was born. I know that his date of birth is 1908, and that he lived in Madison County during the early 1900s. He married Hannah Louise Merchant in 1932. Do you have any information you could send me on his place of birth?

Be certain the child includes a self-addressed stamped envelope with his or her letter, to make it easier for the librarian to send any information.

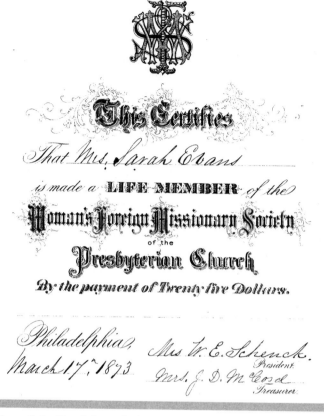

Figure 2.4 Church Record of Ancestory

CENSUS RECORDS

A census is a count of the people who live in an area. A state census would tell how many people lived in that state at the time, and a national census would tell how many people lived in the United States during that year. Every 10 years, a federal census is taken to help decide how many representatives for the United States Congress each state is allowed. There has been a census every 10 years since 1790.

More information is included in a census than just how many people live in an area. Census takers, for example, list the names, ages, and relationships of all persons living in a household, as well as the county of residence. If a student can match an ancestor's first and last names with a place of residence and an approximate decade (such as 1920–1930), a child might be able to discover more information—the names and ages of brothers and/or sisters, or a husband's or wive's full name, for example.

Many public libraries have copies of census records on microfilm, which (with the help of a librarian) students will be able to examine. Remind your students to think about their questions before they go to the library, and to take all information they already have about that ancestor with them before they begin their search.

If an ancestor lived at a time when census records are unavailable or considered "confidential," a person can still request a copy of a specific document related to his or her own family from:

Bureau of the Census Office
U.S. Department of Commerce
Pittsburgh, KS 66762

If the ancestor the child is inquiring about is alive, the child must have that person request the record. If the ancestor is deceased, the child must send a copy of that ancestor's death certificate with his or her request. If a state census exists for the period being researched, the information contained in that census may be helpful. Ask the public librarian if a state census is available. As a matter of fact, *whatever* the ancestor-related questions are, ask the librarian! They often think of unusual places to look for genealogical information.

OTHER PLACES TO LOOK

If your students tried all the suggestions here, and *still* do not have the answer to their ancestor question, don't despair. There are more places they can write to for information. If students write to any of the agencies listed here, be sure they ask for the proper forms needed to process their requests, and remind them to include a self-addressed stamped envelope. The following agency has the largest collection of genealogical records in the United States:

Genealogical Society of Utah
50 East North Temple Street
Salt Lake City, UT 84150

The following library contains the second largest library genealogical collection in the country:

Allen County Public Library
Genealogy Department
900 Webster
Fort Wayne, IN 46802

Also, *The Directory of Historical Societies and Agencies in the United States and Canada,* published by the American Association for State and Local History, Nashville, Tennessee, may be able to help you with names and addresses of genealogical societies in areas of the country.

If students know that their ancestor served in a branch of the military during World War I, World War II, the Korean War, the Vietnam War, or the Gulf War—especially if they know which branch (Army, Navy, etc.) and the approximate date—tell them to write to:

National Military Personnel Records Center
9700 Page Blvd.
St. Louis, MO 63132

If the ancestor served in a war that occurred before any of these wars, students may write to:

National Archives
Central Reference Division
General Services Administration
Washington, DC 20408

If their ancestor was an immigrant who arrived in America by ship between the years 1820 and 1945, suggest the student write to the National Archives. For ancestors who arrived before 1820, there may be records at the actual port of entry, or in the state archives for that state. Here are some books that may help your students begin their search for an ancestor who immigrated:

Passenger and Immigration List Index: A Guide to Published Arrival Records, by
   P. W. Filby
A Bibliography of Ship Passenger Lists, 1583–1825, by H. Lancour

If your public library does not have these books, ask the librarian to borrow them from another library.

If none of these sources contains the information your students need, try writing to a museum with a collection of ship's logs. The museum staff will be better able to help if the name of the ship the ancestor arrived on is known. The names and addresses of museums that have ship's logs collections can be found in the Appendix at the end of this book.

■ Trying It Out

Family Trees

Cindy Stiver wanted her second-graders to have an understanding of what constitutes a family. She read aloud *Amelia Bedelia's Family Album* (Parish, 1988) and *Me and My Family Tree* (Showers, 1978) to students. After the books had been shared, Cindy asked students to brainstorm a list of family terms they had learned from these stories, and to discuss how family members help one another and depend on one another. Then she introduced the concept of family trees, showing students a large poster depicting her own family tree, and discussed each "branch" and what it means. The children took home a family-tree form to be filled out with the help of a parent and, when these had been returned, the class as a whole graphed the number of family members in each child's family. In this way, the children could begin to see diversity within the concept of "family" within their own classroom setting.

What's in a Name?: Intermediate

Deborah Hudson wanted her sixth-graders to have a strong sense of their background. "I wanted them to seek answers from family members so they have a better idea of their origin," she says. "I started the lesson off by asking the students to think about their names." Deborah had brought in a paperback book on choosing names for babies, which had lists of names for boys and girls and their meanings. The students used this book to look up their own names.

"Does anyone know what his or her name means? How did you get your name?" she asked the students. Deborah acknowledged, "There's no special story of how I got my name, so I told them the story of how my husband and his brothers got their names. We had a super discussion on name meanings and wonderful stories on how a few of them got their names. The students could not wait to get home to find out whether there was a story behind their own name. . . . One student was so anxious to get started that he asked to use the payphone to call his mom!"

Once she had the students' attention and interest, Deborah proceeded to talk about family trees, and how sometimes people get their names by being named after relatives, such as a great-grandfather or an aunt. "I put an example of a family tree on the overhead projector, and passed out blank paper copies to every student. They were to complete the family trees at home, with the help of family members. On the back of the family-tree form was a worksheet where they could indicate the origin and meaning of their names (and related stories behind their names, if there are any). I gave the students several days to complete these two assignments and bring them back to class."

Not all students completed both forms, but Deborah found that even those few who never seem to return their homework had something to contribute to the discussion that developed from this assignment. "Students really love to talk about themselves and their families—even sixth-graders," she adds. "They are also eager to learn more about their families and themselves, if given the opportunity."

Deborah created a bulletin board display highlighting her students' artistic depictions of their own families. Following their discussion of family tree charts completed at home, and stories surrounding how they got their names, students were invited to draw their families. Resulting artwork was mounted on colorful construction paper and displayed on the bulletin board. Students also had a chance to give a brief oral description detailing each family member's characteristics.

Later, Deborah created another bulletin board display of her students' homes. This time, students were asked to stuff brown paper lunch bags with newspaper and fold them across the top. A piece of construction paper folded into a roof shape is stapled to the top of the bag. Students use colored paper and "found" materials to decorate the exterior of their houses. "Try to make them look as much like your house as possible," she told them. When students finished decorating their houses, these were tacked to the bulletin board and "connected" by a curving "road" made of brown butcher paper. Each student labeled his or her house with name and address, if desired.

When she does this project with another group of students, Deborah says she "will try to find ways for the students who do not have much family support to find a way to discover this information and be proud of who they are." Ideas for doing this include: giving some students extra time to complete the assignment, sending preliminary letters home to secure parental cooperation, and suggesting that students consult extended family members when possible. "Some students were disappointed when they were unable to fill in their entire family tree."

What's in a Name?: Primary

Cindy Stiver's second-graders took a different slant on the "What's in a Name?" activity. Cindy brought in Lauski's (1991) *The Best Baby Name Book in the Whole World* and had each student look in the book to find out what his or her name means and its origin. She gave students a worksheet called "My Name" and had them write the meaning of their names on the sheet. They took the worksheet home, where it was necessary to interview their parents to complete the remaining information. As the children brought the completed "My Name" worksheet back to school, Cindy gave them a piece of posterboard and instructed them to use classroom stencils to print their names "in big letters." The children looked through magazines to find illustrations depicting the meaning of their names, cut these out and glued them to the posterboard, and displayed them in the hallway.

As an extension to this activity, Cindy taught her students how to do acrostic poems by writing their names vertically on a large sheet of paper and composing a phrase about themselves that begins with each letter of their names.

At My House . . .

After Cindy Stiver read *A House Is a House for Me* (Hoberman, 1982) to her second-graders, they created models of their homes. "First," Cindy says, "they brainstormed the kinds of dwellings people can live in. Then we listed these ideas on a big house shape made from bulletin board paper." To further stimulate interest in homes as dwelling places for families, Cindy had her students take home a "House Scavenger Hunt," which listed items usually found in homes (e.g., refrigerator, table, TV, lamp, chair, etc.) and asked students to find and count the numbers of these items in their houses. "They tallied the numbers, and brought them back to school. Then we compared numbers of items within groups, and created a graph to represent the total numbers of items for the entire class."

The next day at milk break, Cindy was ready to help her students build models of their own homes. As she passed out full cartons of milk ("Don't open these," she cautioned), Cindy placed cans of ready-made cake frosting, graham crackers, and other edible decorations on tables for each group. Students used plastic knives to "frost" their milk cartons, broke the crackers into appropriate shapes for roofs, doors, windows, and other decorations, and "built" their house. The students had 10 minutes to complete their creations, then they held them up and told other class members about their homes. When everyone was done, the students drank their milk and ate the outside of their houses!

Family Roles

Barb wanted her second-graders to understand and explore the make-up of their immediate and extended families. She began by asking the students to talk about their grandparents. The children responded eagerly. Many of them had fond memories of staying overnight or several days with their grandparents. "They help with homework, and they read you books," Aaron suggested. "We go on walks, and we buy stuff together. They even taught me how to swim!" Andrew contributed. And Summer remembered, "He taught me how to play cards, and he tells me stories."

This discussion was a lead-in to Cynthia Rylant's book *When I Was Young in the Mountains* (1982). Barb showed the cover of the book and commented on the fact that it received an award for its pictures. Then she told the class that the story "is about some memories that someone had about growing up with their grandparents." During the story, Barb and the children talked about how it feels to do things with your grandparents, such as those seen in the book illustrations, which show a child and grandparent sitting out on the porch, snapping beans. The children concluded that grandparents make them feel secure, loved, and cared about. Barb and the children discussed the things in the story that show what children can learn from grandparents: how to snap beans, read, sharpen a pencil with a knife, pick berries, listen carefully, and so on. They also discuss what things children can help their grandparents with, such as reading when their eyes are poor, running errands, picking things up from the ground for them, and helping them walk down steps.

After reading the book, Barb led her students in another discussion. She says, "We then discussed the ways that all people in their family can teach the others new things and help each other out in different ways. (The kids found out that most parents don't have as much time to spend with them as grandparents do.) We listed these things on a large chart with pictures of children, parents, and older relatives. We filled the chart quickly and easily."

Following the chart activity, Barb had her students move into smaller groups and create a collage of all the different age groups of people that could add something to the family unit. The students' collages, along with family photos brought in by parents, were used to make a bulletin board about how families work together.

Barb feels that an important benefit of this experience is that she learned something about the community her students live in, as well as specific things about each of their families. "I learned that most of the children in my room have families that are close," she says. "The community that I teach in is small and close. Their families centered mainly around the parents and older members of the family." It surprised her to learn that, prior to this experience, her second-graders did not visualize themselves as contributing members of their families. "Many of the children did not feel that they could contribute within their families. [Through discussion about family roles, however,] the children did become aware of everyone's role within their family. Most had very good memories of grandparents, but some did not know theirs very well because of distance."

For teachers who replicate her collage activity, Barb recommends, "Split the groups up a little smaller so each child can add more to the picture, and to cut down on noise and confusion." She further recommends that teachers be familiar with Rylant's book before sharing it with their students, especially the dialogue. "I would spend more time on the culture and dialect shown in the book," she admits. "The kids [who live in the midwest, and are unfamiliar with mountains] seem to be very interested in the way the people talk and what they wear. Next time, I might even find someone with a southern accent to come in and read the book and tell about how they grew up. A family interview would also fit in well. Family members could be asked how they believe they help the family to function. They could talk about the jobs they do now [for the family] and the jobs they had when they were young children growing up in their own family."

Family Tree Graphs

Dawn Hamlin wanted her kindergartners to learn more about their families—who their family members are, and the special relationships they have with members of their families. She started the lesson by having students brainstorm as many family members as they could (e.g., mother, father, brother, sister, aunt, uncle, grandmother, grandfather, and cousin). As students brainstormed, Dawn made a list on the board.

They reviewed their list before beginning the next activity, which was the making of family trees.

Students took home a form intended to help them and their parents cooperatively complete a simple family tree. When these were returned to class, the students had a discussion about the size of families—the fact that some people's families have more members than others—as they looked at each student's family tree chart. Dawn led them in a graphing exercise showing the number of people in each family for the class. The children drew a stick figure for each member of their families. Some wanted to include grandparents and aunts and uncles, but, because of time constraints, Dawn decided to limit the graph to those family members who live in the same house.

Then Dawn commenced a series of lessons focusing on one member of the family at a time, using Mercer Mayer's books *Just Me and My Mom, Just Grandma and Me, Just Me and My Little Brother,* and others. Since her school had access to the CD-ROM for *Just Grandma and Me,* students explored this topic using the computer. Each student was invited to bring in something special representing the family member being studied on particular days, such as a photo, a special gift from that family member, a letter or postcard, and so on. On the first day, one girl proudly displayed her mom's shot-glass collection. Another mother permitted her daughter to bring her Precious Moments collection to school.

After introducing the topic, Dawn placed her students into small groups, where individual students discussed with others the things that they do as a whole family and the things that they do with the particular family member being studied. Each student then drew a picture and wrote (with assistance) a brief description of something special that he or she does with that particular family member alone. After Dawn and her students completed this series of lessons on individual family members, the students' drawings and text were collected into a big book for the whole class to enjoy again and again.

Dawn readily admits that the family tree activity can be "sticky." "I made some mistakes that need to be corrected," she says. "The family tree that I used did not leave spaces for stepfamilies. These are an important part of many families, and young children want to include them." Being close to her own family, Dawn was also surprised to learn "how many students did not know the names of their parents and grandparents. Some of them also did not know which grandparents belonged to their moms and which belonged to their dads. I intended for students to do the family tree at school [at first], but it turned out that they had to take it home and have someone help them fill it in." These kindergarten students learned much of the information required to pass the proficiency test to be promoted to first grade through this series of experiences.

Dawn discovered many things about her students' lifestyles, and how those lifestyles differ from her own and what she had come to expect persons in her community to do. "I also did not anticipate that several of the students have no contact with their grandparents. Some of the students have grandparents that live very far away, but they still talk to them and receive holiday gifts. . . . But some could not recall having ever met or talked to their grandparents. When we did the [lessons] for grandparents, these students had the option of doing it for a special older person that they know, an aunt or uncle or family friend."

Some aspects of this project were difficult for Dawn, as well as for her students. She reflects on these experiences, and what they mean in terms of using these activities again. "I had one girl whose father is in the service and he had just recently been transferred out [to an uprising in the Middle East]. She cried when we were working on the section about dads. The other kids were very good about it and tried to help her feel better. . . . At first, I wondered if I would ever do this type of a project again [in kindergarten]. . . . But the more I thought about it, I realized that that is the very reason for doing it. The family structures have changed so much recently and these kids haven't been able to keep up with it. I think it really helped the students to examine the relationships in their families."

Other suggestions arising from Dawn's experiences include sending a letter home explaining the series of lessons on individual family members and listing possible examples of objects students might bring to class a week to several days before the series of lessons actually begins, and allowing students to graph immediate family members not living with them to allow for separated parents and/or stepfamilies. Finally, since the book *Just Grandma and Me* is available on CD-ROM, teachers with reluctant readers may find the CD-ROM format serves as an extra motivation for these students.

Family Tree Project

Sandi Herman teaches fourth grade at a parochial school. She decided to have her students do family trees to help them "see their relationships to the generations before them; learn the names of their great-grandparents, and create a dialogue between parents and students about their families." The Family Tree project was assigned as a culminating activity to the Family Scrapbook project (see page 60) because, as Sandi says, "Many children have asked about and become interested in their earlier generations through the Family Scrapbook project."

Sandi's students began by defining a family tree, using what they knew about Abraham's genealogy (from the Bible). They created a family tree for Abraham on the board. Then they discussed how the concept of family trees might have originated, and how they could develop a family tree for their own families. "What information will we need?" they wondered, and listed as many items as they could. Finally, each student drafted an initial family tree for his or her family, based on information already known. The students took these drafts home to correct, clarify, and add to them with the help of parents and other relatives. Completed family trees would become a part of their now ongoing Family Scrapbook.

Sandi says of the Family Tree activity: "For the most part, the class was enthusiastic and I found that they knew a great deal about genealogies . . . and had so many ideas for how to find information that they needed (other than just asking their parents). Some of the students really got into the genealogies in the Bible, and had a hard time moving on [to their own]. My worksheet needed more spaces for great-grandparents, and there was no way to indicate whether a great-grandparent was maternal or paternal [on the original worksheet]. I had to be sensitive to several family situations. . . . One boy just did his dad's side of the family."

When she uses this activity with her students next year, Sandi says several changes could improve implementation. For example, doing family trees early in the Family Scrapbook project might prompt memories needed for family stories and photographs. Sandi also would have a certain parent share the work he has done on his family's genealogy, since he could answer procedural questions the students might have. Her send-home worksheet already has been improved, but she would like to design it in such a way that it looks like a tree with branches for each side of the family.

Chapter 3

Family Artifacts

Historical artifacts, especially those with personal significance, become powerful motivators in the hands of capable teachers. These teachers know how to use artifacts and memorabilia to their greatest advantage as learning aids. Recommendations from national social studies standards and recent literature on the topic of artifact use suggest that when children are "active constructors, not passive receivers, of meaning," they are motivated to learn new information and build on what is known. They must be given opportunities to become physically involved through hands-on experiences, to ask questions, and to talk about what they are experiencing (Field, Labbo, Wilhelm, & Garrett, 1996; Oldfather, 1994; Perkins, 1994; Brooks & Brooks, 1993).

What are artifacts? Objects or realia from the material, educational, or artistic culture of a society can be considered artifacts, including such things as food, clothing and accessories, tools, weapons, items related to lodging and shelter, transportation, household goods, personal possessions, items representing play and recreation, folk arts, fine arts, and anything related to everyday life. Paper artifacts, while not as enduring as those made of many other materials, can yield a wealth of information about everyday life in a particular era. Items such as wedding invitations, food labels, postcards, ticket stubs, deeds, certificates, and stationery all invite students to explore "rescued fragments of history" (Rickards, 1988).

In addition to providing primary source information, the use of artifacts in the elementary classroom can help encourage the habits of mind that lead to a love of learning and intellectual inquiry (Martinello & Cook, 1994, p. 26). These habits of mind include providing a mental set for learning, attending, and persevering; thinking flexibly and fluently; following hunches; creating metaphors; taking risks; working collaboratively; and finding elegant solutions (Field et al., 1996). Instructional approaches that lead to the development of these habits encourage children to consider the practical uses and personal values associated with a particular artifact, to consider these within the context of the object's original setting, to set the stage for making cross-cultural comparisons for similar artifacts, and to explore how these objects have changed over time.

Until quite recently, artifacts were considered more appropriate for museum or anthropological study than for lessons for young children. The current emphasis on experiential, hands-on learning and exploration through inquiry has inspired a number of teachers to look for new and interesting ways to use artifacts in the classroom. The next several activities provide some appropriate examples of artifact use.

Grandma's Attic Trunk

Remember grandma's attic—and the curious treasures found there? This activity capitalizes on the fascination of heirlooms and memorabilia, enticing students to indulge their curiosity and imagination, encouraging them to learn about their own recent family history. And it all begins with a mysterious trunk.

PREPARING THE TRUNK

Collect photographs, pictures, old newspapers, postcards and greeting cards, magazine and/or newspaper clippings, school yearbooks, catalogs, family trees (often found in family Bibles), marriage and birth certificates, and anything else small and reminiscent of family life, and place these items in an old (preferably battered) trunk or large suitcase. Ask neighbors and relatives to contribute to the collection, or haunt flea markets and antique malls for inexpensive (and anonymous) samples. Wrap some of the items lovingly in fabric or doilies (as grandmother might have done). Place all of the items in the trunk or suitcase, and close or lock it tight. Take the trunk to class and display it on a table.

TEACHING PLAN

The presence of the trunk should engender some curiosity. What is it? Why is it here? What could be inside? Who is it for? Where did it come from? Ignore students' questions at first, heightening the suspense. At some point during the day, "give in" to the mystery of the trunk by postponing any immediate plans and devoting some time to talking about the trunk and its contents. You might begin with questions such as these:

"What do you think is in the trunk?" (Allow time for numerous responses.)

"Why do you want to know what's in this trunk?" (Accept any answer, then focus students' attention with the next question.)

"Why is somebody else's 'junk' of interest to us? Are you saying we can learn something from what other people left behind?"

Provide time for a brief discussion on this topic, remembering to ask thoughtful questions rather than provide specific information. Finally, share this bit of information with the students:

> We are a part of history. History is not made by "other people"; it's made by people like us. All history starts with families and communities. You and your family live and work in a community. Your parents and grandparents and great-grandparents all lived and worked in a community. Perhaps they ran a blacksmith shop, or grew corn and took it to the gristmill to be ground, or built the local schoolhouse or church. They were the foundation of the America we know and live in today. They made history. If we are lucky, they kept records of their lives, so we could learn about what it was like to live then.
>
> I call this "Grandma's Attic Trunk." The things in Grandma's trunk might have been put there by your grandma or your great-grandparents. They show what it was like to live in this community a few decades ago, when your parents' parents were growing up.
>
> An attic is the space between the ceiling of a house and its roof. Not everybody has a space like that where they can store things—some people keep things like this in their basement or a spare room or a closet. But Grandma's trunk was kept in the attic, and she stored special papers and heirlooms there. Let's see what's in Grandma's Attic Trunk.

Show students the items in the trunk, and talk about how these items can help them learn about life from that time period. Now you are ready to begin the unit of study.

UNIT DEVELOPMENT

The unit will last between six and nine weeks, making it an ideal project for a complete grading period. Ask students to bring in family objects and memorabilia to display and discuss. (Reproduce the form shown below to help students structure their presentations.) Make maps to depict the geographic origins of articles brought to class. Display the items (if possible), reports, and maps in the classroom.

Have the students pinpoint the geographic location of specific objects on a large world map hanging in the classroom. Use colored pins to mark the spot. Attach yarn or string to the pin and print the student's name on a small piece of paper at the other end of the yarn or string. Staple or tape the identifying piece of paper to the bulletin board or wall beside the world map.

■ Trying It Out

Grandma Stiver

Cindy Stiver wanted to try the Grandma's Attic Trunk activity with her second-grade class. "My objective," she says, "was to get the children to think about the importance of learning about their family history."

Cindy had inherited an old cedar chest from her grandmother, which she used at home for linen storage. One weekend, Cindy took the linens out of her cedar chest and filled it with as much family memorabilia as she could find: a beaver coat

FAMILY ARTIFACT REPORT

Name _____ Date _____

Name (or description) of historical article found:

Who owned the article?

What historical period is the article from (for example: the 1920s)?

What do you know about the life and times of the person who owned this article?

Which well-known people also lived during this time period?

What famous events occurred during the same period?

What other interesting or significant information can you provide about this article and/or the time period in which it was used?

from the 1950s, postcards, an autographed softball and trophies, her own wedding cake topper, her first stuffed animal, her baby album and first pair of baby shoes, an article of clothing brought from Vietnam by her father, wedding pictures of various family members, graduation invitations and cards, a college sweatshirt, her own high school and college diplomas, a family Bible, and school yearbooks. Then, with the help of her husband, Cindy took the chest and a rocking chair to her classroom over the weekend.

"When my students arrived [on Monday morning], they were welcomed by Grandma Stiver," she recalls. "I was dressed in an old dress with an apron, a gray wig, and old glasses." A majority of her students didn't even recognize her! They had lots of questions: Who was she supposed to be? Why was she dressed like that? What was the trunk for? Cindy told them only that she was "Grandma Stiver for the day" and that they would have all their questions answered later.

"They crowded around the chest and sat in the rocking chair," she remembers. Some students even went out to bring in children from other classes to "meet Grandma Stiver." After the first school bell rang, Cindy called her students to order and asked them to gather around her and the cedar chest. "I started off by reading a silly book called *I Unpacked My Grandmother's Trunk* [Hoguet, 1983]. Some of the things in the trunk [in the story] were a bear, a dinosaur, a snowman. . . . I asked if all of the twenty-six things listed in the book could be packed in a trunk." The children all laughed and said, "No!" Cindy asked them what things *could* be packed in a trunk. A discussion ensued in which Cindy and the children talked about trunks, souvenirs, attics, and family history. When Cindy asked the second-graders what the word *history* means, their response was, "Stuff that happened a long time ago." Cindy told them they could learn a great deal about their own family's history by looking through old pictures, newspaper clippings, and family Bibles.

"I slowly opened the chest," she says. "No one could see in it. One at a time, each child came up and peeked in." As the children "peeked" at Cindy's family memorabilia, each one was allowed to choose one item to show the rest of the class. "It was interesting to see the expressions on their faces when they finally got to look in [the chest]," Cindy states. "One little boy came up, peeked in and said, 'Oh my goodness. Look at all this cool stuff!'" As each student selected an item to show his or her classmates, they had to try to predict something about Grandma Stiver. They also had to tell why they thought "Grandma" had decided to keep that particular item for a long time. "By the things that I packed," Cindy says, "they could tell that I was married and the date I married. They learned that I loved to play softball, and my team won lots of championships. They discovered who my friends were in high school and college. They also decided I had traveled all over the U.S. and to three other countries."

When the students had examined all of the items in Grandma Stiver's trunk, they concluded that if the pictures had been dated and had the names of the people pictured on the backs, it would be easier to find out more information about the special people in Grandma Stiver's life. They also decided that by examining objects saved by family members, they could find out what jobs and hobbies these family members had valued in the past.

After everyone had spent an additional 15 minutes rummaging in the trunk and trying on the beaver coat, Cindy gave them a homework assignment: For a family project, students were to bring in a "trunk" of their own, made from a shoe box or other small box, with at least 10 items in it related to their family's history. "I sent a letter home to parents explaining that we were studying family history, and that we would like them to become involved." Students and parents had one week to work on their "trunks" before bringing them to class.

The students brought their collections in shoe boxes, picnic baskets, paper bags, and large cardboard boxes. One student made a treasure chest from materials valued at over $60 (with the help of his father) to hold his collection. "The kids were so excited to tell the stories behind their goodies," Cindy says, "and they were eager to hear the other kids talk, too." All students wrote about the contents of their "trunks" in class; these descriptions became part of their display.

CONTENTS OF JON'S TRUNK

Magnetic match-up game

Magazine article, "Sunday's Child"

Recipe for macaroni and cheese

Pictures of Jon's family, Scout the dog, Jon and Heather fishing, Brad and Scout, the final adoption celebration, Jon and cousin Aaron, Jon and Heather in costume, and Jon and Brad making Halloween cookies

CONTENTS OF SARA'S TRUNK

Family pictures

Friends' pictures

1st-grade awards

Wedding bouquet from parents' wedding

Newspaper article

Earrings and necklace

Stuffed tiger

Toy dolphin

Grandpa's hat

Postcards and pictures from family trips

"Grandma's Attic Trunk got the children thinking about and interested in their family history," Cindy concludes. "Their excitement was one of the best parts of this little unit. I will do this worthwhile activity again next year!"

Family Heirlooms

Read *The Patchwork Quilt* (Dial, 1985) by Valerie Flournoy. Talk about family heirlooms that have sentimental value, but not necessarily monetary value. Ask students (or their parents) to bring a family heirloom to class. Discuss each item's sentimental value to the family, and how it is similar to the patchwork quilt in the story. Make a classroom quilt by having each student bring in a precut piece of fabric. You may want to use "liquid embroidery" markers on plain colored fabric for students to draw an image that represents themselves and their contributions to the school and the classroom. The quilt will then become a "class heirloom."

■ Trying It Out

My Family Treasure

Susan Livensparger introduced her second-graders to the concept of family heirlooms by reading the book *Song and Dance Man* (Ackerman, 1988), which tells the story of grandpa's days as a vaudeville dancer. When the children visit their grandpa, they can always count on his taking them up to the attic, where he digs in an old suitcase containing his old top hat and cane used for dancing. These, and other items saved from his vaudeville days, are his "treasures." Susan wanted her students to explore the "treasures" that exist in their own homes and memories, so after reading *Song and Dance Man,* she displayed an old suitcase containing some of her own family treasures. Susan states, "The children listened very quietly to *Song and Dance Man.* They wanted to share their experiences about grandparents. I had brought one of my own family heirlooms to school—an old silver soup ladle. After reading the book, I sat with the children around me as I usually do and, holding the silver ladle lovingly to my chest, I said, 'This is my treasure. . . .' I paused to make sure I had everyone's attention. Then, 'This silver spoon was given to me by my mother, who got it from her mother, who got it from *her* mother. This is my treasure because it has been in my family for a long, long time. My great-grandmother used this silver spoon to dip homemade soup out of a big pot. It's called a *ladle,* and it's made out of real silver.' I held the ladle toward the children, saying, 'My treasure is very, very old. I love it and someday I'll give it to my daughter or daughter-in-law. I want to take very good care of it and make sure it lasts a long, long time.'"

Having gained her students' attention, Susan shared other family treasures from the old suitcase: an egg beater, ice tongs, and her own baby picture. "The students were very curious about my treasures. They wanted to touch them. So we passed most of them around," says Susan. "The egg beater and ice tongs were a big hit. They wanted to try both!"

The sharing of treasures from the suitcase, and the family stories behind them, led to students' sharing their own family's stories. But part of what Susan wanted her students to learn involved respect for treasures from the past, especially those in museum exhibits. She admits, "I didn't pass my baby picture around because I said it was my mom's treasure and she wouldn't like it. They accepted that. We discussed not touching things in a museum. We just didn't have enough time to share all their stories! So I made the assignment to bring a treasure from home and two pictures that represent their history. They had so much to say I could hardly get down the hall to get them to lunch!"

After lunch, Susan's students were still interested in the contents of her old suitcase, so she arranged an exhibit on her desk that could be viewed throughout the afternoon. The children left school in a spirit of excitement, and returned the next day with a variety of "treasures." Susan planned for them to write about their treasures after finishing their reading class. "They could hardly do reading because they were concerned with their treasures," she recalls. The students were instructed to write one description of each treasure they brought, using Who, What, Where, When, Why, and How. Cherron's description is shown in Figure 3.1; descriptions written by others follow:

> "My baseball card is special to me because it is a Frank Thomas runs batted in card. I got it three days ago. I keep it in a book so it doesn't get bent. Becaus it is worth at least a doller." (Nate)
>
> Desiree wrote, "My treasure is a seal. I had it for a long time. I was in texes win I got it. My dad got it for me. He said win I hug it he would feel it. Win I am far away. I love it very much." (Desiree)

"We are going to make a museum to show off our treasures," Susan told the children after they had displayed and talked about their special objects during sharing time. The museum exhibits were set up on their desks, including baby pictures and recent pictures, family and personal treasures, and the descriptions each student wrote. They talked again about how not touching museum treasures would help them remain intact for others to enjoy. According to Susan, "We all wandered around—no complaints, just interested talk!" They planned to spend more time shar-

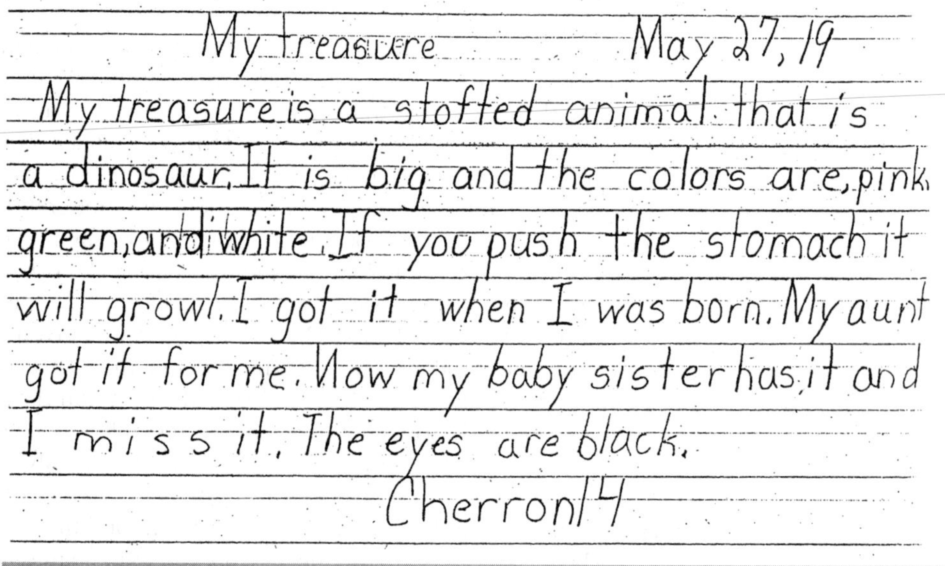

My treasure   May 27, 19
My treasure is a stoffed animal that is
a dinosaur. It is big and the colors are, pink,
green, and white. If you push the stomach it
will growl. I got it when I was born. My aunt
got it for me. Now my baby sister has, it and
I miss it. The eyes are black.
                    Cherron/4

Figure 3.1 "My Treasure"

ing and viewing exhibits the following day. To Susan's surprise and great pleasure, the children suggested they be allowed to represent their exhibits on videotape. She got out the camcorder and taped them, then they invited another class in to view their exhibits.

Susan's students learned that heirlooms have personal appeal and are associated with emotional attachment. They were exposed to the diversity of treasures, or heirlooms, present in their own classroom, and, when their classmates from another class visited, they learned of even more diversity (and that beauty is often in the eye of the beholder). The students who visited the "museum" were inspired to do their own "treasure" project, and talked of their visit so much that Susan's students were asked to leave their museum exhibits in place for one more day so that the two other second-grade classrooms might visit also.

Susan's suggestion for teachers who wish to replicate her heirloom project involves assisting children with writing their descriptions (many of her students were low-achieving second-graders; teachers who want to do this project with beginning first-graders or even kindergartners should utilize aides and/or parent volunteers). "I learned some new ideas about where I want children to go as far as their values concerning their own history," she states. In the past, Susan and her students had done time lines as a way to bring history to life, but "I loved the curiosity and interest that sharing family artifacts garnered," she admits. "I learned that these ideas could make a whole semester or year of excitement for students.... This project lends itself to subjects all across the curriculum."

Artifact Logs

Karen Jorgensen and James Venable (1993, pp. 39–41) planned mini-lessons based on artifact collections organized on tables throughout the classroom. "I ask students to discuss what they know [about a topic] and set up artifact centers around the room," Karen says. She encourages students to talk about the artifacts so that they exchange ideas and theories in conversations with one another as they move about the room. "I usually ask students to write what they know...in a history response log," she notes.

"We introduced the logs the first year [artifact centers were used], thinking that they would provide a convenient place for children to write down the information gathered from the centers and to express their reactions."

While some students thoroughly enjoyed expressing their thoughts and theories in the logs, "writing profusely, carrying them from center to center, and referring to their collected notes whenever they wrote a story or an informational piece," other students disliked the process and neglected their logs days on end. The second year the logs were used, teachers were prepared with a somewhat more structured log writing process.

Before students investigated a set of Native American artifacts, for example, they were asked to write down what they knew and what they wanted to know about the tribe. These log entries became the basis for a class discussion, and the entries and questions posed helped both teachers understand that students harbored embedded stereotypes about Native Americans. Most students knew only what they had seen on television.

Karen and James talked about how they could help their students see the Ohlone tribe as a rich and distinct culture, rather than as a media-stereotyped image. They reorganized their artifact centers to show (1) the kinds of indigenous plants, nuts, seeds, and shells tribe members used for medicine, personal hygiene, and cooking; (2) animal skins from animals the Ohlones might have trapped or hunted and used for many things; (3) games and other forms of entertainment; (4) utensils used for cooking; and (5) a collection of Ohlone myths on audiotape for students to listen to.

Karen recalls, "The students examined and discussed the artifacts with each other for five days. We looked and listened as they tinkered with and talked about the various objects. We also captured student talk by putting a tape recorder at one of the centers. We knew that if we stood nearby, they would say what they thought we wanted to hear. . . . I sensed they often forgot about it and talked to each other as if we were not there."

Karen then describes a portion of one of the tapes in which a conversation ensues among Christina, Nicole, and Victoria as they examine toys and games used by Ohlones. Christina and Victoria make predictions about the artifacts and their usefulness to Ohlones; Nicole confirms these predictions by repeating them and then making connections between the artifacts and her own life. The three students begin to role-play to discover and verify the toy's function.

Students' artifact log entries became much more thoughtful and analytical with the teachers' new approach. The questions asked by students gave Karen and James additional insight into where students were in their understanding of the historical milieu the artifact collections were intended to represent. This increased level of understanding provided the two teachers with much-needed information that allowed them to reconstruct or reorganize available artifacts and decide whether additional artifacts were needed to enhance student learning.

Chapter 4

Family Rituals and Traditions

Traditions have to begin somewhere, and it may surprise your students that some of the traditions people now observe began as *family rituals*. These practices were adopted by other families, who perhaps carried them to another community when they moved away. Eventually, no one seemed to know *who* started the ritual (or even why), and a tradition was born.

It may surprise your students to learn that not all traditions are practiced by all the people who live in a community. While interviewing an immigrant from England, for example, a college student was surprised to hear her informant say, "Of course we don't celebrate the Fourth of July—why *should* we?!" Not everyone celebrates Christmas festivities; some students and their families prefer not to observe birthdays with parties and gifts; a few feel offended by the Halloween practice of going door to door in costume. Help your students begin to realize the diversity in commonly recognized traditions.

The holiday season is a good time to talk about rituals and traditions. As students and their families prepare to celebrate Thanksgiving, discuss the history of the holiday. After Thanksgiving, ask students what holidays they and their families will be observing next. Whether they celebrate Christmas, Hanukkah, or just get together with their families during the winter break, students are likely to have memories of Decembers past to share.

Family Holiday Traditions

Begin your study of family traditions as students return to school after Thanksgiving. Here's how to get started:

Did you share a special meal with your family this weekend? Why was it special? Don't answer out loud—but think: What did you eat at this meal? Think again: Have you ever had this particular food at a special meal before? When was it? What made it special?

When people share a certain experience like a special meal on Thanksgiving, and decide to share that experience together again, they are creating a *ritual*. And if enough other people like to practice that ritual, it may become a *tradition*. Giving each other valentines on February 14, for example, is a tradition. Sharing Thanksgiving dinner with your family or friends is a tradition. But as we discussed recently, we didn't always have a Thanksgiving—somebody had to start that tradition. Every tradition starts with real people.

Your family has its traditions, too. Maybe you always go to grandmother's house on Thanksgiving. Or maybe your family always goes out to eat. Foods can play a part in traditions, such as turkey being associated with Thanksgiving, but perhaps *your* family always has ham—or even tofu. Think about your family's traditions. Which ones have to do with Thanksgiving? (Discuss these traditions.)

Some people celebrate holidays with their families in the month of December. Does your family have traditions associated with Christmas or Hanukkah? What are they? How does *your* family celebrate special times? Write about your family's traditions.

Continue the study of family rituals and traditions by having students observe happenings at home to discover everyday traditions—those not associated with holidays or special times. For example, Kathleen Kennedy, daughter of Robert Kennedy, once described a Kennedy family ritual in this way: "Every morning, each child was required to recite three current events, and on Sundays the older children were expected to make a speech about a personality in the news." She went on to relate that the family's favorite football cheer was, "Clap your hands! Stamp your feet! 'Cause Daddy's team can't be beat." Using these examples may help your students come up with examples of their own. Record these in the family folklore scrapbook.

▧ Trying It Out

Family Traditions

Virginia Thorpe and her students decided to explore family traditions as a follow-up to their research on children's pastimes throughout the generations. Virginia says, "Holiday times such as Thanksgiving are good times to have your students reflect on their family traditions. Maybe they always go to grandma's house and have turkey with all the trimmings. Maybe they celebrate Christmas on the stroke of midnight." When asked how she adjusts her family traditions assignment for students who may not celebrate these holidays, Virginia suggests making a class family traditions book divided in some way other than by common holidays. She says, "Students should share their tradition by writing and possibly illustrating what their family does together. Stories can be laminated and placed into a classroom book. Time order could be emphasized by having your student editors responsible for the story arrangement in monthly or seasonal sequence."

Family Recipes

Bring in some cookies or other simple food made from one of your family recipes. Share the recipe with students, as well as any related stories involving the recipe and/or food. Then ask students whether there is a "family recipe" that has been passed down through the generations in their families. Pass out 4" × 6" lined recipe cards (for younger students, you may want to write categories such as *title, ingredients, directions,* and *source* on the card itself). Give students several days to come up with a family recipe and write it on the card. Instruct them that if any stories are associated with the recipe or food, they should be prepared to tell these, also. When this assignment is completed, create a "Class Recipe Book" using the family recipes. (Be sure to credit the appropriate family members for their contributions!)

My own mother, who recalls helping her mother make the lye soap used to do the family wash (and sometimes their hair!), contributes this nostalgic family recipe:

EDITH SULLIVAN'S LYE SOAP

1 can Red Devil lye	1 cup ammonia
2 3/4 pints cold water	handful of Borax
5 1/2 lb. warm grease (lard)	2 oz. sassafras oil

Mix lye and cold water in an iron skillet with a wooden stick. Solution will get very hot. Let stand about 1 hour. When the solution has cooled to almost lukewarm, pour it very slowly into warm grease and stir until mixture reaches a consistency of honey. During this stirring process, add 1 cup ammonia and Borax. When the proper consistency is reached, pour mixture into pans (old cake pans 9" × 13"). Cover with cloth so they don't cool too fast. Let stand about 24 hours. When set, but not too hard, cut into squares and remove from pans.

Family Calendars

Give each student a generic calendar and have each child fill in the dates for the year, including recognized national holidays. The students then have an opportunity to share their calendars with their families, finding out and filling in special family dates, including birthdays, anniversaries, graduations, family reunions, weddings, vacations, ethnic holidays, religious observances, and so forth. Students return the completed calendars to school, where they share their own special days with classmates. All students then decorate their own calendars and present them to family members as a gift.

Ethnic Celebrations

Peoples of all cultures and societies celebrate or commemorate special times in their lives. Sometimes these celebrations are confined to immediate or extended family (such as what a particular family does to celebrate Thanksgiving), but at other times, much or all of the local community may be involved.

Weddings are one example of celebrations that all cultures have in common. But families of various cultural/ethnic backgrounds in the community may celebrate wedding traditions in different ways. Challenge your students to find out how families in the community (including their own) celebrate wedding festivities, and if or how ethnic backgrounds influence these practices or traditions.

▪ Trying It Out

Weddings around the World
I worked with a group of students as they collected oral history interviews with women immigrants in the local community. Many of the women talked about their own weddings, or how their family celebrates weddings and related events (such as engagements). Excerpts from these interviews follow, demonstrating how such research can supply students with a wealth of information about celebrations in the local community.

LORE (GERMANY)
Our wedding was a two-day wedding. I don't know how many guests we had, just 25 or so, just family. And then there was a supper with meats and all that. At midnight there would be another meal, with little bread and tidbits, cold. And the next day, it was the same thing again. And then all the neighbors and friends that brought gifts would be invited the *next* day, for coffee.

FARAH (IRAN)

[When] I was seventeen, sixteen, we all had to go to bed and sleep at 10 o'clock. And I couldn't go out to party, not that many times. Maybe somebody's birthday like twice a year, but that somebody's birthday had to be somebody that my dad knew, my mom knew. And I couldn't go out with anybody, go to movie or anything with any guy. I knew a lot of guys because my family was one of the families that was very educated and had freedom. My parents went out of the country a lot. Still, I couldn't do anything.

First time I saw my husband I was about 13 years old. I knew him about 3 or 4 years. I never talked to him. He never talked to me. Everybody in my city . . . at that time we were living in a very small city at the border of Russia and Iran. Very pretty city. Everybody in the town knew it, that he loved me. We went that far. But we never talked. We never talked. Just think about it! How can somebody love somebody else when they never talk?

And it took us 7 years to get married. I got married when I was 18 years old. Actually, I was in twelfth grade when I went out with him [for the first time]. Most of the time my sister went with me. And every time I came back, he had a big problem with my dad. He said, "I don't want her to go out with him because I don't know where she is or what she's doing." I couldn't go anywhere, do anything without my sister around me all the time. . . . But other dads are worse than him. I think he was good because he told him, "You want to see my daughter, you want to talk to my daughter, you come in my house. I let you guys sit in my living room and talk all you want. But you guys are not gonna see each other anywhere but my house." And that time I was like 16 years old. And that in Middle East, especially in Iran and Turkey, they don't do that. In most of the Middle East countries and Arabic countries, they don't [permit] that.

My mom got married when she was 12 years old. And she had me when she was 13 years old. My grandmother got married when she was 16 years old. My sister got married when she was 19 years old. Thirty? No, you too old [then], they don't get married. That's exactly what it is. They don't [find a spouse] after 25, [people say] "There's something wrong with her." Then you have to watch. It's the same with guys. My husband was 23 when we got married. When 27, they're gonna ask questions. "What's wrong with that guy? Why he's not married yet?" You know. I think 18 is the best [age to get married] in my country. Most of the time they get graduated from high school and they get married.

MARY (ROMANIA)

We got married in my [Protestant] church, but I never knew my husband was Catholic. Yeah, he was Catholic, but he never talk, I never knew that until after we got married. So he was going to [his] church once in a while and I go to [my] church, and I didn't know when we had kids where they were going to Sunday school!

[After our wedding] we had a big dinner, sit-down dinner. All the ladies, bunch of ladies got together, you know . . . my mom was in charge of it. Got all the ladies got together and they all helped. They cooked; they had roast chicken and soup. Oh yeah, we had music, Romanian music.

UMAMA (PAKISTANI AMERICAN)

A lot of kids don't live on their own. You live with your parents. I know even [Pakistani] kids in the United States, kids that I grew up with, first-generation, live at home until they get married. If you do live alone it's when you go away to school. When you get done [graduate] you come back [to your parents' house] until you get married.

In my culture kids get married early, especially the girls. We get married from 19 to 21, really young. Girls my age going into higher education [are] now getting married at around 22 to 24. They finish their education and then get married. But decisions about moving away, that would be a joint decision [between parents and child]. We would listen to what our parents have to say, their input would mean a lot. A lot of my decisions are based on what my family would agree to. Even like a decision about marriage.

We have arranged marriages. Like I am engaged right now and that is arranged marriage. . . . In Pakistan, the parents choose [a spouse], and then they present [him] to you. You actually have the final choice, but usually the kids agree to what their parents have to say, because there is a lot of trust and respect toward the parent. So if your parents say, "This is a person you should really consider seriously," for the most part, you agree.

My parents' marriage was like this: My grandparents made the decision, and they [parents] got married. They didn't see or talk to each other before they got married. Mine is different. I talk to my fiance a lot, but I don't date him. I have never gone out alone with him. But I have talked to him. We talk on the phone and I have known him almost since I was six or seven years old. But it wasn't arranged then. I think it was in both our parents' minds a long time, we just never knew it. Three years ago, his mom seriously asked him [to consider Umama as a wife]. He would consider it if he could talk to me. So his mom asked my mother; my mother asked me. At first I said, "No, I don't see him that way and I don't want to do it." [But] I thought about it for a while, and a lot of other relatives talked to me. . . . So I said, "Fine." I talked to him for about a year. Then he asked me and I said, "Fine." So it's an arranged marriage, but I had a lot of input.

MARY (GREEK AMERICAN)

When I asked [husband] to get married in a Greek church, he agreed to do that because he respected the fact that because, you know, I basically said, "As much as I love you, I would never want to hurt my parents." And if I got married outside of the Greek church, they would have been devastated. And he agreed to that which was . . . totally in Greek. He didn't understand a thing they were saying! We didn't exchange vows, we didn't talk to one another for an entire hour. The priest does all the sayings and the readings, and [the groom] didn't know what was going on. There was a course that we took so that he would know what was going on step by step, but he didn't know what the priest was actually saying. I'm sure he misses not having a traditional marriage ceremony.

MARIA (GREEK AMERICAN)

My parents, well, we have different ways [from American expectations]. We don't go out and do what the common American does. Like we don't date, we don't have boyfriends. You don't go out [socially]; you go out with your family, not with your friends.

My parents are old-fashioned. See, they came [to the U.S.] in the 1970s and they hold the morals and beliefs and the way of life of the 1970s, in Greece. But Greece isn't what it was. But that is how we were raised. We were raised as if we were in Greece in the 1970s era, but things [there have] changed.

If I wanted to get married, let's say I would go [to Greece] next summer, and I would say, "Listen, I am such and such an age—do you know someone?" My uncles or relatives would look into it. You would tell your family. . . . You wouldn't go up to someone and say, "Hey, I want to get married" [laughing]. You would tell your family, and they would ask around.

Things are done very traditionally. If . . . a girl is constantly going out and "doing things," they start talking about her. If she gets a certain reputation, she won't be able to get married. "Well, that girl was out [until] four o'clock in the morning. . . . " So there is a tradition to it.

ANGEL (MEXICAN AMERICAN)

The sweet sixteen birthday party [is] like a debutante [ball]. Well, ours is when you turn fifteen—and it all started because in Mexico it is really hard to bring up so many children, so when your daughter becomes of age you want to introduce her to society [and find her a husband]. You say, "Okay, here she is, she is available for any young gentlemen to start [courting]." Quienceanos. So you introduce your daughter, and you say, "Okay, anybody you know that wants to court her, she is of age," and that just a way of, you know, telling people that she is eligible now. They can have [the celebration] either when you are fifteen or when you are eighteen, but most of the families have them when their daughters are fifteen so that she can start dating earlier and she can start her family and go out on her own. (That way, you know, you don't have as many children at home then.) But the wealthier families, the more better off families, would wait until their daughter is eighteen, because they could afford to keep her those extra three years. And she would be more mature, and that would like give them more time to actually see who was interested.

It is a huge, huge, huge party; it is typically like a wedding only without a groom. I mean you go to church, you have a reception, and you have the food, you have everything. [My daughter] is going to be ten, so we have five years to prepare for this. I have told [my husband], I said, "Now remember that this is something we are going to do and you know it is just like a wedding. I had mine when I was fifteen and it is just such a special celebration and I have not heard in other culture where they do something like this."

Quienceanos are kind of, I mean people take them very seriously. [The girl's parents] kind of go out and that is when you talk to what is called padrinos (they are your friends) and you go out and say, "Okay, my daughter is old enough now—do you want to make a donation?" So they give you some money—ten, twenty, forty, fifty dollars—and you pull all of the money together the padrinos give you, and that is how you afford it.

I think that that is probably going to be one of the things [my daughter] will remember as part of her ethnic culture. Because I expect to go all out. My mother always used to get mad that in the United States, the daughter, you know the parents of the daughter, are the ones that are expected to pay all of the costs of the wedding. In the Hispanic [culture], it is just the opposite, the parents of the son are really supposed to do most of the financial situation rather than the daughter. But that is changing a little bit, you know with anything, times change. It is kind of like an unwritten law if I go out and ask all of these friends, "Will you sponsor my daughter, be part of her [celebration]?" they will.

JUANITA (MEXICAN AMERICAN)

When a girl turns 15, she goes through, I guess it's equivalent to an American girl's sweet sixteen [party], it is a kind of a coming out. But it's [done] in a big way, though. You would think you were at a wedding. A girl gets 14 girls and 14 guys, and she herself has an escort and . . . the girls wear long dresses. The guys wear either ties or tuxedos, you know, dress up. You'll have your Mass, and then afterwards you'll have the reception, and you'll have like a dance or reception in the evening. Guys don't have this. It's a girl thing.

MARIA (MEXICAN AMERICAN)

One of the traditions that [my mother has] installed in our family is Quienceanos. All seven of us have been in Quienceanos [celebrations with others], and she's pretty happy that the oldest one, her oldest daughter, is turning fifteen this year and that she's gonna be getting her a Quienceanos. And she feels proud that she has installed that in us and that it's gonna be carried on.

The things that they have to do in the Quienceanos is to buy a beautiful gown for them to wear, and a crown that they set onto them, and gifts that they receive. The priest is installing some beliefs that they have to have . . . when she was fourteen, you know, she was a child, but now she's fifteen—she's an adult, and she has to act ladylike. She should follow certain guidelines, and she shouldn't jump into things. . . .

There's fourteen girls and then with the Quienceanos girl, it's fifteen, so that's saying that she's important—fifteenth one. There's a watch, a ring, and a necklace presented by certain people, and each one has a symbolic meaning, like a watch is like for time and a ring is for eternity, and the Bible is important 'cause it should show that you know the Bible, following God's way and things. It matters. The bracelet is to show that when she was younger, when she turns into a woman, when she is married, it's to show her remembrance of when she became a lady.

Chapter 5

Family Storytelling

Family stories are powerful forms of communication that help shape people and establish their sense of who they are. Stories convey information to the listener, and family stories convey a sense of identity and connectedness to family members who tell and hear them. Stories about a person's past are essential to making sense of the person's experiences and present. The use of storytelling is universal, but the form may change from culture to culture. This means that the stories family members tell at gatherings and on special occasions create and maintain a sense of heritage for the children involved.

There are many benefits to students' researching, collecting, organizing, and retelling their family's stories. Interviewing, notetaking, proofreading, and editing skills are learned or polished. Children gain a sense of their family's history that might never have been revealed otherwise. Families reminisce together, forming important bonds. Students are exposed to both the diversities and commonalities of family life in their community or neighborhood. A sense of time and the passage of time is gained as students and teachers examine the influence of events on people they know.

Toni Kennedy (1995) has spent several years involving her students in family storytelling projects. I have paraphrased her helpful advice to help teachers as they consider incorporating family storytelling into the curriculum or community culture of their classrooms:

- The hardest part for students is finding out about the first story—it gets easier after that.
- Older family members usually take responsibility for knowing and telling family stories. Have students telephone or write or visit grandparents, great-aunts and great-uncles, or their parents' eldest sibling to ask about family stories.
- When students start out with a question rather than a general request for a family story, things go more smoothly.
- Bringing in or referring to family artifacts enriches the family storytelling process.
- Occasions involving traditional celebrations or rituals are rich sources for family stories.

■ Students who research and write family stories come to sense their own valued role as a family member (especially when copies of scrapbooks or storybooks are made to give as gifts to extended family members).

Help your students get past that first difficult story with the "Search Me!" activity (discussed next). Then pick and choose from among the other activities and strategies in this chapter to enable your students to become family storytellers.

Search Me!

Introduce students to the idea of family storytelling by having them examine their own stories, or lore, through this activity. Use the worksheet provided to structure this personal research activity; invite students to query siblings, parents, and extended family members as they search for answers to the worksheet questions. After students return the completed worksheet to class, ask them to select one item from the worksheet and write a one-page story about their past or themselves in the present using the information provided on the worksheet.

Can You Top That?

Everybody loves a good story, and one way to immerse students in family folklore is to tell one. Start by recalling a story from your own childhood, then ask students to think of something that happened when they were "little." If kids are still reluctant to share a tale from their past, use this one from *A Celebration of Family Folklore* (Pantheon Books, 1982) to motivate them further:

> *Every time we came home from the store with a new jar of peanut butter, my dad...would write [in it] the initials of the one he thought had been the best that week. And then the next morning—or whenever we'd go to open the peanut butter to put on our toast or something — he'd call the person [and] say, "Oh, look what's here!" And he would tell us that it was the little fairy that lived in the light downstairs, whose name was Matilda...that she had done it. That used to make you be good so you could get your name in the peanut butter.*

Whoever tells it, whatever the subject, family stories belong to a living family—and so they have the potential to help your students learn that history is not just about dead people—it's about the living, the real, and even the familiar. It's continually evolving, and the possibility exists for new stories to be added every day (although you probably don't want to hear family stories every day of the school year!). But even when fantastically embellished, family stories probably have a grain of truth in them, and so they help shape a family's history.

Discuss with the students the differences between *family history* and *family folklore*. During the Grandma's Attic Trunk unit, for example, the children brought in real memorabilia, or family artifacts, and studied the items' impact on family members and society at the time they were used, whereas during the Family Stories activity, they shared oral accounts of family members' experiences. Remind them that a story often changes in the telling, so that the story they shared in class was not even necessarily identical to they way they heard it at home. Even young children can understand that family stories entertain us and reinforce the family's belief and value structure. *Family history* is based on such verifiable facts as birth, marriage, death, and employment records; *family folklore* is based on the ways families experience and preserve their traditions and values. Consider helping your students preserve their own family folklore with "My Family Folklore Scrapbook."

Search Me! Worksheet

I. Official Personal Information

Name _____

Address _____

Age _____

II. Unofficial Personal Information

1. Nicknames

    a. Current _____

    b. Past _____

2. Good Luck Charms

    a. Current _____

    b. Past _____

3. Favorite Games

    a. Current _____

    b. Past _____

III. Memories and Traditions

1. Favorite Foods

    a. Thanksgiving _____

    b. Christmas/Hanukkah _____

    c. Birthday _____

2. Skills/Hobbies

    a. List special skills you have, who taught you, and when you learned them:

    _____

    _____

    _____

    b. List hobbies you enjoy, why you became interested in these, and when: _____

    _____

    _____

    _____

    c. What is the first song you remember? Who sang it? _____

    _____

    _____

    _____

    d. What is the first rhyme you recall? Who said it? _____

    _____

    _____

    _____

My Family Folklore Scrapbook

After students share family stories in class, ask them to write down and illustrate the stories. Provide sturdy paper for this purpose, because as students collect more stories, they will create a scrapbook of stories to add to their family's collection of memorabilia. Have the scrapbooks bound (the local office supply store may be willing to do this for you) after students create their own covers with the title "My Family Folklore Scrapbook" and their family names.

Outside of class, have the students write down and illustrate stories told by other family members. Especially encourage them to contact older living relatives for this purpose. It is a good idea to provide them with these suggested topics:

▦ Stories about how our family survived and/or pulled together during hard times: disasters, illnesses, accidents, emigration, unemployment

▦ Stories of skills or knowledge learned from older relatives: farming, sewing, fishing, needlework, good manners, values and beliefs, old sayings

▦ Stories about funny incidents or practical jokes involving members of our family

▦ Stories of times when parents, grandparents, aunts, and/or uncles were young

▦ Stories about family courtships (what happened when you were dating Mommy?)

▦ Stories of relatives who were (or might have been) heroes, villains, and/or who did memorable deeds

As students collect family stories, they may alter or add to this list. Urge them to include other interesting details, too, such as Uncle Jake's prize-winning chili recipe or the directions for making Cousin Wanda's favorite fishing lure.

▦ Trying It Out

Family History Albums

Sandi Herman's third-graders created Family History Books as a way to "investigate our own family history, see our relationship to our family, to learn more about our family history, and to appreciate our families and their traditions." Sandi set the stage by sharing her own family scrapbook and by establishing guidelines with the students for developing their own family history books. The instructional sheet Sandi gave her students included:

1. Interview someone you would like to learn more about. This can be in person, over the phone, or you can write down your questions and have the person being interviewed write down his or her answers.
2. Bring a picture and write about it.
3. Write a will.
4. Write about a family tradition.
5. Write an author's page.
6. Write about how you see the future—your own and/or the world's.
7. Write about a funny incident that happened to one of your parents in the past.
8. Write about a funny incident that has happened to you.
9. Include a family tree.
10. Other things that may be included:
    a. Describe family members.
    b. Describe the oldest family item (artifact)—tell about its significance.
    c. Tell what you especially remember and appreciate about your grandparents—especially if they are no longer living.
    d. Discuss family words that have special meaning.

> **e.** Describe the oldest family story that is known. It can be about how your family came to America, your grandparent's childhood, how your parents met, and so on.
>
> **f.** Write about your family's way of celebrating "firsts" (first tooth lost, first day of school, first ballgame played in, etc.).
>
> Add pictures and decorate your Family History Book so that it is personally yours!

Students were asked to purchase old-fashioned scrapbooks, the kind with paper pages that can have items pasted to them or photos attached with photo corners, and that can be enlarged by adding additional pages as the scrapbook grows. Sandi used her own scrapbook as an example, and sent home a note to parents describing the type of scrapbook she preferred students use.

Kirstyn's Family History Album was laid out in this fashion: The cover page is decorated, and Kirstyn has written the words:

A Family History
    written by: Kirstyn

The first page of the album contains information from Kirstyn's interview with her grandmother:

> My great-grandma Helen Davis was born in 1916 in Monroe, Indiana. She was 18 years old when she got married in 1934. She had 2 sisters and 4 brothers. Her best friend was her husband. In her spare time she likes to sew. When they didn't have cars they did a lot of walking. Since they didn't have electricity, they used kerosene lamps for light and wood burning stoves to cook on. When the Great Depression came, they had no money and grew their own food. Her chores were to work in the garden, feed chickens and milk cows. Her school was a country school and had 1-8 grades. Her brother was in World War II. She had 5 children of her own and raised them in Decatur.

The second page, which deals with family traditions, is decorated with Kirstyn's drawings of Christmas tree ornaments and is centered by a photo of her family at Christmas time. Below the photo, Kirstyn has typed these words:

> It is a family tradition to always open presents on Christmas Eve. We always have it at my Grandma Davis' house. My aunts and uncles, grandma and grandpa and my cousin are always there. We open presents from youngest to oldest. Afterwards we go to the candle light service. I usually fall asleep during the candle light service. Then I go home and have fun. Then I try to go to sleep but usually I am so excited for Christmas Day to come that I can't sleep.

The third page explores Kirstyn's hopes and dreams for the future:

> My hopes and dreams are to have a lot of kids. I want to have 3 boys and 5 girls. I want to have a nice veical like a Van or a Explorer. I want to be a nurse or a house mom. My hope is to stop violence and abortion and have peace in the world. Every night I would like to read a story to my children. I would like to live in a beautiful house. My hope is to go to college and be a cheerleader there. I want to have a lot of pets.

The fourth page describes a funny incident that happened to Kirstyn and her beloved cousin. There is a photo of the two of them together, taken on the day of the incident. Kirstyn has drawn colorful valentines around the photograph and written these words:

> It all started when me and my cousin Christina were getting ready to go skibobbing. We were scared at first and wanted to go very slow so we wouldn't fall off but then we wanted to go fast. We thought it was so much fun but then we got going a little to fast and fell off. I liked that a lot. We had so much fun. This happened in June 1995.

The fifth page of Kirstyn's Family History Album describes a funny incident that happened in her mother's past. Kirstyn's drawing of a huge softball appearing to whiz through the air dominates the page. She adds these words:

> My mom and her sister and brother and the neighbor kids were playing softball while their parents were at work. A neighbor kid was up to bat and hit a foul ball while a blue bird van was going past. It hit the van but didn't break anything. Then the man got out of his car and asked who was the oldest and my mom was the oldest so she stepped up and said I am. She had to explain that they didn't mean to do that. Then he left and they all started laughing because it was so weird that the ball hit that van.

The sixth page contains Kirstyn's family tree through her great-grandparents. The seventh page shows a photo of a man with a ski cap, scarf, and heavy jacket wearing swimming trunks. The man is standing in snow, holding the hand of a warmly dressed toddler; men in swimsuits on the bank of a semi-frozen river are in the background. The page is decorated with Kirstyn's imitation of bear tracks. Kirstyn writes:

> A funny story about my dad is when he goes polar bear swimming in the St. Joe River on New Year's day. He goes with two other friends and it is freezing cold and sometimes there is ice on the river. They sing the Star Spangled Banner and then they run into the river with about 50 other polar bears. Usually they just run in and get right back out. I think they look silly with swimsuits on when it is so cold. Sometimes they are on t.v. I suppose that's because other people think they're pretty silly too.

The eighth page of Kirstyn's album is devoted to herself. It is centered with her recent school photograph, and contains the following description:

> Kirstyn Heine was born at Park View hospital in Fort Wayne, Indiana on February 24, 1986. She would like to have a lot of children. She is 10 years old and lives in New Haven. There are 5 people in her family. Her favorite food is broccoli and grapefruit. She is interested in collecting American Girl dolls, playing sports and dancing. She goes to Central Lutheran School. Her family is important to her. She has blonde hair and blue eyes. Her friends are Ashley Kidd and Alexandra Rosswurm.

On the ninth and final page, the reader learns of a scary accident that Kirstyn once had:

When we were at the lake I went tubing and it was wavy. I was going a little too fast and fliped off the tube. I went about 6 feet in the air with my armes and legs straight out. I was scared. Then I landed in the water on my head. I though that was scary but fun. When my family saw that I wasn't hurt they all laughted hepterically. I never went tubing again that week but this year 1996 I am going to go tubing but hopefully I don't fall off again like last year in 1995.

Sandi found that her students' parents quickly became very involved in this project. "Many parents really got into this and added ideas [of their own]," she states. One parent even insisted that her child conduct the required interview on video-tape—the child's great-grandmother was quite ill when the assignment was made, and not expected to live much longer. Other parents learned things about their own parents they did not even know as their children interviewed grandparents for this assignment. Sandi's only suggestion for teachers who decide to replicate the Family History Book Project is "I would spread it over an entire semester rather than doing it in one month's time."

Grandma Book

A different version of the family album activity, the "Grandma Book," is described by a sixth-grade teacher (Carter, 1995). John Carter asked his sixth-graders to develop a family history project during a nine-week grading period. First, he supplied them with a one-page instruction sheet describing alternative approaches they might take to develop their project. The instruction sheet asked students to list family members they might write to as they gathered information about the family's history; to indicate a focus or theme for the project (family gatherings at holiday times, family vacations, or celebrations of elderly relatives' birthdays were given as examples); and to write a letter to the family members on their list explaining the class assignment and asking that each family member write a page or two summarizing their memories of the selected theme.

John says, "Some of the first drafts of letters [from family members] were one or two sentences" only, and did not communicate memories or relevant facts about the family's history. "I asked the students to . . . rethink just what they wanted to tell their relatives," he recalls. Students worked together in class to create webs or clusters illustrating their ideas, and "these strategies helped tremendously. Soon, students had well-elaborated letters" to send to the same relatives. This time when they received their responses, students gained firsthand perspectives of an historical event from their own past, through primary sources created by family members.

Once students had received several satisfactory responses from family members, they considered ways to "publish" their findings or present their project to their peers. Students transposed letters from relatives via word processing, using the who, what, where, why, when questions to create newspaper accounts of the event or theme selected. These newspaper articles became a focal part of the family history book they were creating.

Next, students devised informative introductions to their books and wrote original poems about one family member featured in their books. In this way, students were called on to use different writing and editing skills with each portion of the book developed. "I had conferences with the students at various stages of their writing," John notes, adding that students shared their writing efforts in groups of three students each. Students in the group were given a revision sheet and asked to read their group members' papers, focusing on one or two points needing revision.

Most of the students were able to collect and describe a variety of family photographs and candid snapshots during the nine weeks of the project. These photographs became an important part of their family history books. Other artwork or graphic material included a time line of each person's life included in the book, a brief biography of each person included, and original art (especially by students whose families were unable or unwilling to contribute photographs).

After the family history books were edited, revised, and completed, students designed a creative cover that depicted the focus or theme of their project, their family name, and their own name with the date. "Many parents reported...how involved they themselves became as their children worked on the projects," John explains. "One mother told me that she and her husband cried as they leafed through the pages of their son's book called "Christmas at Grandma's."

These family history books provided more than an opportunity for nostalgia for students, however. One student elected to chronicle the life of a relative who lived in seventeenth-century New England. He learned that his relative had been directly involved with the Massachusetts witch hunts. Another student's great uncle supplied copies of his pay stubs from the early 1930s, causing general amazement in the class that not only did people earn as little as $25 a week for 40 hours of work, but that they could support an entire family on this amount.

As a culminating assignment, John gave each student a time line of important events in twentieth-century history, and asked the students to compare the time lines of their relatives (developed during the project) with the time lines of well-known historical events. This comparison gave students the opportunity to "see how someone related to them had actually lived at the time of . . . famous historical events," and provided them with comparative information about local, national, and world history.

Uncle . . . Who??

This activity is designed to help students collect and preserve family stories. Use the following questions or design your own, and provide students with copies as they conduct their family scrapbook research:

1. What do you know about your family's last name? Did it undergo any changes coming from the "old country" to the United States? Are there stories about the name change? What are they?
2. In your family, are there any traditional first or middle names? Nicknames? What are they? What are the stories behind them?
3. What stories have been handed down about your grandparents, parents, or other ancestors? What do you know about their childhoods and teenage years? What kinds of schools did they attend? When did they leave school, and why? What kind of a student were they?
4. Is there a notorious or infamous character in your family's past? If so, who are/were they? What are the stories connected with this person? Are there newspaper clippings or photographs to document the stories?
5. How did your parents meet? Your grandparents? Are there any stories associated with their courtship?
6. Have any historical events, such as World War II or the Depression, affected your family? How?
7. Do any of your relatives have stories about a fortune made or lost?
8. Does your family hold reunions? Where and how often? Are there records of these reunions, such as invitations or photographs?
9. Do any of your family members have family heirlooms or memorabilia that have been kept in the family for generations? What are they? Why are they important? Are there stories associated with these?
10. Is there anyone who—while not being related to your family—is considered "one of the family"? Who is it? How did this come to be?

■ Trying It Out

Family Storytelling Festival
Wenona Hoham and her fifth-graders decided to explore family storytelling using the Uncle . . . Who? activity. Wenona wanted to use this activity to "get students interested in finding out some of their family folklore [and help them] understand that not all 'history' is found in a textbook—that history is made of people, their actions, and

how it is recorded." Family storytelling, Wenona felt, would help her students establish a link with their past.

The family storytelling project took place over five consecutive days of one-hour class sessions. Some of the work (especially background information) was done at home. Wenona introduced the storytelling project one week before students began to collect their own family's stories, first by playing a tape made by a local storyteller about local legends, and second by sharing a few of her own family stories. During the rest of that week, Wenona and her students worked together (in groups of three) to examine the Uncle...Who? questionnaire and to formulate any other questions that might be used to gather information from family members about possible stories to share with their classmates. At first, some students protested, "I don't know any of this information!" or "There's nothing interesting about my family," even though they generally appeared interested in beginning the project.

Once students took their lists of questions home, they came to school the next day bubbling over with many exciting things they had discovered about their families and family members. They reported calling grandmas, aunts, and other relatives they seldom see. There was an air of excitement about the class that day.

Wenona's students write every day as a part of her process writing program, so actually writing a family story after researching it was no problem to them. Some students did request help, however, selecting which of their several family stories to concentrate on. Eventually, a few of them decided to combine two or more related stories into one larger story.

By the second day of writing, most students finished the first drafts of their stories. They began to share their stories within their groups, giving each other helpful comments and suggestions, such as where details should be added to increase story interest, or ways to make a part of the story more clear to the listener.

On the third day, students began to illustrate their stories. Some just wanted to sketch simple drawings, while others thought colorful illustrations would add to their story's appeal. Wenona encouraged the children to include a map in their illustrations, describing something about the story's location. As the students discussed what kinds of illustrations to include, Wenona reminded them that "pictures should illustrate the main points in the story."

Students created story wheels on the fourth day. The wheels were designed to highlight the main elements of the story and were meant to be used as a tool for storytelling (rather than reading the written story). As students practiced using their story wheels, they admitted that they missed having the written form in front of them. Most were comfortable with using the story wheel for retelling by the third trial.

Wenona circulated around the room, suggesting to several groups that they "put the [story] wheel under your chair and tell the story using hand gestures, facial expression, and voice inflection." She also decided to remind a few students of the rules of good listening.

The fifth and final day of the project was the "Family Storytelling Festival." Wenona's students served as "buddies" to students in one of the first-grade classes at their school, and this class was invited to the Festival. One student from each group was selected to tell his or her story while being videotaped in front of the live audience. The students were visibly nervous, but behaved like the good sports they were. They did a good job sharing their stories orally, and the first-grade buddies enjoyed this unique experience. The few students who shared their family stories on videotape wanted a copy to "take home and show my mom/dad."

Wenona suggests that teachers who wish to replicate the Uncle...Who? family storytelling activity plan several weeks in advance so that they can invite parents and other family members to attend the Family Storytelling Festival, some of whom would be prepared to tell a family story, also. Another recommendation is if facilities allow, videotape each child in the class as he or she tells a family story and allow the children to take these videos home at the end of the year. Wenona also suggests some pre- and postworkshop activities:

PREWORKSHOP ACTIVITIES

■ Begin a daily journal writing activity (if not already a directed activity in your class) one week before the workshop.

■ Listen to the audio cassette, "Growin' Up a Hoosier" by LouAnn Homan (or similar local storytelling resource).

■ Begin collecting family memorabilia from students.

■ Hand out family questionnaires to all students one week before the workshop.

POSTWORKSHOP ACTIVITIES

■ Do a final editing and publish the students' work.

■ Invite parents and grandparents in for a storytelling/sharing session. Encourage them to bring a tale to share.

■ Encourage journal writing as a means of preserving family history.

■ Set up a family history center with students bringing copies of letters, photographs, or any other family memorabilia.

■ Arrange a session with a younger class when your students explain the importance of family stories to children in a lower grade, and share their family stories with them.

How I Spent My Summer Vacation

Linda Gibson and her second-graders were working on the purpose and use of sequence in story. They had been introduced to the concept of story sequence, and even analyzed sequence in two stories in their reading series. But Linda wanted to personalize the concept for her students. She invited them to cooperatively write a story on the computer. "Each child was to add onto the story two lines at a time at two different times," she explains. "They decided they wanted me to do a story starter to get them going." Linda's story starter focused on the kinds of stories families often tell each other. It goes like this: "Hi. My name is Stephen, and this is the story of my best summer vacation ever. I live in New York, but I was headed for a great sea adventure." As Linda read them this story starter, she says, "They were all excited and couldn't wait to get to it. They all had their own ideas of how it should go. I reminded them that a story has to have a sequence, or order, to it." The class worked on their group story for a week, with Linda reading aloud to them each day the previous day's work. "We ended up with a seven page single-spaced story that is *incredible!*" she concludes. "I printed out their story and made copies for everyone. Each student made a cover for the story and three illustrations to go with it. They now each have their own book written by the entire class."

What is particularly interesting about Linda's students' project is that it provided the impetus for students to ask family members about vacation stories as they worked to think up new and interesting details to add to the class story. After the sequencing lesson was over, students still wanted to pursue family vacation stories. At the end of the year, Linda's students put together personalized books about "My Best Family Vacation Story Ever," complete with covers and illustrations. This was one of the most valued assignments of the year—parents and siblings all got involved. Not one student left his or her "Family Vacation" book behind at the end of the year.

Nonnie, Chan-Pans, and Nissiles: Family Word Fun

When I was a toddler, I couldn't get my tongue around my Aunt Juanita's name, so she became "Nonnie." Pancakes were a favorite breakfast food, and my mother soon learned that when I chanted "Chan Pans! Chan Pans!" I was hungry for her special pancakes. A friend confesses that as he played war games with neighborhood friends, he pronounced "missiles" as "nissiles."

Your students probably do not realize it, but one more thing that makes their families unique (and adds to family folklore) is the language they and their families create together. Ask students whether anyone they know mispronounced "spaghetti" as a young child. How many students' families *still* refer to spaghetti as "g'spetti" or "pisghetti"—due to their early mispronunciation? Is there a sister who couldn't say "refrigerator," and so now the whole family calls that appliance the "fiddle gator"? Or maybe when someone was sick in bed, Mother took his temperature, gave him cough syrup, and "did the tucky-poo," so that now when it's time to go to bed, children in that family ask to be "tucky-pooed."

Have students collect as many of these "invented words" as they can from family members, and tell the stories behind them. Share them in class—how they came to be and who was initially responsible for creating the new phrase—and consider making them part of the family folklore scrapbook.

Dialects and Accents

Mispronounced and "invented" words are not the only ones that can help motivate your students to research and write family stories. Regional dialects and accents vary from place to place. Examining dialect and/or particular accents indigenous to the community motivates the study of local history as students compare local language usage with standard practice. Help students see that regional word usage and dialects represent how language is commonly used to communicate in a geographic or culturally defined area. For example, the word or phrase for carbonated flavored beverage varies regionally in the United States—whether local residents call it "pop," "soda," "soda pop," "tonic," "soft drink," or the generic "coke," neighbors in the regional area understand what is meant. Also, consider whether technology has contributed to "closing the gap" for many regional accents: Do newscasters or weatherpersons in the Deep South necessarily have southern accents?

I grew up in the Appalachian mountains, where spoken language is often colorful and (to nonnatives, at least) indecipherable. Have students compare this collection of Appalachian terminology and interpretations with words and phrases familiar to them. (One caution: Although such colorful examples may be used to spice up students' creative writing, students should be discouraged from criticizing others' accents/dialects, or stereotyping persons based on the way they speak. A quick summary of former U.S. President Jimmy Carter's international and national contributions after listening to his southern accent during a news broadcast will help them get the point.)

APPALACHIAN DIALECT

acrosst	across
afore	before
aim to	intend to—"I been aimin' to go for a year now."
ain't	am not, are not, is not
anywheres	anywhere
ary	any—"Have you got ary eggs?"
ast	asked
ax	ask
bad to	habitual action—"I'm bad to forget that."
blowed	blew—"The wind blowed mighty hard last night."
borned	born
boughten	bought, purchased—"I woke up late—I guess we'll have to have boughten bread for breakfast this morning."
bound to	must—"I'm bound to have one of them newfangled thangs."
busted	burst
can't hardly	can hardly
childern	children
clum	climbed—"He clum that cherry tree and fell down and busted his noggin."

corn squeezins	illegally manufactured whiskey (also called "moonshine" or "white lightnin'")
don't care to	don't mind, don't object—"I don't care to work hard for my money."
evertime	every time
everwhen	whenever
everwhere	everywhere
everwho	whoever
et	ate
far	fire
fit	fought (verb); temper tantrum (noun)
gimme	give me
go to	intend to—"Evertime I go to fix supper, he comes in wantin' somethin' to et."
growed	grew
gully washer	hard rain
hain't	has not, have not, am not, are not, is not
heered	heard
hern	hers
het	heated
hisn	his
hit	(occasionally) it
holp	help
hunerd	hundred
hunker	squat; (sometimes) "hunker down"
jedge	judge; justice of the peace
jist	just
kindly	somewhat, sort of—"She's been kindly sick."
law!	exclamation of astonishment
mater	tomato
middlin'	tolerable; (often) "fair to middlin'" as a response to question "How are you?"
nary	ne'er a—"Son, I ain't got nary a dollar to my name."
nowheres	nowhere
offen	off of— "We bought our cow offen Mr. Whitlow."
oncet	once—"Oncet on a time . . ."
ortent	ought not—"You ortent to do that."
ourn	ours
pizen	poison
poke	small bag or sack—"Jist gimme a poke to put these maters in, and I'll be on my way."
poke sallet	poke salad, a wild green leafy plant eaten as a green vegetable
ramp	wild edible root plant with a strong taste and odor
reckon	suppose, guess—"I reckon it'll rain soon."
right smart	a considerable amount or distance
school	educate
sech	such
slow pokin'	idling, working at a slow pace —"Now don't you be slow pokin' around."
'spec	expect
'spose	suppose
tater	potato
thang	thing
theirn	theirs
them there	those—"Take them there boards out to the shed."
they's	there are
tommy toe	cherry or plum tomato

tuck	took
twicet	twice
us'uns	we
young'uns	young ones, children
yourn	yours
you'uns	you (plural)

Ask your students to suggest examples of local dialect or pronunciations affected by local accent. Record their suggestions on a chart, adding to the chart daily as students bring in ideas suggested by family and friends. Spend a few minutes each week reviewing newly added words and phrases, and encourage students to consider what this information says about the community's history.

Part

II

Community and Local History

The study of one's personal and family history can be a powerful motivational strategy that inspires students to think differently about history and social studies as school subjects. It is equally important, however, for teachers to help their students learn to place important people, places, and events in some sort of historical context. Studying local history is a good way to begin looking at historical context, especially in elementary grades.

Jorgensen (1993) says that when learning history, children "require meaningful contexts." Meaningful historical contexts are as important to historical understanding as contextual understanding is to reading comprehension—simple memorization of important dates and events produces no historical understanding, just as simply knowing words and sounds produces no meaningful comprehension of what has been read. Local and/or community history projects and activities help children place facts, dates, and events in a context that makes sense to them as citizens of that community.

Leigh and Reynolds (1997) also emphasize the role local and community history can play in extending children's historical understanding beyond self and family. Local historical study should include hands-on and interactive experiences with realia and primary sources, whenever possible. Students are excited "to learn that history involves buildings and landmarks that they pass on their way to and from school each day." Lifelong community residents, photographs, letters, diaries, and old maps can be indispensable resources for classroom teachers who want to involve their students in interactive projects and community field trips.

Before beginning a local or community history unit, spend some time at your local historical society and/or museum, making notes and investigating curricular resources available to local teachers. Make a visit to the local public library, also, where published diaries and letters may be bound or kept in vertical files. While at the library, inquire about old newspaper clippings and historical picture books that provide "then-and-now" comparisons.

At first, the massive amounts of (possibly unorganized) information available at local museums and public libraries may seem impossible to digest, much less incorporate into the curriculum. Look more closely, and keep an open mind. Suppose, for example, you are interested in developing a unit on early pioneers of the area. Materials in local museum and/or public library collections may include such gems as diaries, letters, or transcribed oral interviews (even newspaper feature articles) with early pioneers. There may be descriptions of early schools and churches, accounts of how organizations and businesses were started, even family histories with accompanying photographs and written narrative. Names of influential early settlers will crop up again and again; when you latch onto the surname of a particularly influential founding pioneer, check the society pages of the local newspaper during his or her generation and the next for account after account of dinners, teas, dances, engagements, debutante balls, military service, weddings and receptions, and birth announcements. Such seemingly mundane details provide students with the flavor and texture of life in the early days of their community.

Don't forget to visit the local courthouse, where surveyor's maps, aerial photographs, copies of appropriate legal documents, and advice may be sometimes had for the asking.

Studying Local and Community History: Suggested Interview Questions and Subtopics

I believe that students who develop their own interview questionnaires become more adept at asking good questions and feel a greater sense of ownership for the interview process than those who use a list of prepared questions. Having been a classroom teacher myself, however, I also know that a list of sample questions can go a long way toward encouraging busy teachers to try these projects. In case you are one of those very busy teachers who appreciates specific examples, here are a few suggested interview questions for community interviews, just to get you started. (See "Oral History Technique and the Interview Process" in the Introduction for more interviewing strategies.)

BACKGROUND INFORMATION ON LOCAL HISTORY

Information on these questions usually can be found in local libraries and historical societies:

■ What was the local geographic area like before this town was settled? In the early days of its settlement? Now?
■ What people first settled this area? Why did they come here? When?
■ Who settled here later? When? What drew them to the area?
■ What religious or ethnic groups settled here? Has this changed? What percentage of the current population's roots are from that religion or ethnic group? Other ethnic groups?
■ How did early settlers earn their living? Has that changed? How so?
■ How was the community or town "laid out"—neighborhoods, streets, major city buildings?
■ Which early settlers were most influential? Why?
■ Which local residents have been influential in different eras of the town's history? Why?
■ How were early houses built and furnished? Has that changed over the years? How and why?

■ What industries represent the majority of the population now (i.e., steel mills, electronics, technological manufacturing, farming, dairy farms, etc.)?

■ How was the early settlement of the area influenced by forms of transportation? How is the current population influenced by transportation?

■ How were early settlers influenced by commerce here and nearby?

■ How are we influenced by commerce now?

■ What examples of cultural resources were evident for early settlers? Now?

■ How have the area's land and water resources contributed to its history?

■ What examples of architecture are from various eras in the town's history?

■ Have certain geographic areas been settled largely by one group but not another? If so, why? Is this still true?

COMMUNITY HISTORY QUESTIONS

These questions (and others like them) can be used when interviewing a classroom guest, or by younger children as they interview older relatives or community members:

■ What year did you come here? What were your reasons for coming here?

■ What was the community like when you first came here (or when you were a child)? What did people do for a living? What were their homes like?

■ Think about the way the neighborhood looked when you first came here (or when you were a child). How has it changed? Give as many specific examples as you can.

■ Do the same people or families live here as when you first came? How are things different? Have your neighbors changed in terms of backgrounds, age, interests, careers, concern for the community?

■ What problems has this community faced since you came here? How have those been resolved, or how are they being resolved? What problems have not been solved? Why?

■ Are there any interesting "characters" in this community? What can you tell me about them?

■ Are there any interesting stories about this community?

IMMIGRATION

These questions can serve as a starting point when interviewing recent immigrants or those who came to the United States long ago:

■ What country did you originally come from? When?

■ What were your reasons for coming to the United States?

■ What was it like in your home country before you left?

■ What do you remember about the trip over here?

■ What were your expectations about the United States?

■ What were your first impressions of the United States?

■ How were you treated by others when you first arrived? Has that changed?

■ Were there some things that you had to adjust to? What were they?

■ What do you miss about your old country that you don't see in the United States?

■ Which customs or traditions from your old country have you retained?

WORK EXPERIENCE

Use these questions to interview various people in the community to get a broader perspective of "community helpers":

■ What job do you do? How did you get that job?

■ Where do you work? Please describe what you do there on a usual day.

▨ What special skills have you learned by doing your job? How did you learn these?

▨ What do you like best about your job? Why? What do you like least? Why?

▨ Describe your co-workers. Do the workers there depend on each other? In what way?

▨ What was the first job you ever had? Why did you decide to work at the job you have now?

Other subtopics for community study include:

1. The natural community (stands of forests and clearings; animals and plant life; changes in the natural setting; the impact of humans over time)
2. Government and services (local government; schools, colleges, and universities; churches; business establishments providing community services)
3. Organizations (historical societies; fraternal groups; 4-H; Boy Scouts, Girl Scouts; Big Brothers, Big Sisters; YMCA, YWCA)
4. Agriculture/related industry (farms; ranches; manufacturing; food delivery and preservation; groceries and supermarkets)
5. Roads and transportation (major and minor roads; roads of the past and roads of the present; how roads are built; buses, trains, airports)
6. Monuments and landmarks (cemeteries; natural landmarks; statues)
7. Recreation (parks; playgrounds; waterways; buildings)
8. Traditions (festivals; banquets; sporting events; carnivals; fairs; barbecues or other social events)
9. The arts (writers, artists, actors, singers, and/or dancers from the local area and their work; art or drama about the local area; myths, legends, or songs about the area)
10. Place names (places named after people [and why those people were important]; city, town, neighborhood, or community names and how they got them; street names and where they came from)

Chapter 6

Time Lines and Time Capsules

As with family history projects, time lines of local and/or community history can be the springboard for many more investigations. Developing or using a time line can help students notice trends, consider cause and effect, and become aware of the chronological relationships between and among events.

Find out whether a time line of local history already exists (historical societies or local museums often have copies of time lines available), then work with your students and outside resources to expand and update the existing time line. If no time line exists, telephone or write the state historical association for assistance. In any event, most local history time lines are not as current as teachers would like, so the challenge of creating a new one or expanding an existing one will appeal to both students and teachers.

A Local History Time Line

Working with students, develop a time line showing your town or community's history. Consult some of the local resources and contact knowledgeable resources to make certain the time line is as historically accurate as possible.

Begin the local time line with the first documented relevant date in local history—for example, the date the region was first referred to as a "territory." Include dates of political, economic, military, and ecological interest, along with an annotation or details keyed to a symbolic legend (much like a map legend). Original, primary, and secondary source research may be needed to fill in the gap between 1945 and the current year.

There will be many uses for the new time line. Help students use it to study cause and effect—that is, understanding not only what happened in the past but also why it happened. For example, when students studied lessons intended to teach them about the Wabash/Erie Canal during their local bicentennial, they noticed from available time lines that the decline of the canal system and the advent of the railroad transportation system occurred at about the same time.

Use time lines to study the lives of famous or influential people and their contributions to the local area. Students in Huntington, Indiana, childhood home of former U.S. Vice President Dan Quayle, were able to see connections between activities and educational experiences during Quayle's local childhood and his later recognition as a political figure as they studied a time line of his childhood and adult years.

▨ Trying It Out

Time Line of Monroe County

Teachers and students in one county worked together with university and local historians to develop a local history time line. This particular time line was intended for use by third- and fourth-grade teachers during units on community and state history, and so included information about what was going on in the state as well as the local area. Although the examples that follow detail historical events and important people related to Indiana history, teachers may use these as models to develop their own local time lines and date lines.

TIME LINE: MONROE COUNTY & INDIANA HISTORY

1800–1810	Indiana Territory separated from Northwest Territory. Vincennes became capital, with Wm. Harrison, governor. With Harrison's Purchase, the southern part of Monroe County was obtained from the Indians. The survey line was the 10 o'clock line.
1810–1820	Indians fought with the settlers in the War of 1812.
1813	Corydon became the new capital of Indiana.
1815	David McHolland was the first white settler in Monroe County.
1816	Indiana became the 19th state in the Union. Land in Monroe County went up for sale. Early settlers: Buskirk, Ketcham, Fleener, Graham, Matlock, Parks, Rogers, Stout, Wampler, Woodward. Abraham Lincoln moved to Indiana and lived for 14 years in Spencer County.
1818	Northern part of Monroe County obtained by treaty at St. Mary's, Ohio. Bloomington was founded. First double-log courthouse built (costing $400). Wm. Hardin opened a store with $150 in stock and "wet groceries" (whiskey, the settlers' "cure-all"). First school held in log courthouse with Dudley C. Smith as teacher.
1819	New brick courthouse planned and built by John Ketcham. A well was built on the square for use by settlement. The first church, Presbyterian, was built. A doctor, David Maxwell, set up office in Bloomington.
1820–1830	Indianapolis became the new state capital. All historic papers from capital at Corydon were moved by wagons to Indianapolis and never unpacked (these papers were lost). Bloomington was a "booming town" with 140 people. Businesses were set up: blacksmith, iron works, tannery, horse-drawn grist mill, saw mill, carding mill, gunpowder maker, saddle-maker, general store.
1821	$30 was spent for books for a library in the courthouse.
1822	Bloomington had two newspapers: *The Daily Word* and *The Courier*.
1823	Indiana Seminary becomes the first college (for men) in Indiana.
1825	Main transportation was river routes. Many flatboats carried goods on the Ohio River.

1827	The National Road from Richmond to Terre Haute was completed. It was made of crushed stone.
1828	The Michigan Road from Madison to South Bend was completed. It was a dirt road about 100 feet wide, hacked out of the wilderness.
1830	There were 5,678 people in Monroe County. Most were lumbermen, hunters, or farmers.
1832	After Black Hawks' War, Indians moved west to Kansas. More Indiana land was open for settlement. Since 1700, nearly all inland trade and emigration routes were through Indiana because of available waterways. The Wabash-Erie Canal was started, joining the Erie and Mississippi by way of the Wabash and Ohio Rivers.
1836	Orchard Stage Lines started in Bloomington, carrying mail and passengers to Indianapolis, Columbus, and Madison.

The Indiana Historical Bureau (1992) developed this time line and accompanying activities for classroom use:

Dateline: Native American Removal from Indiana

1820	Most of Delaware Indians gone from Indiana
1824	Bureau of Indian Affairs created
1829	Andrew Jackson becomes president
1830	Indian Removal Act is passed by Congress
1833	Kickapoo removed from Indiana
1836	Yellow River Potawatomi sign treaty and are given 2 years to leave
1837	George Winter, artist, moves to Logansport and begins his sketches of Indiana Indians
1838	Yellow River Potawatomi are forced on the Trail of Death
1846	Miami removed from Indiana
1897	Miami declared to have no tribal rights
1992	Indiana Miami sue federal government for recognition

Focus. After Indiana became a state in 1816, land ownership continued to be at the center of conflict between the Indian tribes, settlers, and the United States government.

From 1795 to 1840, chiefs of various Indiana tribes signed 16 treaties with the United States. The government wanted land to sell to settlers. The settlers were able to buy government lands very cheaply.

The situation concerning the Indians was very complicated. United States Indian policy changed over time. Under President Thomas Jefferson, United States policy tried to teach Indians to farm and be more like the white settlers. If Native Americans began to farm, Jefferson thought they would gradually give up their vast hunting lands to the government. When Andrew Jackson became President in 1829, he wanted to obtain the rest of the Indian land quickly.

Points of View. Native Americans in Indiana and other states lost out to white settlers' desire for land. [Words and images from a newsletter] present various points of view on the removal of Indians from Indiana.

> *In August 1821 there were treaty negotiations in Chicago, Illinois. Metea, an Indiana Potawatomi said that whites were taking Indian lands so fast that "the plowshare is driven through our tents before we have time to carry out our goods and seek another habitation"* (*quoted in Edmunds,* The Potawatomis, *p. 220).*

> *Governor James Brown Ray negotiated treaties with the Miami and* Potawatomi *at Paradise Spring in 1826. He said to the Miamis: "You ask us whether we wish you to live or perish. . . . If we did not wish you to live, and had not a due respect for you, why should we come to you to negotiate with you peaceably.—The numbers of the white men are like the trees in the forest, and our power is equal to our numbers.—We could take possession of your country by force and hold it, if we did not respect your rights (quoted in Riker & Thornbrough, eds.,* Messages and Papers Relating to the Administration of James Brown Ray, Governor of Indiana, 1825–1831, *(Indiana Historical Bureau, Indianapolis, 1954, p. 146).*

> *President Andrew Jackson in his 1835 message to Congress said that the removal of Indians beyond the Mississippi River was nearly finished. The plan should be carried out "as fast as their consent can be obtained. All preceding experiments for the improvement of the Indians have failed. It seems now to be an established fact that they can not live with a civilized community and prosper" (quoted in Richardson, ed.,* A Compilation of the Messages and Papers of the Presidents, 1789–1897, Vol. 3, *(Government Printing Office, Washington, DC, 1896, p. 267).*

Activities.   Try some of these:

- Discuss these points of view. What does each quotation mean? Write these points of view in your own words. What is your point of view after reading these quotations?
- Form discussion groups. Each group could discuss one quotation and then present it to the whole class. Another group could discuss how the [accompanying] pictures affect the viewer's point of view.
- Select one quotation and write a brief essay expanding its point of view.
- Refer to the [pictured] map. . . . Where are you located in Indiana? What Indian tribes lived in your area based on the treaty description?
- Investigate your local history to see what your part has been in the history of Native Americans in Indiana. See also the [pictured] map . . . , which has 1990 Native American population figures for each county.
- There are many Native American sites in Indiana marked with monuments, plaques, and markers. Locate those in your area and create a tour map.

Young Children Celebrate a Centennial

Judy Finkelstein and Lynn Neilsen (1985) wondered how to help their first- and second-graders understand 100 years of history when their local community celebrated its centennial. "To the young child . . . participation in home town centennial, or in some cases bicentennial, festivities is cause for anticipation of seeing a parade . . . eating favorite foods . . . generally having a good time." When children in primary grades participate in such festivities, the motivation can be "a catalyst for much content learning. Personal history, cultural awareness . . . [and] association, classification, and problem solving can appropriately be introduced."

How should teachers organize the study of centennial or bicentennial history for young children? The first important thing to remember is to limit the choice of content and concepts—cover less material in more depth. Second, create opportunities for children's backgrounds and experiences to be a part of the learning process by including family homework projects. Third, help children express what they have learned through creative language experiences: "writing, acting, speaking, producing, and drawing . . . that they might organize and record their ideas for personal reflection and sharing."

The following activities are offered as ways to help young children comprehend and appreciate their community's 100th or 200th birthday (Finkelstein & Neilsen, 1985).

What Is a Hundred?   Bring in containers of small objects for children to count (e.g., paper clips, dried beans, buttons). Prepare 6" × 6" inch squares of colored construction paper. Divide the class into small groups. Have each group count to 100 using their small objects, and place the 100 objects on a square of construction paper. (For advanced students, or as an extension, have students divide objects into groups of 10 each, with each group placed on a colored square, and count to 100 by tens.)

Within groups, have students decide on a small object that group members can easily collect (e.g., seashells, bottle or milk jug caps). Set the collection goal at 100, and display these items prominently in the classroom as they are brought in by group members. Create a chart for each group to record the number of items as they are brought in. Each day, discuss how many items have been brought in, and how many more are needed to reach 100. (Perhaps the first group to reach 100 could be recognized in some way to provide added incentive.)

Family Book.   Students and family members work together on stories and anecdotes describing 100 years of their family's history. The completed book will have five sections: family history 1 year ago, 5 years ago, 10 years ago, 50 years ago, and 100 years ago. Illustrate the stories and anecdotes with photos and drawings of people, events, and artifacts.

Scavenger Hunt.   Involve students' entire families by sending home a letter describing a community scavenger hunt. Challenge students and family members to find community artifacts that are at least 100 years old: Houses, buildings, organizations, churches, schools, parks, and flags are some of the possibilities (they may think of others). The public library and local history museum may be consulted. Students must bring in the artifacts (if these are in the family), or photos or drawings of them, along with written descriptions of century-old community resources. These reports are then displayed on a "Scavenger Hunt" bulletin board.

Classroom Museum Day.   Introduce the museum concept by taking a trip to a nearby museum. Inform curators ahead of time that your students are studying the past 100 years of the community's history, so appropriate artifacts and resources will be demonstrated or available for examination on the day of your field trip. While at the museum, encourage students to compare and contrast items seen with similar items or functions in modern times.

After the field trip, begin planning a Classroom Museum. Brainstorm on items 100 years old or more, and decide which of these items students could bring in for a museum display. Send a letter home explaining the project and informing parents that extreme care will be exercised in the display of valued family heirlooms.

As you prepare for the Museum Day, have students design and send out invitations (invite 100 guests). The children could serve 100 cookies and 100 cups of punch or juice. Grandparents could be invited, and would bring many memories of items displayed that might not otherwise be available.

Community Map.   Show students how the community was laid out 100 years ago by drawing a simple map on the board: Where the mall or shopping centers are now, what was once there? Where the school is now, what did the location once look like? Put x-marks on locations where students now live, to show their current homes' proximity to woods, meadows, farmlands, and so on, of 100 years ago. Show expansion of the original settlement by drawing dotted lines around it.

Centennial Newspaper.   Help children write a "child's eye view" of what the community was like 100 years ago, and try to get it included in the centennial edition of the local newspaper. Allow students to suggest departments or subheadings for the newspaper article, such as local/state/national news, sports, comics, weather, social events, advertising, photography, and editorials. After subheadings have been identified, divide students into groups and assign (or have groups volunteer for) these topics, one per group. Their writing should emphasize the contrasts between what the community was like 100 years ago, and what it is like now (have other subheading groups work with the photography group to decide what photos will be needed). When subtopics are completed, use a page layout computer program to create newspaper-width columns, and carefully proofread and edit each entry before sending it to the local newspaper editor.

Time Capsules

Children have trouble conceptualizing the passing of time, especially younger children. Time lines can help students visualize the passage of time in a linear fashion, but they do little to increase understanding of the *nature* of various time periods. Since children have fewer experiences than adults, they have fewer reference points to help them comprehend the change aspect of time. Turner (1989) suggests that children "better understand time and how it relates to the development of human events if it is put into concrete sensory form" (p. 124). Time capsules and similar "containers" of time's passage offer instructional aids that help children develop experiences and understandings related to sequence of events, relationships among events, and how these events fit into the overall scheme of historical time. Shoe boxes, crates, egg cartons, soft drink cartons with dividers, coffee cans, oatmeal boxes, and other similar containers can be used to collect and store materials and memorabilia related to a specific event or era. Activities employing "Time Stopped in a Bottle" or "Time Wrapped in a Box" (Turner, 1989) are summarized here:

Generation Bottles: Colored water (use food coloring) is stored in clear plastic or glass bottles to represent life times of individual family members. The person who has lived the longest is represented by a bottle full of colored water; the next younger relative is represented by a bottle almost full, and so on down to the youngest family member (represented by a scant amount of colored water in a bottle). These bottles are arranged in order from almost empty to full. Label each with the family member's name and age.

Good Year Bottles: Collect many bottles of different sizes and shapes. Each bottle is decorated to represent a "good year," depicting significant events that happened in that year. After choosing or being assigned a specific year, students or groups of students select pictures, news headlines, cut-outs of people's photos or products and decorate the labeled bottle.

Bottles of Time Pills: Each bottle represents a specific year. "Time pills," or rolled/wadded strips of paper, give a brief description of an event from that year. Students take turns pulling time pills from the bottle and identifying events from the descriptions given. When a student has correctly named all events from the time pills, he or she may create another "time pill" for that bottle.

Bottle-Time Dioramas: Remove one side from a large plastic bottle (e.g., a 2-liter soft drink or bleach bottle) and have students construct a scene inside to represent a favorite event for a particular year or topic of study.

Message Bottles: Much as sailors once dropped bottles containing notes overboard, hoping they would be found and read, students can pretend to send messages from the past. Students pretend they are marooned time travelers stuck in a particular year. They decide what messages they would like to send to the future, place these messages rolled up in bottles with tight-fitting caps, and float them in a large tub of water. Other students "find" these bottles, read the messages, and respond with messages of their own from the present.

Stacking Time Boxes: These are made from similarly shaped, lidded boxes, labeled by students with a particular time sequence (e.g., 1950–1959). Students consult magazines and newspapers from the time period (if possible), make copies of articles representing important issues from that time period, and arrange these "clippings" chronologically in the box. Filled boxes are stacked in chronological order and used as a basis for discussion or for writing activities.

Years of Our Lives: These boxes contain artifacts (paper and otherwise) that students consider important representations from particular periods in their lives. The student's birth month should be marked on the box, and all boxes arranged chronologically by month of the year. Each day for 12 consecutive days, one box is examined and discussed by class members.

Generation Boxes: A stack of three or four boxes is used to represent the generations alive in a student's family (one box per generation). Boxes are labeled with the birthdate of the individual representing that generation (e.g., the student, his or her parent, grandparent, and great-grandparent). Students fill boxes with items and information relating to each generation represented. This activity can be a data gathering activity prior to developing a family history album.

Century Boxes: Groups of students are assigned a century. The group gathers information related to significant events and persons from that century.

Decade Boxes: This activity is similar to Century Boxes, except groups of students are assigned specific decades. Use this idea when researching background information about the local city or community.

Trying It Out

Time Capsule Books

Toni Whitney recalled that her high school graduating class from the 1960s had made personal time capsules to share at their tenth-year reunion. She decided to use her time capsule to get her sixth-graders interested in recent history. Over the weekend, she "buried" her time capsule on the schoolyard, made a "treasure map" leading to the site, and began her activity when students returned on Monday.

Toni advises, "Put students into small groups and give each group a map and a set of directions. Each group will begin at a different starting point and are instructed to go to each of the seven points that are indicated on the map. The seven points are determined according to the written directions and measurements each group is given. Clues or directions should be developed to suit your surroundings. Once everyone has reached point seven, they are instructed to find an unusual object or treasure. This can be buried in a waterproof container or hidden."

She continues, "Once the capsule is found, it should be opened and the students should be given time to examine the objects. A large group discussion should follow to determine the decade in which the items came and how they may or may not have affected their lives today."

"Discuss the purpose of a time capsule and brainstorm what students could put in a time capsule to represent the present decade. Students can then make books showing what they would like to include in their time capsule and write an explanation as to how it would represent them or their family. An alternative method to this would be to use shoe boxes and have students create their own time capsules using actual objects. The students could also make a class time capsule to be opened at a later date."

When Toni's students "discovered" her buried time capsule from the 1960s, everyone was interested in seeing what was inside. "All the way back to the building, students kept asking what was in the box—I told them they would have to wait and see," Toni says. Once the items had been examined, students had a great many observations to make about the time period known as the "sixties." "They thought the clothing and the hairstyles of the 1960s were hilarious, and said they would *never* dress like that!" she recalls. But then they began to talk about how many of the styles are coming back, such as striped pants and wide-heeled shoes, and realized that some fads do "recycle."

"We discussed many of the famous people and events of the sixties, and students realized that they knew more about the sixties than they thought they did," Toni relates. "Many students had heard of Malcolm X . . . and even have clothing with the X symbol on it, but they didn't know what Malcolm X actually did. Racism became a heated debate among the students, and they shared their views on how people should learn to work together. Not all shared this view. I could really sense the values of their parents when they were sharing."

Toni's class also discussed representations of the Vietnam War contained in her time capsule. Some students wanted to tell stories about relatives who had fought in that war. Amish students in the class strongly voiced their opposition to all war, while other students said they felt war was sometimes necessary "to keep order." Finally, as discussion began to wind down, the students began to look through recent magazines for ideas to include in their time capsule books.

Some of the items that students decided to include in their Time Capsule Books were clothing, shoes, pictures of hairstyles, pictures of famous people, photographs of special events, models of popular automobiles, games, lists of important events, books or newspapers, job descriptions, toys, recipes, music, medicine, architectural designs, and different types of useful appliances and current technology. A sampling of students' Time Capsule Books reveals both the wealth of diversity in students' backgrounds and their perceptions of "important things in my life."

Niva Jean thought it was important to include the following in her Time Capsule Book:

> I am doing this Time Capsule because I want to show how we live. I want to have it opened at the year of 2099.
> ■ (Unbecoming photo of President Bill Clinton). Bill Clinton. He is our president. He became our president in 1993. He allows abortion.
> ■ (Black and white photo of Amish horse and buggy with two passengers.) Horse & Buggy. The Amish transportation is a horse & buggy. My culture is Amish. We wear plain clothes and wear caps. We have no electricity.
> ■ (Magazine cut-out of a white, plain christening dress.) This is a dress that the Amish new born babies wear.
> ■ (Magazine cut-out of a slice of blueberry pie.) Blueberry pie. I like to cook and bake.
> ■ (*Time Magazine* cover photo of popular country music artist Garth Brooks.) Garth Brooks. Garth Brooks is a country singer and country is my style. His latest hit is called "That Summer."

Monica writes:

> My time capsule represents my family and myself, during the early 1990's. I made this time capsule so people could remember what my life was like [as] a kid. I would like to have someone find and open this time capsule in 10 years.
> ■ (Magazine cut-outs of three different women's hairstyles.) Hairstyles. The Hairstyles that were in were long and straight, or short and curly. You will usually have long bangs.
> ■ (Magazine cut-outs of blue jeans and a white blouse.) Clothes. Clothes had to be baggy. Blouses and jeans were the things to wear.
> ■ (Magazine photo of Michael Jordan, athlete.) Michael Jordan. Michael Jordan plays for the Bulls. He plays basketball. He is the hottest player in the NBA.
> ■ (Magazine cut-out of a red convertible.) Cars. Sports cars are in. Such as convertibles, Mercedes, and Corvettes.
> ■ (Magazine close-up photos of a dog and a kitten.) Animals. I like animals. But our animals are dying because of the pollution we are doing to the earth.

Nathan's Time Capsule Book is decorated largely with Nathan's own drawings (see Figure 6.1). The cover page has "Time Capsule" printed in a capsule-shaped object on wheels. The next page contains these words:

> Time Capsule made by Nathan in the year 1993, not to be opened before 2093. This time capsule was made to remember the people from the year 1993 so they are not forgotten. [in red] Warning—If time capsule is opened too early it <u>will</u> self-destruct!!!!!!!!!!!
> ■ (Drawing of a large-screen television with antenna on top.) Television or TV. TV sends sound and pictures into homes by screens and speakers. After school, I like to watch TV.
> ■ (Drawing of a figure shooting a basketball into a high basket.) Basketball. A sport played where the object is to get a ball into a hoop. This is my favorite sport.
> ■ (Drawing of a slimline telephone.) Telephone. A device used to communicate between people. My family and I like to talk to people far away on the telephone.
> ■ (Drawing of the Nike trademark.) Nike symbol. A popular symbol of a company that makes shoes and sportswear. Nike is my favorite kind of shoes.

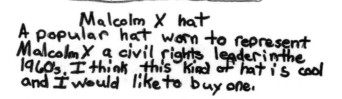

Figure 6.1   Sample Entries for Time Capsule Book

■ (Drawing of a baseball cap.) Malcolm X hat. A popular hat worn to represent Malcolm X, a civil rights leader in the 1960's. I think this kind of hat is cool and I would like to buy one.

Ivan's Time Capsule Book opens from left to right, indicating his left-handedness. The first page of Ivan's book states:

This time capsule relates to my family and me. Some of the things in this time capsule I have at home. Some of the others related to my cultures. Do not open untill Jan. 1, 1999.
■ (Magazine photo of three kittens being fed.) Cats make good pets as well as good mouse catchers.
■ (Magazine photo of a dog.) Dogs are used as pets, garddogs, and farmdogs. One of the things that farm dogs do is heard livestock and gard dogs at night.
■ (Magazine photos of farm horses and work horses.) Horses are used to pull buggies, carts, and wagons. They are useful on the farm. Some people keep them for riding or as pets.

- ■ (Magazine cut-out of a roasted chicken in a baking bag.) We own a chicken house. We have 14,000 chicks at one time. We sell them when they are 6 weeks old.
- ■ (Magazine photo of a richly detailed wooden chest.) My dad makes furniture. I probly have to help him some day too.

Toni says that sharing her high school time capsule from the 1960s helped students learn "more of what it was like to grow up in the 1960s [than commercial materials provide] and see what their parents may have experienced. They also realized that no matter how unimportant they might think they are, everyone is a part of history. . . . It seems that students at the sixth grade level have no concept of time. To them, the sixties seemed like it occurred 100 years ago, and they found it hard to believe that society could change so much in such a short period of time. When students designed their own time capsules, they wanted it to be opened in the year 2000. After discussing this, students realized that this was only a few years away and suggested that it should be opened at least 20 years later. This would allow more changes to occur in the world and then their items would be more interesting to those opening the time capsule."

When she uses this activity again, Toni will invite students to create a "class time capsule," with actual items representing their experience together as a class to be placed in a box and sealed.

The Year in Review

Help your students understand their participation in the history-making process, and the place their community holds in recent and current history, with this current events activity.

Videotape the local and national television newscast one night, and show it to your students the following day. Talk about the events covered and issues raised by the newscasters. Discuss the impact that state or national events have on your students and their families. Talk about what is meant by "current events" (if this is a new term for your students), and announce that the class is going to begin a collection of current events documentation.

Each week, have the students bring in newspaper articles depicting the local area. They must also bring at least one article that depicts a state, national, or world event or issue that affects themselves or their families. Each week, different students are selected to compile a "news review" of articles collected by all students during that week. These students produce their own newscast—video or audio version—and present it to the class.

Following their "newscast," students paste or mount the collected newspaper articles in a large notebook or photo album. This process continues until the end of the year, when all students should have had the opportunity to "tape" and present a newscast. At the end of the year, have a "Year in Review Day." Go through the album and recall important or memorable news stories and the effects on students and their families. (Donate students' completed news album to the school library for others to enjoy.)

Chapter 7

Local Geography and Landmarks

People's interactions with the places they live change their environments in some way. At the same time, the choice of a place to live and work may place physical and/or cultural limitations on people's everyday lives. When students study the local community, they also should study interactions between people, places, and environments—in other words, geography.

The Joint Committee for Geographic Education (1984) identifies five overlapping themes that teachers should use to plan appropriate instruction for students of all ages. Consider these themes as you plan for the study of the local community: location, place, region, human-environment interactions, and movement. *Location* answers the question of where something is; *place* describes the unique (physical and human) characteristics that make an area recognizable; *regions* are defined by characteristics that make them uniquely functioning and delineate them from larger surrounding areas; *human-environment interactions* describe humans' relationships with the spaces they occupy; and *movement* is the exchange of goods, services, people, and/or ideas from place to place.

Children can study the significance of local landmarks as they locate them during their geographic investigations. Cemeteries, statues, parks, and historical buildings often have fascinating stories attached to them. These stories, and related historical facts, serve not only to motivate further investigation about the local area but also to help students see connections between events, people, and the landmarks themselves.

Map Packets

Develop your own resource package for teaching about local maps and geography by making a Map Packet. A Map Packet is an original, teacher-created instructional resource designed for elementary school children to use independently or in pairs. It includes an assortment of maps, related activities for students, a self-checking answer sheet, and an inventory.

ITEMS TO INCLUDE IN A MAP PACKET

A local city street map

A state road map

A regional map (e.g., southeastern states)

One or more "novelty" maps (e.g., Disney World, national parks, another country)

Six or more related activities

Several related activities

A self-checking answer sheet for all activities

An inventory

These materials should be stored in a large manila envelope with clasp closure, a cardboard storage folder with string tie or elastic band closure, or a large pocket folder. Decorate the outside of the envelope or folder with map-related cut-outs or illustrations and words.

Introduce the Map Packet to your students at the beginning of their study of the local area. Explain how individuals or pairs of students may use the activities in the packet to learn more about map reading, map making, and local geography. Place the Map Packet in a learning center or interest center, where it will become a daily attraction as students study the local area. You may wish to create a chart of some sort for students to keep track of who has completed specific activities contained in the Map Packet as a form of assessment.

Local Geography Map

The geography of the local town or community is an important part of its history. For example, a town with one or more important rivers may have been settled as people or businesses transported goods for sale down the rivers. A community surrounded by mountains may be largely supported by families who live on those mountains and conduct their business in the "valley." A community with fertile soil and temperate climate may have attracted people who liked to farm or who knew a great deal about agriculture, and so became a place largely supported by farming.

To understand the geography of a town, students must identify its major physical features. For example, are there rivers, mountains, forests, cliffs? Divide the class into small groups according to zip code (or, if your town is small, by street names or subdivisions). Have students complete a homework assignment using the directions on the Local Geography Worksheet.

■ Trying It Out

Learning about Maps

Nancy Bergstedt wanted to assess what her second-grade students already knew about maps and map reading, and wanted to teach her students how to draw a useful map. She began the lesson by showing students several types of maps, such as a weather map, an atlas, a road map, a U.S. map, and a globe. They talked about each kind of map—its purpose, when it would be useful, and what it was called. "We then made a chart of the things that were alike about the maps and the things that were different," Nancy says.

After this introduction, Nancy asked students to draw a map of the classroom (see Figure 7.1). "I purposely did not give specifics as to what should be included in their maps," she recalls, "because I wanted them to draw what they knew." When students had finished their classroom map assignment, Nancy handed out a worksheet describing a fictional newspaper route and inviting students to draw the route on the street map provided. This worksheet was taken from the recommended social studies textbook resource book, so Nancy felt that it would be on her students' instructional level. "Instead," she reflects, "almost every student expressed confu-

LOCAL GEOGRAPHY WORKSHEET

1. *Take a Walking Tour of Your Neighborhood:* Using a notebook or sketch pad and pencil, take a walking tour of your neighborhood, sketching geographical features, such as hills, creeks, wetlands, meadows, and woodlands. If these places have names, write in the appropriate name for each. Some may have been turned into a park or park-like area for the enjoyment of local residents. Try to determine what features of the area make it different from other neighborhoods.

2. *Make a Neighborhood Map:* Bring your drawing to school, and compare it with others in your group. Did your classmates find features you missed? Did you see features others did not? Pool your findings and make a large map describing your neighborhood on the butcher paper or poster board your teacher gives you. Then use the following recipe to make a model of your neighborhood:

INGREDIENTS

Plasticine

Some sponges or spongeboard

A cookie sheet or baking pan with very low sides (preferably an old one)

Small rocks or pebbles

School glue

Directions

Cut a sheet of paper the same size as the bottom of your pan. Draw the physical features you want to portray on the paper, placing such features as hills and lakes exactly where you want them to go on the model. Use this drawing as your "blueprint" as you make the model.

The cookie sheet is the base of your model. Use the plasticine to form the physical features of your neighborhood (a hill is a mound of plasticine, some pebbles represent rocks, etc.). A field or flat area would be represented by plasticine smoothed flat on the cookie sheet. A creek or river is made by digging a groove into the plasticine and filling it with a little water when the model is finished. Trees can be represented by shredded sponge pressed or glued onto the plasticine. The plasticine will not get hard, so you can change the model several times until you and others in your group are happy with the way it looks. Label the model and share it with others in your class.

3. *Study Human Effects on the Environment:* Now think about the human effects on the geographic environment in your neighborhood. Do any of the creeks or rivers have bridges over them? How about covered bridges? When were these built, and by whom? What did the neighborhood look like during that era? What was it like to live here? What kinds of changes (for the good and the bad) would a human intervention like a bridge have on the neighborhood?

Look at aerial views of the county if you can, or maps of property owned and settled in the area from 30 to 50 years ago. In which areas did housing developments spring up? Why were they built there? In which areas were malls or shopping centers built? Why? What changes did these human interventions have on the neighborhood? On the environment?

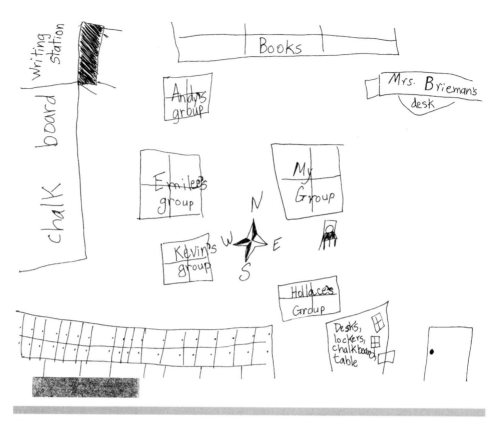

Figure 7.1 Classroom Map Drawn by Student

sion; they claimed they didn't know what to do. I quickly changed my plan a bit, and we went over the worksheet together, in detail. This cleared up most of the confusion, but not all of it."

Next year, when she decides to assess map knowledge with her new students, Nancy says she will do things a little differently. She plans to start by showing students a simple picture and asking them to copy it. Then she would make an analogy between the drawing they had just made and a map. "In thinking back," she states, "I do not think the students really understood that basic concept—that a map is a picture of something else, be it the world or the classroom."

Walk-About Map

Like Nancy Bergstedt, Cheryl wanted her students to understand that a map is a picture of a part of their world. She planned that her first-graders would be able to verbally and physically locate land and water on a map and on a globe, to know that there is more water than land on earth, and to draw their own maps and orally identify land and water on their maps.

The difference between Cheryl's and Nancy's lesson is that Cheryl used a large, 6' × 9' floor map that children could walk on in their socks. "It is very popular with all students," she notes. "The younger ones love to jump from continent to continent, or dance on the equator, or pretend to freeze if they are standing in the Antarctic Ocean.... This is a very kinesthetic geography tool." Cheryl remembers that when she was an elementary school student, only the teacher was allowed to touch the map or globe. She says, "When the first-graders walked in and saw the map on the floor there was a lot of excitement.... In my opening, I showed them a stuffed panda and a model car. I was trying to teach them that the toy objects looked just like the real objects, only smaller." Upon reflection, Cheryl says this is still a very abstract way of teaching first-graders about maps as symbols or representations of something larger, but it did get them to thinking about the nature of maps.

Since the map is large, five or six students at one time can be involved in map activities while other students watch. Then these students become observers, and another group performs the activity. Cheryl told them, "Step on the map and have both of your feet in the water. Pretend you are swimming until both feet are on the land. Now put one foot on the land and one in the water. Now have both feet on the land, with just your toes in the water."

If one group seemed to have trouble understanding these simple directions, Cheryl gave more directions and prompts until all students in the group had their feet on the appropriate spot. She believes that all students need at least two opportunities to try this activity before they can demonstrate their understanding of land and water on their own maps.

Neighborhood Maps

Have each student make a map of his or her neighborhood for a class bulletin board. Students who live near each other can do their maps cooperatively. Display a picture of your school in the middle of the bulletin board, and arrange the students' maps around it to represent the areas covered by your school district.

Another variation of the Neighborhood Maps bulletin board is to place a map of the city or county on the bulletin board with the appropriate community highlighted. Students' maps then represent detailed views of the highlighted community.

▣ Trying It Out

Neighborhood Walking Tour

Cindy Stiver and her second-graders took a walking tour around their school as a way of developing better understanding of and appreciation for their community. Cindy asked the children to notice street names and the composition of particular streets (the original bricks show through portions of pavement on area streets), types of homes, and types of business locations. "What names of things can you find that are named after famous people?" Cindy asked the students. She took special care to point out parks, buildings, schools, housing developments, and streets named after local and national famous people. When they returned to the classroom, Cindy helped the students make a list of the things they remembered named after famous people. "Who are/were these people?" she asked. Groups of students were assigned persons to research, and asked to bring to class a paragraph telling about that person and why he or she is famous. In Cindy's class, parent volunteers who visit each week assisted the groups with their research.

Following the walking tour, students took home worksheets inviting parents and other family members to assist them in listing and describing information about the communities they grew up in. The worksheet included these questions:

1. Where did you grow up (city and state)?
2. What was the name of the street you lived on?
3. Describe the house or apartment you lived in as a child.
4. Describe any special places children played in your community.
5. Describe other special places in the community of your childhood.
6. Were there special events or celebrations in your childhood community? Describe these, and tell about your participation in them.

The information gathered from family members energized students' discussion of their own community and its many aspects—of which they were now aware. Cindy suggested they make an "All about My Community" book as a cooperative project. For each group, she stapled together nine large sheets of paper, labeling seven sheets in the following fashion: A Famous Place, Where People Live, Transportation, Where People Shop, Having Fun, Where People Work, and Facts about My City. Students drew pictures and wrote one or two sentences related to the topic on each page. The first sheet was used as a cover page, and the last sheet as an author page.

Going on a Treasure Hunt

Linda Lucenta gave her fourth-graders an opportunity to review map reading skills and knowledge about maps near the end of the school year with an activity based on treasure maps. "I introduced the book, *The Seven Treasure Maps* (Byars, 1991), to activate their schemata and interests about treasure hunts and maps," she says. Linda read the book aloud to her students (this took almost an hour of class time). Students discussed the book's contents and the use of treasure maps in groups as Linda prepared a projection of a local street map on the overhead projector. Students would be using this map to complete the treasure map activity, so Linda had them practice finding compass directions on the map in small groups as a way of orienting them to this new map.

Next, students used a Treasure Hunt Worksheet Linda had designed, along with a copy of a section from the projected map to discover various locations, using treasure map-type clues. She introduced the assignment, then let students choose a partner to work with while completing the directions on the worksheet. "I encouraged students who did not live in the neighborhood [where the school was located] to find a partner who did," she recalls, "so they would not be at a disadvantage, since the map they would be working with was a street map of the area surrounding the school."

When all pairs of students had completed the assignment, they came back together in a large group. Linda used a different color marker to mark the locations each pair had "discovered" on the larger projected map. To provide closure, she allowed each pair of students to devise their own original "treasure hunt" with their particular map section, then swap treasure hunts with another pair of students. This was all in fun, and Linda told students that if they completed their treasure hunt activities by the end of the week, "I would use one of the treasure hunts for their end-of-the-year party and make copies of the others' treasure hunts for the whole class to use and enjoy over the summer."

Learning about Our Town

Stacie wanted her third-graders to become more familiar with the environment around them, especially their community. She also intended that they learn how to read and use local maps. She began with "what they know," as all good teachers do, by dividing the class into three groups and having one group draw pictures of their families, one group draw pictures of their houses, and one group draw pictures of their neighborhoods. After the pictures were completed, Stacie brought the large group back together and asked, "If we were to put all of these pictures together in one book, what could be the title of the book?" Students decided to call their book "Our Community," and Stacie bound all the drawings together as a class album.

Next, she displayed photos of various kinds of communities (e.g., suburban, rural, farming, urban). Students discussed similarities and differences, which Stacie listed on the board. She introduced the terms *city, suburb,* and *town,* showing photographs representing each term. "What can you tell me about each of these kinds of communities?" she asked the students. Using the overhead projector, the class made a web of identifying characteristics for cities, suburbs, and towns.

Finally, Stacie brought students' attention back to the familiar when she asked this question about their own community, "What is Huntington—a city, suburb, or a town?" Students discussed and debated which term best described their community, then, in groups of four, listed all of the qualities that make Huntington a town. Lists were shared orally with the class as a whole, and students were encouraged to talk with family members at home about their town.

The next day, Stacie's class resumed their study of the community by considering these questions: Has our community always been the same? Does anybody know how it has changed over time? How do communities begin? How do they change? How do they stay the same? Then, using a book written to help children learn about their local area and working in three groups, students read about (Group 1) immigrants to the area, (Group 2) Native Americans in the area, and (Group 3) learning about their town from senior citizens. They discussed their readings within their respective groups, then presented to the large group their major findings. What has

TREASURE HUNT WORKSHEET

You are a messenger for your school, Croninger Elementary School. The principal has numerous errands for you to run. You need to pick up a package at the post office, deliver letters to other schools in the area, return books to the library, and pick up pizzas for the class.

Use the map and the following clues to find all the places you need to go. You will need red, blue, green, and yellow markers or colored pencils. Fill in the compass rose before you get started.

1. If you live in this neighborhood, locate where you live and make a yellow dot there.
2. Croninger Elementary School is on Trier Road. Find it and color it blue.
3. Use your finger and travel east on Trier Road until you find Maplecrest Road. Turn north onto Maplecrest and continue until you find Stellhorn Road.
4. The post office is in Northwood Plaza, which is on the northwest corner of Maplecrest and Stellhorn. Find it to pick up the package, and circle it red.
5. You decide to eat breakfast before you continue your errands. Burger King is across the street from the post office. It's on the northeast corner of the intersection. Make a yellow dot to show where it is on the map.
6. You need to finish your errands after breakfast. Go north on Maplecrest until you find St. Joseph Center Road, and turn east. You should see St. Joseph Elementary School. Drop off a letter and color the school blue.
7. Continue traveling east on St. Joseph Center Road until you find Arlington Elementary School. Drop off a letter and color the school blue.
8. You need to continue east on St. Joseph Center Road until you find Wheelock Road, and turn south. You will find Jefferson Middle School on the west side of the road. Drop off a letter and color the school blue.
9. You have some extra time, so you decide to play golf at Arlington Golf Course. Find the golf course. It is southeast of Jefferson Middle School. Color its flag green.
10. Time to go back to work. Return to Croninger School and drop off the package from the post office. The principal gives you two more letters to deliver and books to return to the library.
11. The library is in Georgetown Plaza, which is south of Croninger School. Try to find Georgetown Plaza. What street is it located on?

_____

    Make a red dot for the library.
12. You need to deliver letters to Blackhawk Middle School and Haley Elementary School. Both of these schools are near Georgetown Plaza. Find them and color them blue. What streets are these schools on?

_____

_____

13. Little Caesar's Pizza is on the northeast corner of Maplecrest Road and State Boulevard. Go there to pick up the pizzas for the class party. Make a yellow dot to show where Little Caesar's is located.

CONGRATULATIONS! YOU HAVE FINISHED YOUR ERRANDS, AND CAN GO BACK TO CRONINGER SCHOOL FOR THE PIZZA PARTY!

been the impact of immigrants and Native Americans on our community? they pondered. To bring closure, Stacie asked students to consider how their town has changed, and how it has stayed the same.

For the next lesson, Stacie tied the reading of *Ramona and Her Father* (Cleary, 1988) to how students can learn about their community from senior citizens who have lived there a long time. In the book, Mrs. Swink (an elderly neighbor) teaches Ramona "how things used to be." Students were invited to discover and share stories from their parents or grandparents to demonstrate how something in the community has changed over time. (These stories were not written down, but upon reflection, Stacie recommends that students work with parents or grandparents to write and illustrate these stories, which would be bound into a class album.)

To culminate their study, Stacie invited a special speaker from the local historical society who would entice her students to learn more about their community with a slide collection and historical photographs. Then they took a bus tour of the community and visited two of the featured sites. Following the field trip, Stacie planned lessons and activities involving the formal use of local and state maps.

Geography of a School

Younger students, or students with limited map reading and making experience, can benefit from a geographical exploration of their own school as a precursor to more sophisticated study. Murphey (1991) suggests teaching children about the five themes of geography by having them explore the school as a geographic site. Materials needed include a U.S. map, a map of the local area, a compass, and chart paper or overhead transparency and markers. Students should be equipped with paper, graph paper, pencils, crayons, and pens. Since groups may need to leave school property during some portions of their investigation, plans should be made to have an adult chaperon accompany each group.

To introduce the topic of school geography, ask students to brainstorm the many things people read: books, newspapers, magazines, advertisements, signs, and so on. Tell them they are going to learn to read something new: a landscape.

Divide the class into five cooperative groups, with each group member being assigned a specific role (e.g., reporter, recorder, time keeper, instructions reader, map/direction reader). Each group will investigate and collect data on questions related to one of the specific geographic themes. Remind all students that everyone has a second role to the one they have been assigned: Everyone also is an information gatherer. The objective is to gather as much information as possible, with everyone in the group working together. Give the following directions to the large group before separate groups begin their investigations: Each group should read instructions, record findings, and come back to the starting point within 30 minutes. At that time, groups will be able to work together for the next 30 minutes to rewrite, edit, or complete their assigned tasks.

Once all groups have returned from their investigations, reporters for each group share their group's findings. The teacher or a parent volunteer records findings on the overhead projector or on chart paper, under the appropriate title (location, place, region, human-environment interactions, movement). As reporters share individual group's findings, discuss with students how and why some areas overlap. When all groups have reported findings, and overlapping areas have been discussed, have students write a geographic description of their school, using examples from the large group chart. Share these aloud when finished, and compare students' descriptions with those in the school yearbook or other descriptive literature.

Instructions for the Five Groups

Location: Location is either absolute or relative. It answers the question "Where?"

1. Find the approximate location of our school on a U.S. map. What is the latitude? What is the longitude? What is the city, or the nearest large city? What major cities are north of the area? South? East? West? Which major landmarks are nearby?

2. Go to the front door of the school. Use the compass to find out which direction the front door faces. Write down the direction.
3. What is the nearest street or highway intersection? Walk to it, recording names of all streets and roads you pass. Look for landmarks, such as drainage ditches, homes, stores, fire stations, and so on, and record these.
4. Continue with your walk until you reach a street or intersection recorded on the local map. Find this location on the map.
5. Now walk quickly back to the front door of the school building. Using your compass, the local map, and the information you have gathered, find the school's approximate location on the local map.
6. Draw a map of the immediate area of the school site, including streets, landmarks, and other important details. Indicate the route your group walked by marking this map with a colored marker.

Place: Place explains the unique physical and human characteristics that make an area recognizable; it tells how an area looks.

1. Walk to the front of the school. Walk on until you have reached the front edge of the school property. Observe and record the following: shape of the land, type of surface(s), colors, objects, buildings (type, material, age), people and their activities, traffic and traffic patterns, air quality, plants, animals.
2. Walk to the back of the school property. Record your observations of this area (use categories above).
3. Go to each side of the school property, and describe your observations from both those perspectives.
4. Using all information gathered, work together as a group to draw a detailed picture of the school site. Divide drawing paper into sections, and assign each person in the group a section to complete. Label the drawing with descriptive words.

Region: A region is defined by characteristics that make it a uniquely functioning area, and that delineate it from larger areas.

1. Go to the front door of the school. Walk to the nearest intersection. Half the group should go in one direction, and the other half in the opposite direction, as you observe and record information about the following regional types:

   Economic: Is it residential, business, agricultural, or recreational?

   Cultural: What can you tell about religions, languages, education, sources for food, and so on?

   Political: What can you tell about law enforcement, mail delivery, sanitation, cities cars come from?

   Environmental: Describe the climate, local landforms, visible plant and/or animal life.
2. Go back to the school property. List all the regions you can identify. Do any regions overlap? Each half of the group should draw a map or illustration showing what it found out about regions in the area.

Human-Environment Interactions: Human-environment interactions deal with relationships people have with the space around them and resulting changes.

1. Walk all around the school property, looking for and recording information about boundaries or barriers (property lines or fences), open spaces, safety features and/or hazards, evidence of litter or vandalism or beautification, sounds (both natural and human-made), any evidence of change to the site (and effects of that change), air quality, land use, building types, evidence of economic use of the land, evidence of cultural use, kinds of plants and/or animals and their effects on the local environment.

2. Go inside the school building. Observe this environment as though you have never seen it before. Record your observations about human interactions with the environment inside the school.

3. Work together as a group to write a short essay or report about your findings. Decide which important details you want to communicate to the rest of the class, and include these. Have the group recorder write down the group's ideas, and work together to edit and rewrite.

Movement: Movement is the exchange of goods, services, people, and ideas from place to place.

1. Walk around the school grounds. Pick an area with a lot of activity. Observe this area for a few moments.

2. List the types of movement you observe. Using this list, assign a movement type to each person in the group, who will observe related activity for five minutes while counting (e.g., *walking*—17 people and one dog walked past). As a group, make a graph showing the types and amount of movement observed in this area.

3. Go inside the school building. Pick two or three key people and interview them, asking questions such as:

    How do people and things get to this area?

    From how far away do people come? What is the nearest location they come from?

    Think about the number of people at this site. Are there more, or less, here now than a year ago? Why?

    What goods are used here? How do they get here?

    What services are used here? How are they brought here?

    Who pays for the goods and services? Who decided that these goods and services would be received? Why?

    Does this site produce any goods? Any services? If so, where do these go? How are they moved from the site?

    Are ideas exchanged with others outside the site? How is this done?

4. As a group, write a summary of your findings.

On the Street Where You Live

Have each student draw a map of his or her own neighborhood, including street names and landmarks. Display a drawing of the school and school property in the center of the bulletin board or hallway wall, and put students' maps up around the drawing. (Try to approximate geographic accuracy.) Pass out uniform strips of colored paper and black markers, and have each student write his or her name on the strip of paper. Students then pin their name tags to the areas on the display representing the street where *they* live.

With older students, display the entire "map" on white or lightly colored bulletin board paper. Have students research the layout of the neighborhood and gradually fill in the missing areas covered by their school district, creating a complete map of the community.

Alternatively, or as an extension to this activity, have students explore a street in their town or city and draw an accompanying map. (You may wish to display a city map, or have students list prominent street names on the board, to facilitate students' selection of a street to explore.) Suggest to students that they choose a street in their neighborhood or town that has stores, public buildings (such as a town hall, library, or museum, if possible), and perhaps a restaurant or office building. As they take a walking tour down the street with their sketch pad, buildings on each side of the street should be noted, mapped in, and labeled. Monuments, parks, train tracks, bus stops, and the like should be included, also. Have students bring their street maps to school to share with classmates, representing "Our Town Today." Tell students, "The next task involves a bit of detective work—What is the history of this street? What did it look like before you were born? Before your parents were born? How can we find out?"

Ask students to visit their streets again, this time as "street detectives." As they walk slowly down the same street, encourage them to look carefully and closely at each of the buildings. Are there plaques or dates engraved in the buildings or walkways that would give a clue as to when the building was erected? Do signs exist that give information about the building's history? Can you find a cornerstone with engraving on it? Have students record any pertinent dates on the maps next to the appropriate building.

Some buildings will have no information about their histories on the outside. Students may need to go inside the building and ask someone for information. Practice approaching other people and asking investigative questions in class to prepare students for this eventuality. Questions such as the following may be appropriate: "Hello, my name is _____. I'm researching the history of this street for my class at school. How long has this business been here? Was another business in this building before yours? When was the building built? Do you know anything else about the building? What was here before this building? Thank you for your help." Tell students to write down everything that is said in these interviews, including the person's name and telephone number in case additional questions later arise. Suggest that students use courteous behavior at all times, and that they wait until business people are less busy before asking questions or return at another time.

A third way students can explore their assigned street is to interview senior citizens or older relatives who have lived in the city for a long time. Ask them to describe what the street was like long ago. Invite senior citizens to recall what life was like in the city or neighborhood in years past, and write down or tape record these memories. If old photographs exist showing the street as it used to be, or the area before some or all current buildings were built, have students try to get copies of these or bring them to class (placed in a protective plastic sleeve) as "evidence" from their detective work.

This "detective" activity is a great lead-in to the creation of Baggie Books.

Baggie Books about Our Town

Use activities such as the ones detailed in this chapter to help students research the history and geography of their city or town. Important items to be researched include (among others):

■ When our area was first considered a town
■ How our town got its name
■ Who were the first settlers
■ What problems were faced by early and later settlers
■ Local landmarks
■ The first modern factory or other industry
■ Cultures and ethnic groups represented in the community
■ Schools and colleges or universities
■ Important news events

Use this information to make "Baggie Books" (see page 34 of the October/November 1990 issue of *The Mailbox* for illustrated instructions). Align "zip-type" storage bags on top of each other (determine ahead of time how many will be needed for your class project). Staple the bags together at the end opposite the sealable end. Cut two pieces of poster board slightly larger than bags to make a cover for each book (poster board should be at least one inch longer and one inch wider than bags). Cover poster board with wallpaper samples or fabric, using rubber cement. Bind, using the "W-Score-and-Fold" method:

1. Score and fold approximately one inch of an end of each cover. Fold back folded piece to make an accordion pleat. When two covers are placed together, folds will form a W.
2. Place stapled-together bags in between two covers. Staple covers to bags along spine.
3. Securely paper clip covers together at top and bottom corners nearest spine.
4. Cut piece of wallpaper or fabric the length of spine and several inches wide. Cover spine with this piece using rubber cement, remove paperclips.

Students will design their "Our Town History" stories on paper precut to fit Baggie Book pages. When completed, slip the finished story pages into the bags.

Sites of the City

Obtain several official maps of your city (often available from the Chamber of Commerce, local banks, Welcome Wagon representatives, or AAA Motor Club) and laminate them. Divide students into several small groups. Give each group a laminated city map.

Write the names of landmarks and other prominent sites on small pieces of paper, and make enough sets to give one to each small group. The groups must work cooperatively to find a way to get from the school to a particular landmark, writing out the directions on a separate sheet of paper. Members of one group will then read their directions aloud to the other groups to see if they can find the city site by following the directions given.

An alternative to this activity is to place students in pairs and have one student give the directions while the other student tries to follow directions to find the appropriate site. This is an excellent listening activity, as well as good practice in map reading and giving clear directions.

■ Trying It Out

City Sites

Michelle Yantz's third-graders worked on map reading skills as they learned more about landmarks in their city. Michelle obtained several city maps from the local Chamber of Commerce and laminated them. She divided her students into groups of four; each group received a laminated city map. Then Michelle passed out sheets of paper on which she had written the names of city landmarks (with appropriate addresses). Each group was responsible for finding a way to get from the school to the landmarks. They used washable colored markers to draw the route, and wrote narrative directions on paper. After all groups had finished, each group challenged the others to find its landmark by listening to the written directions and looking at their own maps. "This can also be used as a great listening activity between partners," Michelle explains. "One partner gives the written directions while the other partner follows them, using the map."

Visitors' Guide for Our Town

Leanne Bailey wanted her second- and third-graders to have a better appreciation of their community and its history. As a follow-up to the students' field trip to several historical locations, Leanne designed an activity intended to help them personalize what they had learned from their outing. Her objectives: "Students will plot important locations on a map, identify qualities about each location that give it relevance, and work cooperatively to create a 'Visitors' Guide.'"

After providing several reference books with colorful pictures and photographs relevant to the local area, Leanne guided the children to identify and brainstorm what they knew about seven community locations. She used an opaque projector to display a city map, and assisted the students as they identified and located the places in their list. Each location was assigned a number (1 through 7); the students counted off, numbering themselves 1 through 7, and thus received their "assigned location" to draw and describe.

"I wanted the students to review what they had learned about their city, and then use that information to make the connection on a map," Leanne states. "The culminating activity would be a tourist-type book, which I hoped would give added purpose."

The seven locations researched included Headwaters Park, Little Turtle's grave, the Old Fort, the Cathedral, the French Fort, Edsall House, and Kekionga Village. As students brainstormed what they knew and/or had recently learned about these locations, Leanne wrote their responses on the board, such as the following:

HEADWATERS PARK	THE CATHEDRAL	EDSALL HOUSE
Newest park	Oldest church in Fort Wayne	Oldest house in Fort Wayne
By a river	On Calhoun Street	No street addresses were used—only people's last names
Pretty		Made of brick

Students worked in groups using the resource books (found in the local library and the Chamber of Commerce) to ferret out more information about their "assigned location." Then individual students drew, labeled, and described their location on paper specially provided for that purpose, which was then complied into a class book titled "A Guide to Landmarks in Fort Wayne, Indiana" (see Figure 7.2). Bobby drew Little Turtle's grave, labeled with the date of death, the slogan "memorial," and the information that "his mother buried him—no actual grave [exists]." Donna drew the French Fort, with the information "The French Fort was attacked by the Miami Indians near the St. Joe River." The teacher drew a street map showing the appropriate downtown area on the overhead projector and, after drawing in the compass rose, asked students to help her place landmark symbols on this map for each of the seven locations researched. Then an expanded map legend was drawn on the side of the map, with each pictorial image labeled.

History Skyline

Help your students come to understand that history exists all around them by encouraging them to examine primary sources and local historical sites to gain first-hand information about life in the past in their community. For this activity, the following materials are needed: pictures/photographs of buildings (from postcards, brochures, and/or magazines); camera and film (Polaroid camera preferred); sketch pads and pencils; and loose paper and crayons.

Show the students the pictures of buildings. Ask, "What can you tell about this building by looking at it? Does it have a history? If this building could talk, what would it say?" Invite and discuss responses, in preparation for a walking field trip in the neighborhood.

Take students on a walk around their neighborhood or town. Concentrate on areas with interesting buildings. When students come upon a building that piques their interest, have them take a photo and/or draw it on their sketch pads. Assist students in finding out more information about the building by politely asking the people who live or work there. If permission has been obtained, have some students use paper and crayons to make rubbings of the exterior materials from which the building was constructed. (Be sure to label the rubbings with the name and/or location of the building.) Continue the walking field trip until several buildings have been investigated, and photographed or sketched, and labeled.

Ask students to inquire at home that night whether other family members (especially older relatives) know anything about the buildings they saw on the field trip.

Figure 7.2 A Page from "Visitors' Guide"

They may ask questions such as "Do you know/remember when it was built? What was the area like before the building was there? What changes have been made to the building and/or surrounding area over the years?" On the next day, encourage students to share their findings with others in the class. Assemble all data (photographs, drawings, stories, anecdotes, important names and dates, etc.). Mount photos and drawings and label each one. Organize relevant findings for each building, place those findings behind the mounted photos or drawings, and bind them into a class book as a record of your research.

■ Trying It Out

And Don't Miss the Covered Bridge!

Deborah Hudson's sixth-graders developed tourist brochures describing points of interest in their hometown. Deborah introduced the activity by posting a large city map divided into four quadrants. Then she divided the class into four groups, and assigned each group the job of "covering" one of the town's quadrants. "This will require careful map reading, as well as your use of the city directory and these pamphlets from the Chamber of Commerce," she told the students. Students were also encouraged to arrange on-site tours of relevant areas of interest to gather even more information. "Get your parents to help you set up a visit—maybe your whole group could go together on a Saturday," she suggested. Tour packets and brochures were developed by each group, who then had the opportunity to "take the rest of the class on a 'guided tour' of their part of the city." The students liked this activity so well that they wanted to take their annual field trip to one of the sites.

As their interest in their own town grew, Deborah's sixth-graders began to keep a Current Events Scrapbook. Deborah purchased a large (expandable) scrapbook, and groups of students took turns reading the daily newspapers, cutting out relevant articles, and pasting them in the scrapbook. At the end of each week, the groups responsible for that week's news coverage gave oral presentations on the articles they selected as newsworthy.

Kids' Eye View of Our Hometown

One fourth-grade teacher decided to involve her students in a research/writing project to "sell" their local community (McCarty, 1994). After seeing a magazine produced by gifted and talented middle school students, Diane McCarty wondered how her students could become involved in a similar project to celebrate their school's Computer Learning Month. She enlisted the help of the school technology consultant, and called the local Chamber of Commerce to get guidance for seeking financial support for the project. She says, "I visited the head of the Department of Tourism and shared my vision of a brochure that would promote our community. I felt that my students might have a whole new outlook on their community that would be fresh and appealing to others. They loved it!"

The Department of Tourism committed $500 to the class project, and offered to contact a local printer. Back in class, Diane introduced the community brochure idea to her students. They began to brainstorm a list of places in their community that should be included in the final product. Being trained in good writing techniques, the students wondered, "Who is our audience?" It was decided that, in this case, kids would write for other kids—the local community brochure would be designed to appeal to children who might be visiting the community with their parents.

The Chamber of Commerce sponsored a class field trip to help students begin their research for the brochure: a bus tour of the downtown area, narrated by a local historian. Diane was somewhat nervous about how her fourth-graders might behave during a 90-minute narrated bus tour, but, as it turned out, "the tour was the best thing to do to excite the students about the project," she says. Students seemed to develop a sense of purpose while listening to stories about their community as they looked and examined local landmarks and historic sites.

After the bus tour, students made a list of 85 local places and events that might be included in their research. This list was narrowed down to 20 items by class vote. One team worked on historical research, and the rest of the class worked in pairs to "write about current establishments and events in the community," Diane recalls. "Each child specified his or her top three subject choices, and from there, the pairs were made." When Diane was notified that a local printing company was willing to donate its time and 5,000 copies of the finished brochure, she and the students began to get down to some serious work.

Next, Diane used information about the history of the county from a packet supplied by the Chamber of Commerce to round out students' general background knowledge. This packet contained extensive, adult-level, reading material, so she condensed it to small increments that individual students could read and report on to the larger group. "The students had to read for only 10 minutes about any historic site that interested them," she reflects.

As an example of what kinds of writing the paired teams might be doing, Diane shared an article from a state magazine. "We discussed it and discovered what made it a good article," she says. "We talked about different forms the articles could take to add zest to our brochure." The class wrote a rap about the local public library as a practice activity for writing about their community, and liked it so much they included it in their brochure.

Student teams spent almost two weeks constructing and editing short articles about their selected topics. Diane feels this phase might have gone somewhat faster if her students had had better keyboarding skills (all preliminary writing was done in the computer lab). "Some students, of course, finished their stories earlier than others, so they began the illustrations," she notes. Students' drawings could represent any of the topics being researched, not just their own. They used pencil sketches to make it easier for the printing company to reproduce their illustrations.

When all teams had completed their articles, Diane put all computer files onto one disk and loaded these onto the hard drive of the classroom computer. "This is where final proofreading and editing took place," she says. "Articles were arranged into a logical layout, and they were checked to be sure all information was accurate." They were finally ready to take their brochure to the printer.

Students and teacher alike were pleased with the graphic artist's design of their brochure. After several telephone discussions and visits from Diane, the printer was ready to run the first copy. Almost all the student-created illustrations were incorporated into the brochure design, which was printed on special paper with a crayon-flecked appearance to appeal to young readers.

Diane and her students could have ended their project here, but they looked for more opportunities to learn and to involve the community. "The fourth-graders and their parents were invited to the printing plant after school to see the brochure being created," Diane recalls. They took a tour of the printing press, beginning with the printer's computer where they watched a demonstration of students' artwork being scanned, color being added via a computer graphics program, and ending with the actual brochure being printed and folded. Students learned about career opportunities they might never have considered, and watched their project being turned into a product the whole community could appreciate.

The 5,000 copies disappeared quickly. Each student took home 5 brochures; 500 were sent to a local bank to include in packets given to people who had just moved to the area and opened new accounts; professors at the nearby university asked for copies to include in packets of local information given to candidates interviewing for teaching positions. "Local businesses love it because it's free advertising for them. Realtors think it's great, too. And every Chamber of Commerce in the state will receive a copy. It will be used in more ways than we ever dreamed!" Diane states.

Local Ecology: Is It Our Problem?

After completing one of the geographic investigations described in this chapter, or perhaps after reading one of the several thought-provoking books on human-environment interactions (e.g., Brown's [1991] *The World That Jack Built,* Cherry's [1992] *A River Ran Wild,* Leedy's [1991] *The Great Trash Bash,* and Van Allsberg's [1990] *Just a Dream*), have students express their thoughts and ideas using one or more of the following creative writing formats:

Pollution: Am I Part of the Problem or a Key to the Solution?
Take a stand on an ecological issue. What message do you wish to communicate? Choose one of the following to voice your position:

Poem: Write a poem about your concern for our environment. Consider using a particular style, such as limerick or haiku.

Story: Develop a story around a situation created by an environmental problem. Who are the main characters, and why are they involved in the situation?

Song: Compose a song that will help people understand what is happening to our environment and how we can help. Get your friends to help you sing it, and record it on tape.

Political Cartoon: Look at some recent political cartoons found in the newspaper. Think of a way a political cartoon could address an ecological issue. Draw a cartoon to send to our local newspaper.

Play: Write a play that shows how we abuse our environment and what might happen if we do not do something about it.

Magazine Ad: Create a magazine advertisement to make people think about ecological issues. Pretend you represent the Environmental Protection Agency.

TV Commercial: Write and act out a TV commercial about conserving our natural resources. Get your friends (or family) to help you make a videotape for the class to watch.

Bumper Sticker: Design a bumper sticker with a short but powerful message about ecology.

Radio Announcement: Write and tape record a public service announcement about ecology that might be heard by radio listeners. Contact the manager of a local radio station to find out if the station would like to air your announcement.

Fable: A fable is a short story with a special message called a "moral." Sometimes the main characters are animals who behave like humans. Write a fable that contains a moral about ecology.

T-shirt: If you could wear a T-shirt advertising something about our environment, what would it be? Design an "Ecology T-shirt" and wear it to class.

Newspaper Article: Pretend you are a reporter who has been given the assignment of writing a newspaper article that will alert the public to an ecological concern. Which will it be? What will you say?

Comic Strip: Design a comic strip that will make people aware of the dangers of being unconcerned about our environment.

■ Trying It Out

Reuse Your Junk

Barbara wanted her second-graders at a rural school to be aware of ways they can show care for the environment. She used the book *Just a Dream* (Van Allsburg, 1990) and the adopted second-grade social studies textbook.

Barbara began the lesson by reading *Just a Dream* to her students and showing them the illustrations. "The book showed them what the earth could look like if we don't do something to stop pollution and waste," she says. Then she called students' attention to their social studies book and the chapter on recycling and reuse. "They did not know as much as I expected them to know about either subject," Barbara recalls. "From our discussion, I got the feeling that most of the children did not recycle or reuse things at home. . . . We had a good discussion about the types of things that could be recycled, and where recycling centers were [locally]," she remembers. At this point, students were ready to talk about what they, as a class, could do to help save their environment. They decided to try saving milk jugs from home to take to the local recycling center, since everyone's family used milk. Barbara made a Milk Jug Recycling Chart to help students keep track of who brought how many milk jugs to school to be recycled.

When her students realized that they personally could do something that would help the environment, "they were a lot more excited than I had expected," Barbara reflects. Students were familiar with the word *recycling* from watching television, but showed no signs of recognition when Barbara read aloud the chapter subheading entitled "Reuse." She shared some examples of reuse, such as giving toys to the Salvation Army to be used by other children when students became tired of them, instead of throwing the toys in the trash. During their discussion, "We also decided that we could reuse things such as cloth napkins and plastic cups," she says. They'd learned something about recycling through their class milk jug project, but how could she interest them in the concept of reusing, Barbara wondered? "I told them to go home and look around the house, especially in trash cans, and see if they could find some junk to make into something useful."

Students' response to the Reuse Your Junk project was tremendous. Children and their parents or siblings worked together to make flower vases from bleach bottles, pencil cups from cans, percussion instruments for the classroom rhythm band from plastic containers and dried beans or rice, and so on. Both these projects were considered a big success by teacher and students. "Every child participated in each project in some way," Barbara says. "Some have even convinced their parents to start recycling.... They even watch me very carefully, to make sure that I recycle everything I can, too." Students' Reuse Your Junk project received a good deal of attention from other classes at their school when these projects and accompanying descriptions were displayed in the hallway. "The kids were very proud of themselves, and liked the feeling that they were helping the environment," Barbara notes.

"When I do this project next year, I will send a note home to the parents to see if they would be willing to do a trial week of recycling, with students keeping written and graphic records," she reflects. "They might want to concentrate on cans and glass or plastics at first. I think that once the parents see how much their children care about this issue, and how easy recycling is, they may start doing this on a regular basis."

War Memorials

Do you have any war memorials in your town (see Figure 7.3)? If so, introduce students to the local memorial by reading Eve Bunting's *The Wall*, about the Vietnam Veterans' Memorial (see Chapter 12). Memorial Day is a particularly good time to share this book. You may wish to make a visit to a nearby cemetery, where students can do a rubbing of a gravestone to get an idea of what the character in *The Wall* did when he created a rubbing from the memorial. Some students may know of or be related to someone listed on the memorial, or who served in the Vietnam War. Allow them to share this information with the class, and/or invite relatives or family friends to come to class to share stories, photos, and other memorabilia with the students. With this type of introduction, students should get much more from a field trip visit to the local war memorial.

Tombstones and Cemeteries

In virtually every town, large or small, some of the least used historical resources can be found in one or more cemeteries. The place may be a splendidly landscaped commercial lawn, an ancient graveyard, a small family plot, or a well-tended church-yard, but it will be filled with clues about people who lived and died in the commu-

Figure 7.3 Postcard of War Memorial

nity. It also may contain information about important events in the history of the local area or nation, and about the values of the community or subgroup.

Your students can become tombstone detectives during a cemetery visit. Encourage them to consider the cemetery as a place of wonder and historical interest, not as a scary place to avoid. They may even find adults there, looking for information about their own ancestors and family trees, which could result in fascinating conversations about family history.

Not only will your students research and collect historical data during their cemetery visit but they can also use the data and experience to develop skills in reading, language arts, and math as they analyze it back in the classroom. They can learn to "triangulate the sources" as professional historians do, by checking dates, hunches, patterns, and other clues with newspaper archives and civic or local historical societies.

To help prepare your students for a visit to an area cemetery, share with them the preceding information and display pictures and drawings depicting interesting tombstones and grave markers. For example, markers for children's graves often contain slogans or cherubic figures representing the surviving family members' feelings about losing a child. Markers for people who served in the military or who were killed during wars or national conflict frequently display some record of those details. Particularly large or ornate markers may lead one to believe that the deceased was connected with a wealthy family. Photos and drawings such as these will help motivate students' interest in the coming field trip to a local cemetery.

Research prior to the field trip might take the form of finding out when the specific cemetery was created, how long it was/has been in use, who has responsibility for caring for it now, which community groups were permitted to bury their family members there and (if relevant) which were not and why, how large the cemetery is now and how large it was intended to be when it was created, and whether any person of special historical note is buried there.

Once at the cemetery, students should behave with respect for the people buried there. Have a discussion prior to the field trip about what constitutes proper cemetery etiquette. Make a list detailing what was discussed, and display the list in the days before making the trip.

Prepare assignment cards ahead of time to distribute at the site, or have students select assignments before departing the school, but *do prepare*. Instruct students each to carry a notepad and pencil for sketching and making notes. You will want to bring various weights of art paper and wax crayons for "rubbings," but wait until the appropriate moment to distribute these materials to avoid any danger of defacing cemetery property. Assignments on-site might include:

- Make a site map of the cemetery. (This activity can be divided among several students or a cooperative group by creating a mental grid of the location and assigning one person or group to each grid, if the cemetery is large.) Include marked gravesites labeled with names, lanes or avenues for walking about or driving, park-like areas or benches for sitting, tombs or mausoleums, entrance and/or exit gates, and so on.
- Read information on grave markers. Note the names, dates of birth and death, epitaphs or slogans, and any other information provided. Divide your paper into four sections per page by drawing a cross, and include information for four grave markers on each page of your notepad. Afterward, look for patterns, missing information, or information of historical importance to share with your classmates. What do some of the words mean? Check the dictionary after returning to class; sometimes *s* was carved like an *f,* and sometimes on older grave markers archaic or old-fashioned words were used that are not in common use now. Do you find examples of these? What other information can you determine about the deceased, besides dates of birth and/or death? Are names of other family members or husbands/wives mentioned?
- Decipher cemetery symbols and decorations. Explore the cemetery, looking for graves with both headstones and footstones, for graves marked by table-

stones (large flat markers raised on four stone legs), and for graves marked by larger markers such as tombs. Search each marker more closely to find symbols of death (such as a death's head with wings and blank eyes, a skeleton, a skull with crossbones, arrows or darts, a crowing rooster, or pickaxes and spades). Look also for symbols of belief in Resurrection of the Soul (such as rising sun, trumpet, torch, angels or winged cherubs, open Bibles). Symbols were used to depict certain religious beliefs (such as arches as the gateway to Heaven, lambs as the innocence of a young child, willow trees representing the ending of life on Earth to begin anew in Heaven). Look for portraits or images of the deceased, or of something beloved to them (such as a pet). Look also for symbols depicting particular wars fought or served in by the deceased (such as a circular shield for the Revolutionary War, G.A.R. [Grand Army of the Republic] or C.S.A. [Confederate States Army] for the Civil War, full cross for the Spanish American War, an American Legion shield for World War I, an eagle for World War II).

■ Preserve artwork of the cemetery. Explore the gravesites, looking for examples of raised or carved artwork. Place a sheet of art paper carefully over a section of the artwork, and, holding the paper perfectly still, rub a crayon (using the side of the crayon) over the paper until a pattern emerges. If you are very careful and patient, you may be able to "rub" the entire pattern represented. On each art representation, write the name and other vital information from the grave marker with your pencil. Divide your attention among two or three artistic representations, and remember to label each one. Be careful not to rub crayon onto the marker itself.

After the trip to the cemetery, use the data collected in your class lessons. With data on dates of birth and death, for example, have students work in groups to determine:

The average lifespan of all people buried in this cemetery

The average lifespan of males compared to females

The average lifespan of people who died before 1920 (or any year) and people who died after that year

The total number of deaths in a given year

The total number of deaths in a given decade

The fraction/percentage of deaths of children under the age of 18, 12, 6, and 2

What conclusions might be drawn from children's deaths about health care or nutrition or disease in a given era

As groups of students complete their calculations, come back together in a large group, pool findings, and compare results. Discuss issues or historical facts and events relevant to your community in light of these findings. What can you learn about the history of your community or town by visiting a cemetery?

■ Trying It Out

Gravestone Rubbings

Cindy Stiver took her second-graders on a walk through a nearby cemetery, where they did tombstone rubbings and researched the age of the oldest marker. Armed with crayons and plain white paper, and accompanied by a few parent helpers, they walked through a cemetery where people who occupied the first established settlement of their county were buried. "Most of the dates [on tombstones] are worn off and hard to see," Cindy told the students as they began their tour. "Put a piece of paper over the tombstone and use a crayon on its side to rub lightly," she said, demonstrating with her own paper. "The numbers and letters on the stone should now show on the paper."

After all students had tried their hand at tombstone rubbing, they returned to the school. There, Cindy focused on the dates they had gathered in their rubbing activity to help students determine how long these people were alive. They also shared their rubbings with each other in groups to find out whose rubbing had the earliest recorded date (some were in the 1700s). The students also discussed the kinds of materials from which these tombstones had been constructed: marble, granite, metal, and wood. They were challenged to find out what materials are used for tombstones now, and why these might differ from the ones they saw at the ancient cemetery.

Chapter

Using Community Resources to Teach Local History

Communities are the wider world of the school. Refurbished ideas in the hands of skillful teachers become creative curricula. The teacher is the catalyst. (Miranda, 1983)

This quote epitomizes the wealth of contacts, information, and resources for teaching local history available right in the community. When teachers increase their sensitivity to resources in the community, explore unconventional local sources or use conventional sources in unconventional ways, increase their local networks, effectively incorporate local guest speakers into the curriculum, and consistently follow up when speakers visit and field trips have been completed, available community resources increase exponentially.

Elementary classroom teachers can use these recommendations to increase available community resources by increasing school-community ties. For example, consider the following:

1. *Increase Sensitivity to Community Resources:* Start to view the people you know in a new light. Notice what interests them, and keep a running file of names, addresses, telephone numbers, and related interests/experiences. This reference file can help you build a pool of possible contacts and begin to consider possible interrelationships between and among the contacts.

2. *Explore Unconventional Local Sources or Use Conventional Sources in Unconventional Ways:* Listen to children's conversations and comments about parents and family friends or neighbors with renewed attention; you may learn of new contacts to add to your reference file. Peruse the local Yellow Pages for other possible contacts—one teacher found an amateur theater group that enjoys performing for children. Another discovered a senior citizen's group that was willing to be interviewed about their experiences in local one-room schools. The possibilities are endless!

3. *Expand Your Local Network:* Communicate your interest in helping children learn about their local community when talking with friends and possible contacts. Rather than just saying, "The kids just love special speakers," express your own interest in the other person's activities, and be specific about your curriculum objectives. For example, you might say, "That's really interesting! How long have you been doing that?...You know, this topic really fits in well with our study of the local community. Would you, or someone you know, be interested in helping my students learn about _____?" When dealing with bureaucracies, be very professional and cordial, ask that your call be directed to a specific person, and state your request as succinctly as possible. A suggested format: "Hello, I'm Gail Hickey, resource teacher at Seymour Primary School; may I speak with Mrs. Johnson?" (When the specific person or her or his secretary comes on the line, say, "Hello, Mrs. Johnson. I'm Gail Hickey, resource teacher at Seymour Primary School. We are studying the community, and I understand you are the president of First National Bank. We're putting together a roster of local dignitaries to speak to our third-graders about their work in the community. May I add your name to the roster?" (Details about how Mrs. Johnson may become involved with the unit on the local community should follow or, if time does not allow, offer to send a letter explaining local dignitaries' anticipated contributions as special speakers, a panel of speakers, or field trip contacts.)

4. *Make Effective Use of Special Speakers and Field Trip Opportunities:* Prepare special speakers and other classroom guests to decrease possible anxieties about speaking before a group (some have little or no experience). Structure the classroom visit beforehand, inform guests in a telephone call or letter before the visit what the order of the day will be, and prepare students to ask thoughtful questions and behave in a respectful manner. Helpful hints for getting the most out of field trips can be found elsewhere in this chapter; briefly, do your homework, prepare chaperons as well as students for the big day, and introduce the topic beforehand as well as follow up on it after the trip is over.

5. *Follow Up:* As in the suggestion about following up on all field trip topics, be sure to follow up when special speakers visit, guests are interviewed, demonstrations are given, resources are loaned, and so forth. Write an immediate thank-you letter yourself, and use the opportunity for practicing letter writing skills by having students themselves follow up. (Local community contacts, especially businesses, adore receiving original letters and artwork from children depicting a classroom visit or field trip—often these are displayed publicly for weeks.) In any event, remember that closure is needed when children learn new information or skills; appropriate follow-up activities or lesson extensions help provide that sense of closure.

Another way teachers can increase access to community resources is to prepare primary source packages based on particular themes (Leon, 1980). Start by developing one local primary source package; over the years, more packages can be developed based on other themes. Or perhaps you might choose to work collaboratively, each developing a local primary source package on a different theme, and sharing your packages throughout the year.

Possibilities for theme topics are only as limited as your imagination: family life, economics, transportation, government; industry, and folklore are only a few ideas. Consider national and state standards and/or competencies when determining local history themes, so that thematic units on local or community topics is not seen as an "add on" or "band-aid" approach to social studies instruction. One museum curator (Leon, 1980) suggests that when teachers adhere to five requirements as they develop primary source packages, the integrity of the curriculum remains intact: consider skills and values, decide on a theme, select primary sources based on the theme, edit documents as needed, and design accompanying activities. I have elaborated on these five requirements based on my own experience:

1. *Consider Skills and Values:* Evaluate potential primary sources from the perspective of standards, objectives, or learner outcomes first, then consider the interest/novelty value.

2. *Decide on a Theme:* A general unit on "Our Community" or "Local History" is too broad, and may result in disjointed coverage of various topics without a sustained focus or in-depth study of any single topic. For this reason, it is best to decide on a theme or narrow topic when developing a local primary source package. To decide on an appropriate theme, list the major topics or themes covered in the academic year and look for ways these topics and local history converge. Or use one of the 10 themes recommended by the National Council for the Social Studies (1994), and develop your primary source package around that topic. (See the Introduction of this book for a list of the 10 thematic strands, with explanations.)

3. *Select Primary Sources Based on the Theme:* Now that a theme has been selected, decide what kinds of primary sources might best be used to explore the theme. Would deeds and other legal documents, along with old and new maps and photographs, be the best choice? Are letters, diaries, postcards, and old newspaper clippings needed? Do artifacts, such as tools, toys, and household goods, exist that students could examine? Think about what kinds of sources are needed, and focus on collecting these items and/or finding community contacts that will permit instructional use of their collections (e.g., museums, libraries, and historical societies).

4. *Edit Documents:* Some primary sources selected may be usable in part, but prohibitive as a whole. An autobiography or biography of a local celebrity, for instance, will be lengthy and, depending on the theme chosen, largely irrelevant. Portions or excerpts, on the other hand, may be just what is needed to lend an air of personalization to the selected topic. For use in a primary source package, then, this biography should be cited in its entirety, with sections or pertinent excerpts included for student use. Handwritten sources are more easily used by children if they are included as typed transcriptions (a good quality copy of the handwritten original may be featured as a novelty, but the transcription is needed if children are to use the source effectively in their investigations).

5. *Design Activities:* How will these primary sources be used? What teaching strategies will motivate and guide students to learn about their local community's history while using these sources? These are the questions teachers must consider as they design classroom activities and experiences or lessons to accompany materials in the primary source package. The more opportunities students have for hands-on or experiential learning, the better. (Protect all items in the package by laminating, mounting and framing, enclosing in plastic sleeves or zipper-style storage bags. Also, be certain to maintain a file of "originals" in a locked drawer or cabinet so items in the package can be "replaced" as needed.) Design questions for discussion (preferably open-ended questions), plan researching, writing, and creative thinking activities, develop scenarios requiring students to compare and contrast, suggest role-playing ideas or sociodrama topics, and include contacts for subsequent field trips in the package. These, and other original activities, should align with curriculum requirements or desired learner outcomes, rather than being activities for the sake of busywork.

The ideas and resources in this chapter suggest a large variety of strategies for studying local and community history using locally available resources. Use them to develop a primary source package, a thematic unit, or a year-long system of study of the local area.

Planning a Successful Field Trip

USING COMMUNITY RESOURCES
FOR HANDS-ON SOCIAL STUDIES LEARNING

Often, the first use of community resources that comes to mind is the ubiquitous field trip. The traditional class field trip to a factory, museum, fast-food restaurant, or zoo accounts for most students' instructional exposure to the learning resources in their local community. In fact, so many teachers take their students on a field trip in a given year that it seems safe to assume everyone is an expert on the subject. My observation (not to mention my experience!) is that this is not always the case.

Let us turn our attention then to becoming field trip experts. Planning a successful field trip takes more than a phone call and a stack of permission forms. Although most field trips can run smoothly with little advance planning, the adage "An ounce of prevention is worth a pound of cure" certainly applies here. Here are some pointers to help you plan an exciting and safe experience for your students:

■ Make contact with key people at the field trip site as early as possible.
■ Find out whether any other teachers at your school or nearby schools are planning a field trip to the same site. If so, negotiate which jobs can be split up—it's easier when more than one person handles all the duties.
■ Make any arrangements needed to reserve transportation and drivers as early as possible.
■ Send home parental permission slips early; follow up if necessary.
■ Make arrangements for box lunches or stopping for lunch. Collect necessary fees, and ask the parent/teacher group to provide "scholarships" for those students who cannot afford the fees.
■ Seek parent volunteers to serve as chaperons. Some districts have rules about adult-to-child ratios; if yours does not, one adult to every three children is a good formula.
■ Schedule a rain date (if necessary), and inform drivers, chaperons, and contact people at the field trip site of your rain date plans.
■ Make a back-up plan in case you cannot go on the field trip.
■ Contact drivers, chaperons, and contact people at the field site one week prior to the date scheduled to verify all details.
■ Establish rules for proper field trip behavior prior to the day of the trip. Instruct students in these rules, print out a copy and mail to all parent volunteers well before the big day, and have extra copies on hand the day of the trip to distribute to chaperons and drivers. Ask everyone involved to cooperate by enforcing these rules consistently.
■ "Count heads" before leaving the school, the restroom stop (if needed), at the field trip site, and before departing the field trip site.
■ Don't forget camera and film to create memories of the trip.

Preparing Students to Get the Most from Their Field Trip

After all field trip arrangements have been made, the next step in a successful field trip is not the trip itself, but the *introduction*. Prepare your students to learn more while on their field trip. Berliner (1985) says that "well-designed field trips can lead to new learning, reinforce what has been already taught, and aid greatly in the retention of information."

The most important thing to remember as you prepare students to get the most from their field trip is that the trip is *an integral part of the normal curriculum*. In other words, a field trip is an experience outside the classroom walls intended to further children's learning about an instructional goal or objective that already exists.

Teachers use a variety of methods for introducing a field trip topic to their students. At the very least, you should:

■ Discuss the objectives of the trip. Why are you going and what do you hope to learn?
■ Create a bulletin board, interest center, or other instructional display to spark interest and encourage students' thinking about the site.
■ Make a Field Trip Web. Just as you use a story web or a thematic web, a Field Trip Web can help focus thinking and raise questions that can be answered during the trip. Draw a large circle on a piece of butcher paper or light-colored bulletin board paper. Write the place or topic of the field trip in

the circle with a bold marker. Draw spokes, or lines, coming from the circle. Invite students to brainstorm related topics and/or questions in small groups, and suggest labels for the "spokes." Develop a list of questions to be answered, and have students decide which questions can best be answered through preliminary research and which can best be answered on-site during the field trip. Assign topics to be researched from the "preliminary research" list, and assist groups as they look for relevant resources or reference materials. Set a date near the date of the field trip (as close to the actual date as possible) for groups to present their findings to the class.

Field Trip Follow-Up

An excellent window of opportunity exists immediately after the field trip—truly a "teachable moment"—when students are primed for learning and motivated from recent experiences. Do not let this opportunity pass. Plan "post-field trip instruction" before the trip, and write down as much of the plan as possible (in case a substitute is needed). Some ideas for post-field trip instruction include:

- Using the Field Trip Web, discuss the following: What did we want to learn? What did we learn? What information do we still need to know? How can we find out?
- Look at photos taken during the trip. (Go to a one-hour photo developer if possible—the kids will be as anxious to see the pictures as you are!) Talk about what was happening in each photo. Create a class scrapbook of the field trip, using anecdotal comments and descriptions written by students to accompany the photos. Ask, "What about the pictures that *weren't* taken? Can you draw what that photo might have looked like?" Include these (with appropriate anecdotes) in the scrapbook.
- Write thank-you letters to the key person on site, the driver(s), and chaperons. Depending on the age of your students, letter recipients would probably appreciate original drawings of field trip experiences to display for co-workers.
- Create a hallway display communicating to other classes what was learned during the field trip.
- Invite students to respond to the field trip using information from the Multiple Intelligences model: Write and perform an original song, compose and recite an original poem, draw a picture, paint a picture, sculpt a figure, create a model, write a story, write an essay, develop and perform a skit, create a mobile or poster or collage, compose and perform a rap, etc.
- If slide film was used, have students work together to create a slide show (complete with narration, musical background, introduction, and conclusion). Show the slides during a PTA meeting, a school assembly, or to another class.
- Use a computer program (such as HyperStudio) to create a "stack" informing others about the field trip topic/site. Make certain every student has the opportunity to contribute some content to the stack. Use computer graphics, QuickTime animation (especially if a chaperon took along a video camera), sound, voice-overs, photos (may be scanned in), and students' preliminary research to make the stack as informative and interesting as possible.

Historical Photographs

All teachers know the value of illustrations and photographs over text alone as a learning tool. This is true in the study of local and community history as well as in other subjects. Photos of the local area from the recent and not-so-recent past lend themselves to unit or thematic study of family, community, city, state, or topics of local interest. It does not really matter whether these photos are from personal or professional collections—the learning value of the unit is increased by them. But not every teacher has considered how to make the best use of historical photographs as learning aids. Let's look at some ways to use historical photos in the elementary classroom.

Think about the goals or intended outcomes of your lesson or unit. A comparison of old photographs with recent depictions of the same scene or geographic area, for example, will help when students are exploring:

Change over time

Impact of technology

City/Neighborhood planning

Environmental impact of human intervention

Alternative land use

Old or historical photographs of your area may be found at historical museums (check local as well as state museums), government archives, old newspapers or magazines, local libraries or library branches, or through the professional or personal collections of members of historical societies and area historians. (Call the nearest college or university for the names of individuals known for their study of the local area.)

Obtain some aerial views of your town or city (see Figure 8.1) and have them enlarged to use as teaching materials. If possible, obtain aerial views from 10 or 20 years ago, as well as from 50 or more years ago. (See information on obtaining recent photographs for comparison below.) Show students the most current photograph: Can they identify buildings, landmarks, geographic areas that are unique to their town? Have these always been a part of the town? When were various buildings built, or roads mapped out and paved, for example? What features have been added in the last ten years? Five years? One or two years? How can we find out?

Display aerial views of the city from long ago. Compare these to the contemporary view. How have things changed? How have they remained the same? What kinds of things seem more likely to change over one person's lifetime? What kinds of things are more likely to stay the same for two or more generations? Why?

Check with your local library branches and/or the local historical society to find out whether a photographic essay or book of photographs has ever been published about your town. Try to obtain a copy of this if it exists. Perhaps the local historical museum has a collection of old photographs or negatives that were never cata-

BIRDS-EYE VIEW FROM SKY LINE DRIVE, DULUTH, MINN.—9

Figure 8.1 Aerial View of Duluth, Minnesota

logued; select a few of these (10 to 25) and ask that they be developed and copied for use by area teachers.

Make copies of photographs showing, for example, the local "Main Street" (see Figure 8.2) when the town was first settled, and find a photo of the same street taken 50 years later, or 100 years later. Each photograph in your collection should be properly labeled for research purposes and laminated for durability. If photographs are mounted, the label should be attached to the reverse side before laminating.

Ask the same questions about these photographs used with aerial photographs earlier: How have things changed? How have they stayed the same? Why? Consider other questions, such as Why do towns have a Main Street? How and when was our Main Street built? Who were the influential people of the time? What was going on in the state (the region, the nation, the world) at the time our Main Street was being built?

Figure 8.2   "Main Streets" (circa 1930s)

Joseph Kirman (1995) has prepared a list of suggestions for teachers who want to make contemporary photographs of historic scenes for comparative purposes. Consider these questions as you prepare to re-photograph a scene (if you don't feel confident of your own photographic skills, perhaps a local professional or amateur photographer will take on the project):

1. What is the precise location from which the photograph was taken? If you know where the original photographer was standing when the photo was taken, your chances of accurately reproducing the original perspective are increased. If the specific spot is not accessible due to new construction or growth, compromise with the nearest available location. (Hint: Line up the camera's center focus with that in the original photograph.)

2. Was the original photo taken from a ground level, overhead, aerial, or oblique downward or upward perspective? Try to duplicate the original photographer's perspective.

3. Look carefully at the edges of the original photo. What "frames" the top, bottom, and each side of the original? A zoom lens or wide angle lens may be needed to duplicate the area covered.

4. Is the original photo square, rectangular, or circular? If your camera produces a different size or shape photo from the original, enlargement and/or cropping may help duplicate the appearance of the original photograph.

Historical photographs of people can also enhance the study of the local community. Friedensohn and Rubin (1987) recommend the use of family photos for studying women immigrants. This is another way to help students recognize the contributions of women to the history of the community or town. (See ideas for Women's Local History in Chapter 10.)

■ Trying It Out

Local Photo Collection

Leah Moulton and Corrine Tevis (1991) discovered a large collection of unindexed photographic negatives from their community's past at the local historical museum. They wanted to use these resources to help their students learn about the history of the local area. Leah and Corrine selected a basic group of 25 scenes related to their specific community, and developed themes appropriate for their students to research (such as public buildings, famous personalities, homes, schools, transportation, occupations). The museum and their school district's media departments worked together to develop, enlarge, and mount the photographs for classroom use. A brief paragraph was written about each scene, using information supplied by the local museum. These paragraphs were copied and attached to the reverse side of enlarged mounted photos, then the labeled copies were laminated.

Once these preliminary steps had been taken, Corrine and Leah collaborated on a lesson plan that would encourage their students to examine the historical photographs in relation to identified themes, compare and contrast available related information and photographs, and work in cooperative groups. Lesson goals include:

To develop concepts of history and change

To develop observation, inference, and conceptualizing skills

To work cooperatively in a group

Materials needed for the lesson include the copied photographs, each with its description covered, and a Photo Worksheet. First, organize students into small groups of four to six. These groups are split in half (creating "partner groups"), and students in groups are given a predetermined pair of photographs to examine and discuss. Then each student responds to the questions on the worksheet in written

Photo Worksheet

1. What is the first thing you saw in the photo?
2. Tell two things that surprised you.
3. Find and list two things you might *not* see today.
4. Give the photograph a title.

form, and discusses his or her responses with other persons in the group. After completing the worksheet and the smaller group discussion, groups exchange photo pairs with their "partner" group. The process is repeated.

Later that day, or the next, both smaller groups reunite to form a larger one (with a total of four photographs to discuss). All students in the group share written responses and results of smaller group discussion. The group reaches consensus on which of the photographs examined is older (How do you know?) and selects a spokesperson to report the group's findings to the whole class.

When the group's research has been reported orally to the entire class, the teacher removes the cover from the descriptive paragraph, and the paragraph is read aloud. Students discuss whether their findings were accurate, and how they might find out more information. As an extension activity, ask students to write a story about what they believe is happening in the photographic scene. (Be sure to review correct spellings of specific local street names, landmarks, and so on, at this point.) Another extension activity would be to have the groups role-play the scene depicted in their photograph, after researching sources about the era depicted for historical accuracy. (Props from the era, if available, will enhance role-play activities.) Also, groups might write a short play depicting the photographic scene, and act this out with puppets they have created.

Using Photographic Slides

Linda Miculka (1997) collected historical photographs of her local El Campo, Texas, area and had them made into slides for use in her classroom. The source of most of Linda's photos was her 96-year-old grandmother, but a local museum or district school office may have a collection as well. An amateur photographer took good-quality photographs using slide film of the old photos Linda had collected ("The results were fantastic," she says). The Texas Institute of Cultures in nearby San Antonio made some museum-quality copies of prints provided by a local museum, for a fee. All slides were selected for their relevance to a local historical theme; Linda's lesson dealt with early farm equipment.

Linda wanted her students to compare and contrast modern farm machinery with equipment used by local farmers in the past. Each lesson involved the use of only two or three slides; one in particular made use of slides depicting three different machines used to harvest grain: a horse-drawn harvester circa 1910, a four-row header combine from the 1960s, and an eight-row header combine used in 1994.

Students viewed these slides and brainstormed as much information from each as possible. Then they made observations about each slide, deciding on similarities and differences. Next, Linda asked them to hypothesize how and why changes did occur. Last, students estimated what quarter of the twentieth century each photo was taken (they were not informed about dates ahead of time).

As a culminating activity, students wrote essays about what they had discovered, using questions provided by their teacher: What changes occurred? Why did they occur? How did they occur? Do you believe these changes are good, or not? Why? Think about each of the three time periods shown in the slides: Which would you like to live in? Why? Students made use of higher-level thinking abilities and problem-solving skills while completing these writing assignments.

Teaching Local History with Postcards

Postcards provide an inexpensive visual aid and snippets of written information about landmarks, scenic areas, hotels and motels, skylines, buildings, and many other topics related to local history (see Figure 8.3). As a medium, postcards have been around for the entire twentieth century. Postcards featuring local scenes likely have been around since 1890, so you should have no trouble finding enough to start your own collection for teaching about local history.

Haunt local flea markets and antique shows for the best selection. Local libraries may have small collections which, once loaned, can be photographed and turned into prints or slides. Postcards older than 50 years are no longer protected by copyright laws, so feel free to make prints or slides of these to use in the classroom (but be sure to credit the manufacturer, if that information is available).

Figure 8.3 Teaching Local History with Postcards

There are many ways to use postcards in the classroom. Bucher and Fravel (1991) recommend using local postcards to expand knowledge about local architecture, historical scenes, industry, military and shipbuilding activity, agriculture, transportation, tourist sites and scenic views, and the environment. Some suggested activities include the following:

ARCHITECTURE AND HISTORIC SITES

■ Chronicle the development of a local historical site, using words and pictures.
■ Examine postcards showing downtown areas. Record your observations about the architecture of buildings and bridges, as well as the types of transportation, businesses, and styles of clothing.
■ Design a postcard to attract businesses to the local area today. Write an essay comparing your postcard design to one used to attract businesses prior to 1950.

INDUSTRY, SHIPBUILDING, AND MILITARY ACTIVITY

■ Compare and contrast different types of ships and the cargo they carried over the years, using postcards.
■ Write a newspaper article that might have been published in a local paper in the early 1940s, using information about military activities found on postcards.

AGRICULTURE AND THE ENVIRONMENT

■ Study postcards depicting local scenery, and report on changes in the environment evident in the past 100 years.
■ Compare and contrast farming practices and crop exports over the past 50 years, as shown in postcard scenes.

TOURIST SITES

■ Pretend you visited this area in the 1930s. Write a letter to a family member or friend describing the things you saw and places you went, using scenic postcards from the period for your information.
■ Make a bulletin board display, using a local map and old postcards. Connect the postcards to the map with yarn and colored pins, marking the location of each postcard scene.

■ Trying It Out

Postcards: Then and Now

Second-graders in Cindy Stiver's class extended their study of the local community by examining "then and now" images. With the help of parents and community members, and by shopping at local antique stores, Cindy accumulated postcards showing the town as it was 10 to 50 years ago. She displayed this collection of postcards at an interest center designed for the purpose. With the assistance of a parent volunteer, students completed activities such as:

1. Write a story about what is happening in this photograph.
2. Identify the buildings in the pictures.
3. Describe how buildings and businesses have changed.
4. Record your observations about types of buildings, clothing, transportation, and businesses pictured on these postcards. Are they different from modern ones? How are they the same?
5. Using these postcards as a model, make a postcard of something we saw on our neighborhood walk. Write a note about it to a friend or family member on the lines provided, and write their address in the address box.

The stories (with accompanying old postcards) and student-made postcards were displayed in the hallway as a way of encouraging students in other classrooms to learn about their community.

Using Old-Time Radio Recordings

When studying about the local area during the period between 1930 and 1950, old-time radio tapes can be an invaluable resource. This period was known as the Golden Days of Radio, since families all over the nation regularly tuned in to local networks for news, music, soap operas, dramas, comedies, interviews, and even opera. Imaginations were piqued by sounds unaccompanied by visuals, and children and adults of all ages gathered to hear and discuss what they heard.

An increasing number of cassette tapes and compact disks (CDs) of radio programs from the so-called Golden Days has become available through commercial producers, allowing teachers as well as the general public to relive this period in recent American history. These recordings can be used to supplement the study of local or community history, or check with local radio station managers to find out whether archives of local news broadcasts or other locally produced shows were maintained that could become part of your local history resources.

Students can learn about how radio as a medium reflected the tastes, values, even moral character of citizens during the period roughly between 1930 and 1950. The Indiana Historical Bureau (1989) reports that local evangelist Billy Sunday's radio sermons in the 1920s warned millions of listeners that "a price would someday have to be paid for the excesses of the 'Roaring 20s.'" The future of transportation was thought to be directly tied to the passenger blimp until "horror-struck radio accounts of the fiery 1937 crash of the German dirigible *Hindenburg* crushed the lighter-than-air passenger industry." At the local level, news reports from southern Indiana claimed "tragedies caused by the 1937 Ohio River flood brought in millions of dollars in donations" from all over the nation for relief goods and supplies on the behalf of flood victims. During the Great Depression, U.S. President Franklin D. Roosevelt's radio-produced "Fireside Chats" comforted citizens suffering from economic deprivation with the sentiment that "the only thing we have to fear is fear itself." These are only a few examples of the many ways radio broadcasts tie in with local history (see Figure 8.4).

Figure 8.4 Old-Time Radio and Local History

Turner and Hickey (1991) suggest other ways radio recordings may be used in the classroom:

■ Have children identify family members, friends, and neighbors who can recall the days of radio. Then, with the children, work to develop a set of questions to be asked about these individuals' favorite programs and the reasons they were so enjoyed. Obtain tapes of as many of these programs as possible. The public library, as well as local book and music stores, may be good resources. Mail-order houses are another useful source for obtaining tapes and CDs (see addresses in the Appendix). Listen to tapes and discuss with students how listening to radio programs must have been different from watching television today.

■ Stage an "Old-Fashioned Radio Night," attempting to recreate the atmosphere of family and friends gathered about the radio. Make a cardboard mock-up of an old console-style radio to put in front of the tape/CD player. Plan a schedule of radio programs and serve snacks similar to those that would have been eaten during that era.

■ Try to assemble a sequence of broadcasts conveying ideas about the information on events citizens would have received during World War II. The recording "This Was Radio" (*Great Moments in Radio, Volume I,* by Nostalgia Lane Recordings) contains a fine collection of these, or you may choose to develop your own in collaboration with students or other teachers. Such recordings include newscasts, speeches, even home-front appeals on regular entertainment programs. Play a small part of the tape daily. Discuss with students the uncertainties people felt, and their reasons for withholding certain information due to military security and other reasons.

■ Play several old-time radio commercials. "Greatest Radio Commercials (... and now a word from our sponsor)" from *Radio Classics* by Nostalgia Lane has a recording with excellent variety. Discuss reasons for the similarities and differences in historic radio commercials compared to today's television commercials. How do radio programs and commercials compensate for the lack of visuals? How does imagination play a bigger part in perception? Compare the old commercials to today's radio commercials.

■ Play some tapes of comedy programs from the so-called Golden Days of Radio such as "The Burns and Allen Show", "The Jack Benny Program," "Edgar Bergen and Charlie McCarthy," "Fred Allen," and so on. Compare the humor to today's comedy programs on television. Note how the shows' stars participate in related commercials. Discuss reasons for this situation. Point out the way music is used for transitions between parts of the program. Discuss vaudeville and the relationship between vaudeville and radio shows (types of comedy, same short skit and song format for many, etc.). Discuss the fact that many radio performers performed vaudeville first. Ask students whether these shows/jokes/comedy routines are still funny. Why or why not?

■ Have the children work on a series of skits, commercials, and routines to imitate an old-time radio comedy-variety show. It will be necessary for them to research the major events of the era, as well as the impact these events had on local citizens and the local community. They will use this information creatively to develop radio programs, and work on their writing/editing skills at the same time.

■ Have students look for photos from the 1930s and 1940s. Perhaps family members have these in their photo albums at home. Another source is magazines of these decades, such as *Look* and *Life* (public and university libraries usually have bound copies of these classic magazines). Encourage them to look particularly for photos or pictures showing the family gathered around their radio, or pictures and drawings of old-time radios. Examine the photos for styles of furnishings, clothing, activity, and so forth. (See hints on using historical photographs for additional ideas on using these photos.)

■ Select an important event of the era called the Golden Age of Radio— a moment that caught national or even worldwide attention. Play a news broadcast depicting some aspect of the event and discuss how people must have felt as they listened. What did this event mean to them? What did it mean to local citizens? See if children can find one or more local people who recall the event (or details about the event), and remember listening to radio at the time; develop a questionnaire and have students interview this person about his or her memories of the important event (see suggestions in the Introduction of this book on interviewing classroom guests). Possible events include Black Friday on the New York Stock Exchange, October 28, 1929; *Hindenburg* Disaster, 1937; Election of F. D. Roosevelt to an unprecedented third term as President of the United States, 1944; the Japanese Attack on Pearl Harbor, December 7, 1941; V. E. Day, May 8, 1945; V. J. Day, August 14, 1945; the election of Harry Truman as President of the United States, 1948; and the Berlin Airlift Ends, 1949.

■ Play segments from comedy programs of the 1940s. Have children listen to the commercials, and notice how often the commercials are made part of the show with comic segues, involvement of the actors, and the like. They may also listen for different types of propaganda, how often the listener is asked to visualize, or how the other senses are appealed to rather than just listening.

■ Have children use a printed program schedule showing when different programs were aired (Dunning's 1976 *Tune in Yesterday: The Ultimate Encyclopedia of Old-Time Radio, 1925–1976,* from Prentice Hall, is a good source of program schedules). See if they can categorize these as Depression Era, War Time, and Postwar. Can they find some differences in the types of programs aired during these various eras? They might also look at long-running shows (many were aired more than once a week), and make hypotheses about why so many of these radio programs were aired for 10, 20, even 30 years, whereas today only a few television shows survive for more than a few years.

■ Have children listen to some of the themes and musical "signatures" from the days of radio. Discuss why so many programs tried to have a beginning that caught the attention and was memorable to radio listeners. Compare this practice to modern television network practices, and to the use of movie credits at the start of theater films.

RADIO ADS

As students review commercial advertisements from a particular time period, they should find that these ads reveal customs, social issues, political concerns, popular language, and information about the everyday life of local citizens. This information, not readily available from commercial textbooks or reference works, can help children develop in-depth perspectives about life in the local community or town during the mid-twentieth century.

If the basics of advertising and propaganda have not been shared with students, this is the time to begin (see "Ad Grabbers" below for shorthand propaganda techniques). Help students understand that in order to market a product or service, advertisers must appeal to people's perceptions of themselves as they are or as they wish to be. The objective of such an appeal is to capture one's attention by communicating "I have what you want" or "I have what you need." Advertisers look for ways to reflect and relate to everyday citizens' needs, goals, values, aspirations, and social orientations. At different historical times, society's needs and wants may have been different, yet some basic needs and wants remain the same for generations. By studying advertisements, children can discover not only important information about their own period in history, but the socioeconomic and cultural aspects of the recent and not-so-recent past as well.

As an example, advertisements during the World War II period and those of the postwar 1950s provide a study in contrasts. The patriotic push of the war effort was seen in virtually every advertisement during the war years, along with other signs of the times. In the postwar era, ads focused on or promised "the good life," providing evidence that the 1950s were, for the most part, happy times, years of plenty in terms of goods and services, years when people felt justified in taking their leisure. Contrasting radio commercials from the war years and those from the years after the war can provide students with vital clues to the "feel" of that period: How did people live? What were their values? How did they work? What were their interests, problems, social styles? What emphasis was placed on transportation? How did people spend their leisure time?

Use the following suggestions to guide students in their historical exploration of radio commercials from World War II to the 1950s:

- Have students read about U.S. involvement in World War II from a selection of materials available in an Interest Center on the topic. Ask them to think about how the war changed the lifestyles of local people, and to give examples to support their answers.

- Provide a commercially produced recording of old-time radio commercials from 1940 to 1945. Have students listen to this recording to find information about the everyday lives of Americans during these war years.

- Have students make a list of products and services advertised in the old-time radio commercials. Include public service announcements in the list. Which advertising techniques are used for each product or service? How did advertisers appeal to the local citizenry? Do students think these appeals were effective? Would they be effective today? Why or why not?

- Ask students to create an old-time radio advertisement for a favorite product sold today. Have them include appeals, songs or music, even skits that would have been used to sell the product in the 1940s. (Have them repeat this activity after studying radio commercials from the 1950s, and compare the two ads.)

- While students listen to radio commercials from the 1940s and those from the 1950s, have them listen for social, moral, even religious values reflected in the ads. Ask students to keep a log of examples, and discuss these in class after everyone has listened to the recordings. What values are communicated in the 1940s? The 1950s? How are these values communicated? Describe how values communicated from the 1950s are different from and similar to those communicated from the 1940s.

- After listening to radio commercials from the 1940s, write a description of what life might have been like for a hypothetical local citizen: a housewife, a soldier on furlough, schoolchildren, the owner of a grocery store, a woman worker in a munitions factory, a father who didn't go to war, a teacher.

- Have students read about the 1950s from resource materials placed in an Interest Center. Ask them to consider the changes that have taken place in the world, the nation, the state, and the local community since the war ended. How is life different for local citizens? How is it the same?

- As with radio commercials from the 1940s, ask students to listen to commercials from the 1950s and discuss what these ads reveal about the everyday lives of local citizens during this time.

- Have students make a list of products and services heard about in radio commercials from 1950 to 1959. Include public service announcements in the list. Which advertising techniques are used to sell these products and services? Are these appeals similar to, or different from, appeals used to sell similar products/services in the 1940s? What evidence can students give for their answers?

- What local values are reflected by radio advertisements from the 1950s? How are these values communicated? Are they different from the values communicated in the commercials of the 1940s? If so, how? Are values communicated in a different way from those of the 1940s? If so, how? Why do students think this is so? What can they learn about life in the local area during the decade of the 1950s by listening to radio commercials produced during this time?

- ▪ Have students write a description of what a day in the life of a local citizen might have been like in the 1950s if they were a teenager, a factory worker, the owner of a grocery store, a housewife, a father, a teacher, a child in school.

- ▪ As a creative writing assignment, ask students to consider the changes brought about by the ending of World War II, especially changes felt in the local community. Have them pretend they were a young parent in the 1940s, with small children who grew into teenagers during the 1950s. Ask students to write a story or play about the conflicts in a local family brought on by social and economic changes that occurred between 1940 and 1959.

AD GRABBERS

Strengthen students' critical thinking skills by exploring propaganda techniques used in radio commercials of the 1940s and 1950s. How many examples can they find?

Appeal to the Senses: Buy this product because it looks, smells, or tastes good.

Snob Appeal: Buy this product because it will make you a little better than everyone else.

Happy Family: Buy this product because it shows how much you care about your family.

Celebrity Endorsement: Buy this product because a famous person uses it.

Bandwagon: Buy this product because everyone has it and you don't want to feel left out.

Humor: Buy this product because the jokes or laughs used to advertise it make you feel good.

Romance: Buy this product because it will make you appeal to a potential boyfriend/ girlfriend.

Testimonial: Buy this product because an expert recommends it.

Just Plain Folks: Buy this product because people just like you are satisfied with it.

Celebrating a School's Heritage

One of the goals of social studies instruction is to help students appreciate their national heritage. Knowing that the immediate is often more real to youngsters than the abstract, or distant, the wise teacher will plan a study of local historic events and sites before expecting students to comprehend issues of national significance. One way to begin this study is with something very familiar to students—their own school. Braun and Sabin (1986) have published a detailed description of how one school arranged such a celebration. Initiating a unit of study on the history of the local school can be a task that involves the whole community. Begin by announcing that your class (or the entire fifth grade, for example) will be studying the history of the school. Send notices home to parents, contact the local newspaper, and get permission to post flyers around town, such as at the public library and the supermarket. Include telephone numbers for interested persons to contact you and/or the school if they have information or resources to share. Have the students collect as much information as possible from written documents while they wait for responses to the notices.

A list of possible questions to include in letters, announcements, and student handouts might cover topics such as these:

- What educational institutions have existed in the community?
- Who taught in these schools? What were their qualifications?
- What educational methods were used during particular periods in the community's history? Why were these considered important or popular?
- What subjects have been studied in these schools over time?
- Which extracurricular programs or activities existed? Did these programs come and go over a period of time, and, if so, why?
- What rules must students obey over the history of the school?
- What was the pattern of school attendance? Did it vary for some individuals? If so, why?
- What programs existed or exist for non-English-speaking students and/or parents? Gifted students? Students who are disabled? Migrant workers? Racial or religious minorities? Other groups?
- What were students' favorite activities and subjects? (Get supporting details.)
- How was lunchtime handled at various points in the school's history? In what activities did students engage during "lunch"?
- Were library books and/or a library available to students? When and how often? Who was responsible for the library and the books? What were students' favorite books during particular periods in the school's history?
- What was the degree of parental support for each period in the school's history? Were parent/teacher groups active? What activities did parents engage in to show their support of children's education?
- How was the school financially supported by the community? How were taxes and/or bonding issues important? What types of fund-raisers, raffles, festivals, and other activities were useful? Are these still used to raise money for the school? Why or why not?
- How did the community as a whole get involved in children's education? Were particular educational policies, issues, or materials the source of discussion or debate? Do newspaper accounts exist of these? What do these discussions or debates reveal about community attitudes toward education and the schools?

Appoint a committee to handle the organization of the celebration. Parent volunteers and senior citizens would be ideal committee representatives. When you and the students find yourselves deep in paperwork, this committee can catalog loaned materials, copy documents that must be returned to the library or make trips to the courthouse to copy documents that cannot be brought to the school, file responses to your advertisements, correspond with persons volunteering information, and assist students in following up.

Plan an open house (the committee can help with this, too) as a culminating activity for your study of school history. Contact local radio and television stations to publicize the open house. (One school named their open house after the first class to attend the school: "A Reunion of the Class of 1910.")

Solicit the cooperation of local organizations, such as retired teachers, local historical organizations, retirement home residents and staff, and clubs and societies associated with the school (e.g., 4-H, Scouts, marching bands, etc.). If the organizations themselves did not keep primary sources, perhaps individual members did. The most efficient way to find out is to contact the organization and get a list of members from years past.

Include school board members in your search for historic information, as well as invite them to the open house. In many small communities, some school board positions have been held by succeeding generations of family members. Not only will board members appreciate being included but some may actually be willing to share memories or resources. Make the experience as multidisciplinary as possible by having students be responsible for writing or composing thank-you notes to contributors throughout the unit, and by writing and distributing invitations to the open house.

You might include the following in your study of local school history—or come up with your own ideas!

School Song: If one exists, who wrote it? What do the lyrics mean? What do they reveal about the history of this particular school? Where did the music come from? Who decided to use this melody, and why? Do you sing it today? Why or why not?

Murals: Have students create murals depicting the history of the school as it is revealed to them. Display these at the open house.

Slides: Find out if a local photography shop or photographer will volunteer to create slides from the old photographs you and your students collect. Have students use the slides (making sure to include examples of current students, their dress, favorite activities, and examples of their work) to create a slide show (complete with accompanying background music and narration). Show the slides at the open house.

Taped Anecdotes: Students interview former students who live in the community, and capture their anecdotal comments on tape. Interviewees should tell which year or decade the anecdote depicts, and then tell the story in their own words as they remember it.

Time Line: Using a long roll of paper (or a computer program designed for this purpose), students create a time line representing the school from the time it was in the planning stages up to the current year. Include brief descriptions of important relevant events (such as "Kindergarten building added" or "4th-graders took first place in state science fair").

1914 Dress-Up Day: Students and teachers dress as they think their counterparts might have done during the school's first year of existence.

Old-Time Schools

An excellent extension to a History of Our School Project, or one worthy of effort in itself, is an Old-Time Country Schools Oral History Project. Conducting oral history interviews with people who attended old country schools, or who taught in one-room schools, can be a very rewarding experience for students and community members alike. Identify the school or schools to be researched (these buildings may not be still standing), the time period during which they were in use as schools, the specific location, and several people who have personal memories associated with each of the schools. Have the class work together or in groups to compose a list of relevant questions.

Contact the public library and/or local historical museum or association to ask whether any written records or photographs of the school's history exist. Visit the newspaper archives to research news coverage of the school and its students and teachers. Telephone the courthouse to ask whether deeds or other legal records exist, and whether the class may have copies of these. Compile all available evidence prior to conducting interviews—examining written documents and old photographs often enables students to develop more comprehensive and relevant interview questionnaires.

Telephone potential informants at least two weeks before interviews are intended. If these individuals are agreeable to an interview on the telephone, follow up right away with a friendly letter confirming the date, time, and place of the interview as well as the name of the student or pair of students who will conduct the interview. (Enclosing a recent school photo or snapshot of the student(s) who will conduct the interview, if possible, is helpful in getting the interview process off to a good start.) Don't forget to mention again in the letter that the interview will be tape- or videorecorded, so no surprises occur when the informants arrive at the scene.

Then, two days before the scheduled interview, telephone informants again to confirm. (Involve students in these procedures as much as possible—use the opportunity to introduce or sharpen letter writing and telephone etiquette skills.) Interview questionnaires must be finalized well in advance of the scheduled interviews. Each student who will use the questionnaire should be thoroughly familiar with the questions, preferably enough to permit the asking of questions without actually reading them, but definitely enough to avoid stalling or halting over unfamiliar words and phrases. If students have worked in groups, each member of the group should have contributed at least two questions to the effort; questions should be composed in an open-ended fashion to facilitate communication and should reflect students' efforts at preliminary research on the school's history and background. Specific questions will come from resources available and students' research, but some general questions can serve as a guideline.

SUGGESTED INTERVIEW QUESTIONS FOR STUDENTS/TEACHERS OF OLD-TIME COUNTRY SCHOOLS

1. Think back to when you went to/taught at the old school. Remember what it looked like when you walked in the door. Describe the room where you were taught in as much detail as you can.
2. How were the grades arranged in the old school? Who sat where? Was there a "pecking order"? (Did older kids pick on younger ones?)
3. What was the order of the day — that is, what did you do from the minute you arrived until you left each day? How did you occupy your time while the teacher worked with other grades?
4. Remember what you/they did at recess. What games were played? Describe those for me. What did the boys do? What did the girls do? Did the "big kids" spend their recess doing different things from the "little kids"? How so?
5. What songs did your class sing? Will you sing one for me?
6. Tell me about a really memorable event that happened at the old school.
7. Was there ever any controversy about a teacher or a subject being taught? What was it?
8. Did you ever do "special" things, such as art projects, plays, field trips, films, visitors who spoke, or anything like that? Tell me about it.
9. How was the old school different from schools today? What things are not as good now? Why? What things are better in modern schools? Why?
10. Where did you go to the bathroom? How did you get a drink of water? Did you have a "rest period"? If so, when, and how did you "rest"?

Remember to provide a general information form for each informant to complete. These forms add to the available information on the schools researched, and personalize each interview as well. Items to include on information forms are name of person being interviewed, address, telephone number, occupation, birthdate, age when interviewed, year(s) attended the school being researched, and name of school attended and its address or location.

After interviews have been conducted and students have had the opportunity to make some sense of their findings, have individuals or groups of students communicate the results of their research through collages, posters, poems, essays or reports, oral presentations, or Hypercard stacks (see Figure 8.5). Then plan a day to commemorate and celebrate students' research by inviting informants to school to share with their interviewers highlights of experiences in old-time schools. Some ideas to get you started:

■ Read Chapter 1 from *Farmer Boy* (by Laura Ingalls Wilder) aloud in class. Talk about "tin dinner pails" and what children of long ago may have carried to school in their lunchpails. Compare Wilder's experiences with those of the guests in your class.
■ Have informants bring photos from their days in the old country schools to share. As a backup, have a copy of *America's Country Schools* (by Andrew Gulliford) handy to serve as reference. Collect shoe boxes and half-pint milk cartons beforehand; after viewing old-time school photos, have students and guest work together to make models of one-room schoolhouses (use the milk carton to represent the bell tower). Glue on a piece of folded poster board for the roof, paint with tempura, and add windows or other decorations with colored construction paper.

TO PARENTS.

This report is sent to the parents for their inspection. Examine it carefully. If you are satisfied, sign your name in the proper space below. If not satisfied please communicate in a friendly spirit of cooperation with the teacher.

Signature of Parent or Guardian.

1st month	Mr. H. A. Thorn
2nd month	Mr. H. A. Thorn
3rd month	Mr. H. A. Thorn
4th month	Mr. H. A. Thorn
5th month	Mr. H. A. Thorn
6th month	Mr. H. A. Thorn
7th month	Mr. H. A. Thorn
8th month	Mr. H. A. Thorn

_____ Union _____ Township Schools.

District No. _____ 5 _____

Monthly Report of _____ Retta Thorn _____

Grade _____ Third _____

Term Beginning _____ Sept. 5, 1921 _____

Term Ending _____ April 21, _____ 19 22

Period	1	2	3	4	5	6	7	8	Ave. class	1st Ex.	2nd Ex.	Ave. Ex.	Term Stand.
Reading	A	A	A	A	A	A	A	A	B	A	A		
Spelling	A	A	A	A	A	A	A	A		C	A		
Writing	A	A	A	A	A	A	A	A		A	A		
English	A	A	A	A	A	A	A	A		B	A		
Arithmetic	A	B	A	B	B	A	A	B		C	C		
Geography	A	B	A	A	B	A	A	A		B	B		
History	A	B	A	A	A	A	A	A		B	B		
Drawing	B+	C+	B+	A-	B+	B+	B+	B+					
Music	B	C	B+	B+	B+	A-	A-	A-					
Man. Train.													
Physiology													
Dom. Sci.													
Agriculture													
Ds. School	20	20	20	20	20	20	20	20					
Da. Attd.	20	18	20	20	20	20	20	20					
Tim. Tard.	0	0	0	0	0	0	0	0					
Min. Tard.	0	0	0	0	0	0	0	0					
School Citizenship	A	A	A	A	A	A	A	A					

Classification for Next Term _____ Fourth grade _____

_____ Meta M. Vitz _____ Teacher

Figure 8.5 Samples of Old-Time School Memorabilia

(Continued)

Figure 8.5 Continued

- Invite informants to demonstrate a game or song they enjoyed as a student of old-time school (e.g., Red Rover, Drop the Handkerchief, Skip to My Lou, etc.). As a backup, have a tape or CD by Pete Seeger or other folksinger handy to serve as a reminder of the kinds of songs popular in that era.
- Encourage informants to "teach" handwriting skills or spelling to your class during their visit. If possible, have one or more informants bring a spelling or reading text used at their school, and conduct a spelling bee. Or ask informants (in a letter ahead of time) to recall pithy sayings popular when they were children (such as "If at first you don't succeed, try, try again"), and ask them to write these on the board or chart paper for students to use as they practice handwriting skills (keep these as a reminder of informants' visit).

■ Trying It Out

One-Room Schools: Interviews

Cheryl's students interviewed local people associated with one-room schools, and wrote summaries of their findings. They shared their findings orally in class, and discussed similarities and differences in these accounts. A time line helped students make connections between political and economic events and circumstances mentioned in the interviews. Excerpts from these interviews demonstrate the wealth of information that can be learned about daily life in the early part of the twentieth century, and about how values and the emphasis on academics change over time:

Mrs. Dorothy Bartrom was born December 14, 1915. She attended Foster School in Thorncreek Township just north of Columbia City, Indiana. She started as a first-grade student in this school in 1921. She described the school:

> The first thing you notice when you walk through the cloakroom into the schoolhouse is the huge pot-belly stove in the middle of the room. Students in grades 1–4 sat on the left, and the ones in grades 5–8 sat on the right, with the teacher's desk and blackboard at the front. My sister Lois, who was two years older than me, went to Foster first, which helped ease my anxiety about the first day of school!
>
> The teacher I had in first grade was Mr. Robert Forester. He had graduated from high school and took a six-week teacher training course so he could teach that fall. He was a National Guardsman and had to go to camp that summer, so he never did finish his six-week training. They gave him an exam, and he passed it and started a teaching career at Foster School in September, after graduating from high school in May. He later went on to become a principal in Columbia City.

We always kept busy at school. While older kids got their instruction from the teacher, we little ones had lessons to complete at our desks. If we finished before the teacher was ready for us again, we got to practice "ciphering" on the blackboard. At recess, we played ball, jumped rope, or played marbles. We had no playground equipment like they do today. Mostly, all the kids just played together, but sometimes the older kids wanted to play ball or tag without us little ones.

On the first day of school when I started third grade, I had to go home sick. Yes! I was sick, and my sister Lois was, too, because a *woman* teacher had taken the place of our beloved Mr. Forester. Miss Geneveve Shuman took his place. We didn't know what to think about that.

Our drinking water was fetched in a bucket every morning by the teacher or one of the older kids, from a house across the road from the school. And we went to the bathroom in the outhouse.

How are schools now compared to then? Children are so unruly now! Children then went to school and behaved, and never thought to act up. But it's easier to further yourself now, because few people went on to high school and college back then.

Mr. Warren Smith was born in Union Township in Huntington County on April 18, 1910. He started first grade in one of the nine district schools, which were numbered at that time, but not named. He attended the school near Plum Tree for the first two years, and describes it as:

There were two big old pot-bellied stoves in the center of the schoolhouse. Neighbors near the school donated wood to burn. The boys in grades 6, 7, and 8 were the janitors: had to haul wood, pump water, fill the stoves, clean and do repair work—this was just all considered part of their training and schooling.

Now, this schoolhouse was modern—had two separate outhouses—one for the girls, and one for the boys. Had its own outside pump for drinking water.

We didn't get much recess time at school. At noon we all ate our lunch, and if you ate quickly enough you could "run around" a little bit while the others finished. You went to school then to learn, not play.

The teachers back then mostly had a high school education, with a six-week class in the summertime, to get to teach grades 1–8. It was very rare for a teacher to have even two years of college.

In third grade, I went to a new school in District 3. It was the newest school in the county—had separate cloakrooms for boys and girls, and even had a wood-fed furnace instead of a pot-belly stove. Had a real janitor! It closed down after three years, and I had to move to another school. Then they got buses; must have been about 1924. They were real big ones! Could hold 15 kids! Pretty fast, too. Could go up to 15 miles an hour on a good road.

The teachers in all three schools where I went depended on the older kids to help the younger ones out with their work. This was considered part of their learning, too, helping out that way. All lessons were given and completed at school. Very little homework, because we were expected to do a lot of chores once we got home.

The biggest school event I remember was the Spelling Bee. Every family brought a covered dish, and parents, students, and the teacher all ate a meal together. Then the parents all lined up on one side of the room and the students on the other. It was a contest to see who could spell the best! Most of the parents had never been to school themselves, so this was a way they could educate the adults as well as the kids. Even if we didn't have homework, we took our books home in the evenings so when there was time we could "teach" our parents what we had learned at school that day. The Spelling Bees were usually won by the students.

Only about 50% of the kids ever went to high school after grammar school. This was not, mind you, because they weren't smart enough. It was mostly because there weren't any buses for the high school level and, if you went, you had to get there yourself. It was 1930 or later when they started having buses for the high schoolers; more people went then.

How is school now different from then? You use computers now—used your own head then! Kids have no discipline now. Makes it hard for the teachers to teach them.

"Why, When I Was Hired, We . . . "

Tell your co-workers about your students' local and community research project, and enlist their help through student interviews. Assign two or three students per teacher, administrator, or staff worker employed at the school. Identify the person they will be interviewing, and provide a brief description of that person's duties (i.e., teaches kindergarten, helps cook our breakfasts and lunches, keeps our restrooms and hallways clean). Provide time during class for the children to construct interview questionnaires. They may try to elicit information such as changes that have taken place in the school since the worker was employed (in the physical environment, and the learning/working environment), how long the person has been employed at the school, what they like best about the school and/or their job, the one thing they would most like to see changed, which changes they feel represent improvement and which do not, and so on.

Use this opportunity to practice letter-writing skills. Have each pair or group of students compose a letter requesting an interview with the school worker identified, and suggesting possible times students would be available to conduct the interview.

Allow pairs or groups of students practice time to prepare for the interview process. One student should ask the questions while another takes notes or records responses on tape (if approved with the interviewee beforehand). For younger children who are not taping their interviews, three students in a group works well: While one person asks questions, *two* students can be taking notes. After the interview process is complete, set aside some class time for students to share their findings. Chart information on the overhead projector, the computer, or large chart paper to illustrate patterns in responses (e.g., dates of employment, length of service, type of work done, etc.).

As a class, summarize findings from all interviews and write a narrative describing these findings. Provide enough copies of the summary for each student and all co-workers interviewed. Don't forget to have students write thank-you letters to the interviewees, and enclose a copy of the summary.

Mock Trials

Other local resources for studying the community are found in trial records, newspaper headlines or accounts of local crimes, or consideration of whether a local celebrity from long ago was a hero or villain. Some children may have been the victims of misdemeanors themselves, such as having their lunch money stolen on the way to school or having their bikes stolen from the family driveway. When teachers use mock trials to help students examine the broader aspects of a local crime, or enable them to see different points of view, students learn more about the justice system as well as practice critical thinking skills.

Conducting a mock trial can be an exciting role-playing experience for students in elementary grades. Children's natural enthusiasm for play-acting provides a built-in success ingredient, and their curiosity about courtrooms and trials sustains interest. Some basics for conducting mock trials are essential for teachers who have never used the strategy.

Many students already have a great deal of information about trials, usually from watching television shows such as "People's Court." Viewing such a program, or discussing one students have seen recently, is a good opening gambit to conducting a mock trial.

Students should be well versed in the basics of simulation. As a way of assisting their understanding of the process of simulating a trial, have students act out roles from a familiar activity, such as a baseball game. They will quickly identify the necessary roles—pitcher, catcher, umpire, and others. After simulating an inning or two, you can direct a discussion about the necessary rules and procedures in any game. The following questions may be helpful in drawing an analogy from baseball simulation to the courtroom:

1. What roles are necessary in a court room?
2. Are there rules to follow, as in a baseball game?
3. What kind of procedure is necessary? (e.g., Who should go first?)
4. What is the purpose of each role?

Both civil and criminal cases can be used for mock trials. In civil cases, which reflect the most typical conflicts in everyday life, two or more people have a dispute. Each believes he or she is right. Both sides must be argued as strongly as possible to resolve the conflict. Students also may need practice in seeing two sides of a conflict, especially if they are personally involved. When two 9-year-olds are in a heated dispute, they are unlikely to be able to see the other side. The following story can be read as a pretrial activity for helping students see "the other person's side":

OOG VERSUS UGH

A very long time ago, when humans still lived in caves, two cavemen got into a furious argument about who killed "Old Snagglefang," the stubborn saber-toothed tiger. A glacier had moved into the valley below the caves where these cavemen lived. The ice from the glacier had crushed all the berry bushes, and frozen all the fish in the lake. All the animals had died except "Old Snagglefang," who was just too ornery and stubborn to be driven off.

But one day Old Snagglefang paid a terrible price for his stubbornness. A caveman named Oog found Old Snagglefang asleep in the sun on the side of the mountain, and bonked him on the side of the head with a giant rock. Old Snagglefang reared up, took a last few wobbling steps, and fell into a pit that a caveman named Ugh had dug to snare passing saber-toothed tigers. Oog had just tugged and yanked Old Snagglefang out of the pit when Ugh came along. Ugh insisted that Old Snagglefang was his catch, not Oog's. That is how the fight started.

The question at issue here is: Who really owns Old Snagglefang? Oog, who struck the fatal blow? Or Ugh, who had created the pit to snare passing saber-toothed tigers? Ask students which side they would support. What would be a fair decision? Conduct a debate and have students present arguments for both sides.

A preliminary approach to conducting a mock trial involving local history is to put fairytale characters on trial. Familiar heroes and villains take on new and surprising personalities when students give critical thought to issues of justice and fairness. Plan to spend several days reviewing the story, its characters, setting, and plot sequence. Ask students to consider motives, evidence, and possible outcomes of the story for various characters (How would each character be affected in the future by events in the story?). Decide whether a crime has been committed and, if so, against whom? Conduct a trial, allowing students to role-play judge, district attorney, attorney for the defense, the defendant, the plaintiff, various witnesses, and, of course, the jury.

Mock trials involving local or state historical figures become challenging and more interesting when controversial personalities are involved. Which personalities from your local city's early settlement or development can be considered controversial? Are there two sides to the story of a local historical hero (one of which is rarely or never presented)? It will be necessary to obtain accurate background information about the historical figures, as well as facts and hearsay surrounding any scandal or controversy. Students may be divided into "opposing camps" as they research background information and conduct the subsequent trial, or the trial may follow a lesson or unit of study on one or more local controversial figures or issues.

Modern issues and dilemmas can also be the subject of a mock trial. As this book was being written, for example, one local controversy involved whether large old trees along the riverbank should have been cut down to make way for construction of a hiking/biking trail. The local newspapers were filled with headlines, articles, letters to the editor, and political cartoons depicting both sides of the controversy. While local residents are ensconced in intellectual and verbal battle over such issues, students can research the facts from both sides, and conduct a trial using fictional characters to represent each side.

Different Sides of a Story

This is another strategy for helping students understand multiple perspectives. Ask your students to identify three people (in their family and/or the community) who experienced or heard about the same event (e.g., a tornado that touched down, a robbery, a memorable baseball game, a flood, an election, etc.). The students will construct a set of questions to use to interview each of the three people identified, and will interview them separately.

Have students bring the results of their interviews to class. Do people agree about what happened at the same event? Did someone provide information not known or experienced by the other two? If they disagree on a particular point, what is it? Can the true facts be determined? Why or why not?

Set aside some time for students to share their findings (and the answers to the preceding questions) with their classmates. They may also like to invite students from another class to hear about their interviews. Discuss with the students the ramifications of this experience to (1) history making and (2) their own lives by considering questions such as the following:

■ Who decides what goes in history books? How does the public know it is the "whole story"? Why might one person's story be believed over another person's account of the same event? How does this process influence the study of history?

■ Under what circumstances might you hear (or read) one person's account of an important event? How do advertisers use this situation to their advantage? Are newscasters or newspaper reporters ever guilty of depicting only one side of a story? Can you show some examples?

Trying It Out

Local Residents Remember the Past

When my students conduct oral history projects, I encourage them to consider alternate perspectives of the same event or circumstance. As they begin the project, students enjoy working in groups of four or five. Each group identifies its own oral history focus. (I have found that making suggestions based on local history events and/or issues is helpful; students sometimes use these suggestions as springboards for their own thinking and discussion before they identify topics that are uniquely their own.) For example, in one class, groups of students identified these oral history topics: Education Then and Now (interview retired teachers and senior citizens); The Great Depression (interview local citizens who lived through it, and their own relatives who were children during the Depression); Native Americans in Our Community (interview residents of a nearby reservation); and The Life of the Volunteer Fireman (interview volunteers from two local fire departments).

After identifying the focus of their project, students work together in groups to come up with an interview questionnaire to be used by each member of the group as interviews are conducted and recorded. I have found that having a discussion about "good questions" and providing examples of poor questions (closed-ended) and good questions (open-ended questions or statements inviting lengthy, detailed responses) helps students formulate effective questionnaires. As an example, I've included questions used to interview participants in the Education Then and Now oral history project and some responses:

1. *How did you get to school?*

I lived very close to the school. I walked to it. (Female teacher)

Back when I was a little fella going to school I had to walk. I walked about a mile or a mile and a quarter. We didn't have school buses, everybody walked. (Male student)

2. *Were there extracurricular activities at your school, such as baseball or music?*

   I was the coach of the swimming team. There was a basketball team. (Female teacher)

   Newspaper, Latin Club, Honor Society, Girl's League, Cheerleading. (Female students)

   We had morning and afternoon recess. No, there was none. (Male student)

3. *Tell me about the schedule. How long was the school day? The school year? When did you have vacations? What time did you get to school? What time did you leave? When did you eat lunch? Where did you eat lunch?*

   It was the same as it is now, about 125 days. Except we had to put in longer days. We had to stay at school until 4. We lived very close, so we went home for lunch. (Female teacher)

   About the same as it is now, but not as many holidays and vacations. We never started school before the first week of September. I went home for lunch or ate downtown. (Female student)

   We usually started around the first part of September and mid-March we were done. We had to get out and do farm work. This was a farm neighborhood and that was spring plowin' and all that other stuff. You had to get out of school to get to work. We went to school Monday through Friday and school started about ten 'til eight' til around about three. We had Thanksgiving and Christmas off, but that was about it. We had a one-room school house, grades one through eight, and we all sat in rows with the teacher in front. We had to get our water from a pump, and every once in a while one of the kids would stick his tongue against the pump and get it froze fast and we'd have trouble again.... We had a couple of hollers in the back of the school and that was our "bathroom." (Male student)

4. *What type of discipline was used at your school? What happened to students who misbehaved? Can you recall any stories about someone who misbehaved? What happened?*

   Of course, everyone knew everyone. The town was very small. If anyone acted out, everyone knew it. So we didn't have the discipline problems that we have today. (Female teacher)

   Strict! You had to respect the teacher, or you were sent to the office. (Female student)

   A hickory stick. Usually to the hind end, not the knuckles. There was no principal at these schools; the teacher did it. (Male student)

5. *What was taught at your school?*

   The Three Rs. Your arithmetic was far more advanced then. They had some pretty tough problems in there. (Male student)

   Lots of foreign language. (Female student)

6. *What was your favorite thing to learn/teach about at school?*

   I liked English better than anything. (Male student)

   My favorite subjects were English and journalism. (Female student)

7. *How was religion handled? Did you have prayer in school?*

   We always said prayers and the Pledge of Allegiance. (Female student)

   It wasn't taught. No, there were no prayers at our school. (Male student)

8. *Was there a dress code? What did the boys wear? What did the girls wear? What did the teacher wear?*

Overalls and shirts and coats [for boys]. Girls wore dresses. (Male student)

Skirts and dresses [for girls]. No tight sweaters, and skirt at the knee or lower. (Female student)

9. *Is your schoolhouse still standing? Where is it? What is it used for now?*

Yes, only it is used now for a downtown [college] campus. (Female student)

No. The only thing that is left is a clump of trees. It's all gone. (Male student)

Questions and responses used for The Great Depression included:

1. *Do you remember anything about the actual day of the stock market crash? Tell me about it.*

That's when we were planning our wedding and we didn't feel much of the crash because the school systems had enough cash on hand to pay the teachers at that time. And my father was a pastor and he was still on salary....We did notice that people were becoming distraught about everything. There were especially those who had invested and they had lost their investments, and we read more and more of suicides...people who had lost heavily. People would pick up some small jobs and people would do some door-to-door selling, and that went on for years after the crash. Small items—I remember one man who came to the door and was selling...he called "a thimble for your curtain rod," and if you put this on your curtain rod the curtain will slide smoothly. I still have that thimble....He sold these for 15 cents. That was his income. (Female teacher)

I remember the night...when everything fell apart. It was in October....Dad and Mom come in the house. Banks was closed. I remember we didn't own any farmland and we rented. For five hundred dollars a year—we only had part of it paid, and we didn't know how we was going to pay the rest of it. I was in third grade in school and we had Jersey cows. And Dad decided he would go to the city to see if he could find any work. He got a job. Mom and we three girls (we were little) did the chores then. We separated the milk; my sister and I cranked the separator. It was too much for one to crank, so we both cranked. That's where you pour the milk in a big container, and it goes down through these disks, and there's lots of little cone-shaped disks. When the milk goes through there, it separates the milk and the cream. The cream goes in one spot and the milk goes in another. That was some of the stuff we did. (Female)

2. *Were you working during the time of the Great Depression and, if so, what type of job were you doing? If you did not work, what jobs did your family members have?*

Well, I was teaching before we were married in 1932. It was the height of the depression, and of course salaries were very low at that time. We were paid $1,200 for the year and that was paid on the basis of ten months, so we had $120 a month. After I was married, I didn't teach. In fact, there wouldn't have been an opening because the teachers were staying with their positions as much as they could, especially if they were married and their husbands were without work. We were married in January, and fifteen months later we had our first baby. Then I was tied down with the baby and the work I did was just housework and family raising. But they were happy years. We had each other. (Female teacher)

I was farming. We raised a lot of hogs and cattle and most other crops but we didn't sow any corn. We did sell wheat if we had any to sell. One day I took two truck load of hogs to Ossian. One load sold for $2.80 a hundred pound, and the other sold for $2.90 a hundred. (Male farmer)

3. *What were your circumstances for housing, food, and recreation?*

Well, there was some that were farming that couldn't keep on and they lost their farms. Because we farmed we had most of our food so we didn't worry too much. (Male farmer)

Our housing circumstances were unique since my husband was a pastor.... The Lutheran church had a practice of building a bungalow chapel [for their pastors]. There were four rooms upstairs and no partitions downstairs. So, the first floor was the chapel, and we lived upstairs. We had four rooms and a bath. Nice rooms; it was a pleasant living. Much of the work had been done by the men of the church (because of the Depression), and the heating system was not all that satisfactory. In fact, we had to close off the one bedroom in the winter because the goldfish froze into the bowl.

We paid eight cents a quart for milk...I don't know what [the farmers] got for it. I remember that we could buy hamburger three pounds for a quarter on the weekend. T-bone steak was 17 cents a pound, but we couldn't afford it. We bought meat twice a week. I bought a pound of hamburger on Saturday and made meat balls for Sunday and Monday. Our children were very small then so there were really only two adults eating. We had no [more] meat until Friday, when I could buy a can of mackerel for a dime. Fresh vegetables were practically not available at all. We would buy carrots and cabbage and food that was inexpensive.

Our recreation...well, there was no money for concerts. I did go to a movie once because the theater manager gave all of the pastors—believe it or not—a pass to the movies. Will Rogers was one of my favorite performers, and when a Will Rogers movie came to town, my husband gave me the pass and said, "Now I'll stay with the babies this afternoon. You go to the movies." Or we would go out for a ride—not far. Sometimes we would have a picnic. We did have a radio which was given to us as a wedding gift. We used that a lot. But there was just no money for other recreation. My husband was a bowler, but he didn't bowl during that time, and he didn't play tennis because we needed whatever income we had to keep our family going. We had our family and we knew this Depression would eventually pass. We always had a roof over our heads. (Female teacher)

4. *What are some of the effects the depression have had on you? Are you affected by it today? If so, how?*

We're more cautious. There is one thing that I tried not to do.... I know that a lot of kids who grew up during the depression like we did, when they got married they vowed that their children would never want for things like they did. I think that spoils them. We tried not to do that. (Female)

Well, now when I want something, I go get it! [laughing]. Before, I didn't go get *anything*. I didn't! (Male farmer)

Well, somehow or other I don't think I have ever gotten over the feeling that I must be frugal. We were so frugal for so many years, and so very frugal even after the Depression was over because we had six children and my husband being a pastor, we had a rural congregation. That meant a lot of driving and going to the hospital and so forth, because he made a lot of calls. And you bought your own gasoline (in those days, there was no car allowance [for pastors]). We just had to be frugal because the work had to go on.

And I still watch the sales. I figure if I buy a dress now at the beginning of spring at full price, I'll wear that dress for years. If I wait till after Easter when it's marked down I'll buy that same dress for less, and still wear it for years. That has just become a way of life.

We learned to be satisfied with what we had. We just…counted our blessings, and we often had the feeling that the Lord has taken care of us through real hard times and He's never let us down. (Female teacher)

A Senior Citizens' Tea

Another approach that brings together senior citizens and students for mutual learning experiences is described by Alan Sears and George Bidlake (1991), who planned a classroom social event as a vehicle for conducting oral history interviews about local history topics with local senior citizens. "We felt that the older citizens of our community were a vast untapped resource for information about how the community had developed and about specific historical events," they state. These teachers also wanted their sixth-grade students to recognize the significance of multiple perspectives in historical knowledge, that "the same events or developments might have different interpretations, depending on who comments on them."

Alan and George decided that oral history interviews were the best approach for exposing their students to multiple perspectives in history. Planning and hosting a "tea" was a way to get local senior citizens and students in the same place at the same time, thus avoiding some of the scheduling and traveling difficulties often attributed to young children's experiences with oral history interviews. They sent out a press release, telling about the planned oral history interview process, its purpose, and the date of the tea, which was broadcast by local radio stations and published in the local newspaper. In addition, students made and hand-delivered invitations to homes of senior citizens on their neighborhood streets. Parent volunteers and other teachers agreed to help transport senior citizens to the tea if needed. When the project became common knowledge, the entire school got involved: The choir, gymnastic team, and band all agreed to provide entertainment during the social portion of the day.

Teachers and students discussed and practiced good interviewing techniques. As Alan recalls, "Our guidelines included reminders to be overly prepared with questions, be certain the interviewee is comfortable with the topic, take notes if the subject is not comfortable being tape recorded, have equipment, such as tape recorders and microphones, working properly, be courteous, especially if the subject does not want to answer a question, be prepared to deviate if the subject mentions interesting and unexpected information, and arrange to provide the subject with a copy of the final report."

Students interviewed each other for practice after developing interview questionnaires. This experience showed them that they did not have to follow exactly a specific order of questions, but that they should be certain each question on the questionnaire is covered in some way.

Groups of students planned and carried out arrangements for entertainment, baking and serving cookies, making and serving tea and coffee, and setting up tables and chairs in the gym with displays of students' local history projects (both to share with the visitors and to serve as catalysts for visitors' memories if things begin to lag).

The afternoon of the tea finally arrived. Alan relates, "More than forty guests arrived, eager to participate in our project. Our student hosts greeted them and showed them the displays of students' work. After the entertainment by various school groups, the students served the guests coffee or tea and cookies."

Visitors and one or two students went off to set up and begin their interviews. "We expected this part to go well," the teachers say, "but it exceeded our expectations. The students, who had been nervous about questioning the adults, were very excited about the results of their interviews." One student said, "I was worried that my person wouldn't say anything, but the only problem I had was getting her stopped."

Benefits from this oral history project include enhancement of general knowledge about local and community history, extension of understanding about significant events in local history (such as what happened to people and jobs as well as the economy when the town's economy collapsed when the availability of machines changed the logging industry), exploration and interest in the changing role of women in the community's history, and the recognition and comprehension of famed community leaders as real people with real lives. In addition, "a rewarding result of the whole interview process was the enhanced relationship that developed between the visitors and the students," Alan and George conclude. "Some students had stereotyped images of seniors as dull, uninteresting, and uninterested in kids, while some of the older people viewed the children as the little annoyances who tramped through their gardens and across their lawns." Students gained an appreciation for multiple perspectives of historical events, and seniors had a contributory, positive, enriching experience.

A Living History Museum

Another strategy for immersing students in the study of local history is the creation of a Living History Museum. Special people, events, or activities representing your local area are appropriate foci.

A maximum of 10 to 12 "scenes" should comprise the museum. Every scene is related to the central theme, so pairs or small groups of students may be assigned to research, plan, design, and display each scene. Organize scenes according to either topical or chronological sequence. All scenes should emphasize historical accuracy. (A large, open area such as the school cafeteria, library, or gym lends itself more readily to display and circulation than a classroom.) Each scene should include actors (students), and props appropriate to the event. It is helpful to rope off each scene area, leaving traffic areas uncluttered while protecting the "museum." Still poses should last for no more than 10 minutes (with short rests in between); scheduling viewing times for other classes and/or the community helps prevent tiring of the actors.

Pertinent information describing the significance of each scene should be posted at eye level and boldly lettered. A taped speech or vocal explanation will add to the display. Students who are not part of the displayed scenes can serve as guides, providing brief overviews of each scene for visitors.

Local History Simulations

Simulations can be excellent tools to help students master concepts and apply knowledge to real-life situations. There are two major ways to incorporate simulations into the curriculum: as effective introductory experiences (providing advanced organizers) and as culminating experiences (synthesizing information learned). Types and applications of simulations are limited only by a teacher's imagination. Interact and Abt & Associates offer prepared simulations for classroom use, but some teachers may want to create their own. The following information is presented for those creatively minded teachers!

Essential Elements of Simulation. Steps for constructing simulations in the classroom include (Southern, 1993):

1. Select the instructional goals and objectives of the simulation.
2. Specify an appropriate setting for the acquisition/application of the concepts. A setting may contain role specifications with distinct motives for individual actors, or it may provide only broad guidelines as to the nature of participant roles in a setting.
3. State the nature of the conflict between groups of roles explicitly or implicitly.
4. Provide some indication of goals for the individuals or groups in the conflict and methods of ascertaining when these goals are met.
5. Develop an initial situation that provides sufficient motivation for the participants to begin the action.

6. Specify a management system to provide the participants with consequences of moves and decisions they have made. Such systems may include elements of chance and branching trees of consequences. On the other hand, the system may be as simple as having the manager communicate the consequences of actions through reports, diplomatic pouches, or computer messages.

7. Identify a debriefing mechanism in order for students to have an opportunity to synthesize the experiences they have had. Often this amounts to no more than a discussion session at the end of the simulation, though it might be more elaborate and contain critiques of the outcomes by experts. A simple device that allows debriefing involves conducting parallel simulations and asking participants to contrast the different outcomes.

8. In simulation design it is also desirable to provide students with some external paraphernalia that will help them develop enthusiasm and identify with their roles.

A summary of the basic steps in designing a simulation will be helpful, also:

■ First, decide how simulation fits into your curriculum. Is it related to a theme, an event, or a person? Will it be used as an introduction, a culminating activity, or to help students apply what they have learned midway through the unit?

■ Second, determine what the simulation is expected to accomplish for your students. What is the goal? What are the anticipated learner outcomes? State these in language the students can understand, and share the goal with them before beginning the simulation.

■ Third, develop an outline of the structure of the simulation from beginning to end. Take students' developmental levels, the available resources, and time constraints into consideration. Ask yourself these questions:

How much time will be devoted to the simulation itself?

What costumes, settings, and/or props are needed?

What are the essential roles? Secondary roles?

What background research must students conduct before taking on a particular role? Who will be responsible for monitoring this?

What guidelines or standards are required (if any) to protect students from emotional and/or physical harm during the simulation?

What are the expected outcomes? What other outcomes are possible?

How much time will be devoted to debriefing after the simulation?

■ Fourth, the students begin researching background information and real-life situations similar to those in the simulation.

■ Fifth, when research has been completed, roles and character development should begin to emerge; have students choose roles and begin developing their own characters. (Remember, students will have to stay "in character" throughout the entire simulation experience.)

■ Step six relates to preparing the setting, or stage, for the simulation. Prepare all props, setting, costumes, and so on prior to the scheduled day of the simulation. Developing a schedule with specific deadlines for various steps in this preparation (and names of students who will be responsible for each of the steps) will help ease last-minute anxiety.

■ Step seven is the actual simulation. During the simulation, remember that the teacher's role is to guide students: Monitor activities to ensure that all students stay in character, and troubleshoot where necessary.

■ The eighth and final step in conducting a simulation is the "debriefing" stage. This should begin immediately after the simulation. One format utilizes an open discussion of students' feelings. Students may write about the simulated event from the point of view of their character, reacting to situations encountered in the simulation. After engaging in writing activities, students critique the experience for technical and logistic improvements, and end with a discussion of how the simulation fits into their study of local history.

Interactional Drama

Interactional drama is different from presentation and performance dramatics. Instead of simply being members of an audience of observers or actors in the drama, students in interactional drama react to a problem-solving context, "moving from audience member to participant in the course of the drama" (Turner, 1989a, p. 30).

Putting on an interactional drama in the elementary classroom requires three things: a scenario, background packets, and well-prepared actors. The scenario is selected or developed from a particular topic of study—in this case, a subtheme or subtopic of the local history unit. Students and teachers work together to research and collect information relevant to the scenario (to give it authenticity as well as historical accuracy) and actors are recruited. Background packets are developed for each character, and recruited actors are prepared for their roles by familiarizing themselves with information in these background packets.

When the scenario is acted out, opportunities are sought for student observers to become involved in the action. The actual scenario, then, is dependent on students' involvement in and reactions to these opportunities.

In the third and final phase of interactional drama, students reflect on the experience and clarify the meanings of their reactions and decisions during the audience involvement stage of the scenario. The teacher can facilitate reflection by asking questions such as these:

> *What were the real issues at stake here?*
>
> *How could you have reacted differently, and how would that have changed things?*
>
> *How realistic was the portrayal of the characters and the times they lived in, and what does this tell us about those times?*
>
> *If we had been products of that era instead of our own, would we have felt and acted differently? (Turner, 1989a, p. 31)*

Several dramatic devices can be used to enhance the effectiveness of an interactional drama experience. Five are outlined here (Turner, 1994):

1. *Side Setting:* This device preconditions students to take a particular viewpoint or "side" before the actors begin their interaction. The presentation of one-sided data prior to the drama will bias students to definite opinions. Such a procedure may be used to:
   a. Show the influence of preconditioning on objectivity.
   b. Set the stage for confrontation with one of the actors.
   c. Help students more quickly identify with feelings of characters being portrayed.
2. *Freeze-Frame:* This consists of a prearranged signal to the actors that tells them to freeze the dialogue and movement. Freeze-frames allow the teacher to do a "Twilight Zone"-type narration/commentary or hold a discussion with student observers. At another prearranged signal, the actors go on as if they had never been interrupted.
3. *Time Trance:* A device useful for tuning in imaginations and creating the suspended disbelief needed for illusion, time trance puts students in a mindset appropriate for the scenario about to take place. For instance, the teacher tells students to shut their eyes, then introduces what is about to happen. When the teacher tells students to open their eyes, the actors are ready to begin.

4. *Dramatic Suspense:* Plot suspense and tension between characters help problems seem more real, and students become more involved. Meaningful, thoughtful interaction is more likely to occur if students feel the suspense.

5. *Suspended Disbelief:* Every dramatic experience, even those of television and radio, require the audience to believe in the "reality" of what audiences know is not real. One side of the mind knows this cannot truly be happening, but the other side temporarily closes off this belief and identifies with the characters, setting, and events of the drama. It is necessary that students temporarily suspend disbelief in order to be more actively involved in interactional drama.

Chapter

9

Local Folklore

Folklorists study the ways people of different societies in various eras of human existence communicate their beliefs and traditions. These ways often take the form of orally communicated stories or anecdotes, folk dances, and crafts. Folklore contains some of the most ancient forms of human creativity, making the study of folklore very important. Rarely do folklorists find ways to translate their findings into materials and strategies teachers can use in the classroom, yet, as Simons (1990) says, "To know our folklore—the folklore of our country, our ethnicity, our family, our childhood, our age group, and our ethnic group—is to learn to know ourselves in new ways." When young students study folklore, they come to view themselves through a different lens, looking at aspects of everyday existence often undervalued in the academic curriculum.

Folklore, then, can help students know themselves and their communities better. All socially constructed groups—whether identified as neighborhoods, communities, or ethnic groups—develop and pass on ways of entertaining and instructing each other and their children, or lore of the folk. Riddles, children's games, and modern graffiti are as much forms of folklore as proverbs, myths, and folktales.

Six major folklore genres, or forms, are commonly available for teachers to use as instructional tools (Swanson, 1985):

- *Verbal genres* include forms of traditional expression that depend on words, which usually are spoken or sung (e.g., tall tales, fairytales, historical legends, horror or ghost stories, myths, personal experience stories, oral histories, jokes, riddles, rhymes, proverbs, games, regional speech, and words to songs or ballads).
- *Material genres,* or material culture, include representations of everyday domestic life, farming, trade or industry, and the general cultural landscape such as farm building layout. Material culture is evident in the existence of specialized artifacts, such as textiles (embroidery, crocheting, hand-braided rugs, quilts), food (recipes or recipe collections), crafts (chair caning, furniture making, basket making), architecture (old buildings and houses, farm

layouts), and folk art (hand-carved furniture or gravestones, stenciling, hand-made Christmas ornaments and Easter egg decorations).

■ *Belief genres* include legends, myths, weather lore, folk medicine, and magic. Legends and myths belong to both the verbal and the belief genres because they communicate and serve to influence beliefs about values, the supernatural, and mystical or spiritual experiences.

■ *Body communication genres* include ritual behaviors such as kneeling in prayer, graduation or wedding processionals, ceremonies, dancing, games, informal social interactions (shaking hands, bowing), and gestures.

■ *Music genres* include folksongs such as ballads or work songs as well as traditional hymns, and traditional instruments such as dulcimer, banjo, harmonica, or fiddle.

■ *Customary genres* include those folklore examples that are not readily categorized as word or artifact products. *Action* is the operative word for the customary genre: Calendar and seasonal events, community festivals, family traditions, religious celebrations and/or rituals, music and craft fairs, and sporting or school events all are examples of customs.

What sets these artifacts and folklore forms apart from fine art is not their quality. Rather, it is the way that cultural artifacts "are learned informally by imitation and in apprenticeship, and are handed down over generations by word of mouth," often serving utilitarian as well as artistic or decorative purposes (Swanson, 1985, p. 8). Parents taught their children, older siblings taught younger siblings, local craftspersons taught would-be craftspersons, and so on, passing the knowledge and skills of generation upon generation to local citizens at one time or another in their lives.

Folklore, then, fits in wonderfully with the study of local or community history. Both old and contemporary practices communicate valuable information about the area and its inhabitants. Collecting and studying local folklore through the six major genres can develop students' insightful understanding of their own roots, and the roots of their neighborhood and community.

Local Folklore Themes

Introduce students briefly to the six major folklore categories by providing one or two concrete examples of each. Create a display, with each example labeled with the appropriate genre (such as a recording of a local legend labeled *Verbal*). Spend at least one full day getting acquainted with the various genres and examples, then have students brainstorm other examples for each genre.

Divide students into small groups, and have each group select a folklore theme to research locally. Tell students now that they have brainstormed many examples of each genre, they will spend time in the community collecting their own examples to add to the class display. Each group will collect folklore examples that relate to the group's identified theme. (It may help to suggest a few themes, such as Traditions of Our Community, Domestic Life, Legends and Legendary Characters, Farming Life, Holiday Celebrations, etc.).

As they search for and collect examples of local folklore, students will need tape recorders with batteries and blank tapes (these must be labeled with contributor's name, date, and subject of tape); cameras and film; library cards; notebooks (complete reference information is essential if notes are to be useful later—a funny local joke or the instructions for playing a regional game are incomplete if the name, location, and other identifying information about the local contributor(s) are not included in notes); and a list of suggested questions. Help students consider questions they might ask potential contributors for each folklore theme, and encourage group members to carry a copy of these questions with them at all times. (I met a willing and informative contributor for an oral history project when she "dropped by" my parents' house on Christmas evening when I was visiting them. If I hadn't gone armed with tape recorder, and questionnaire, the lady's wonderful contribution to the project might never have been obtained.)

Each student in the group takes responsibility for at least one example of local folklore related to the group's theme: a personal experience story, an oral history interview, an artifact, a song, joke, or game, or folk wisdom saying, for instance. When examples are brought to school, the group works together to create or develop these into appropriate display objects (i.e., mounts or frames documents and photographs, provides a verbal as well as written record of stories or songs, and labels and describes artifacts).

After all groups have completed their thematic folklore collection, develop assignments and plan discussions involving students in looking at, touching, handling, role-playing, and writing about local folklore examples. Use the examples to create a Class Almanac (see next activity for description) by changing or reorganizing categories.

Almanacking

Remember those old *Farmer's Almanacs?* You do not have to be a farmer to appreciate one—or to make one! All the resources you and your students need are right there in the community.

It is a good idea to bring in two or three old almanacs before you get started. Get a recent one at the variety or hardware store, and scour flea markets or used book stores for a couple of old ones (or you might call on the local senior citizens' association to see what they can come up with). Use something from one of them in class, such as a bit of weatherlore related to the local forecast, and then place them prominently in the room and encourage the children to look at them in their free time. After a couple of days of this, you will be ready to help the class develop its own almanac.

First, tell the students they are going to develop a Class Almanac. Then explain how this project fits in with your ongoing attempt to make history "real." Ask the students to list topics and sections usually found in almanacs. List these on the board or overhead projector. Now let them brainstorm topics and sections to include in the Class Almanac. When you have a manageable outline, you are ready to begin. For those who need it, here's a list of possible topics:

SCIENCE

1. Weatherlore, predicting, and "science folklore" (e.g., "When leaves on the trees turn wrong-side-out in the wind, it's going to rain")
2. Herbs and plant lore, kitchen concoctions for household use (e.g., beauty aids, cosmetics, spot removers)
3. Tide tables, moon phases
4. Ecology hints and recycling tips
5. Home remedies

LANGUAGE ARTS

1. Proverbs and wise sayings
2. Silly sayings and silly horoscopes
3. Jokes, riddles, tongue twisters, jump rope rhymes
4. Folk games and songs
5. Poems, ghost stories, local legends

SOCIAL STUDIES

1. Town history time line
2. Maps of the neighborhoods
3. A map of the town or city, with a suggested walking tour route
4. Birthdays and biographical sketches of "famous" locals

MATHEMATICS

1. Tables of weights and measures
2. Mileage between famous local landmarks
3. Puzzlers or brain teasers using numbers

ARTS AND CRAFTS

1. Recipes and/or instructions for making favorite dishes or crafts
2. Patterns and directions for making homemade kites, toys, birdfeeders, pomanders, and/or quilts

Be sure to caution students against trying any of the "home remedies" they learn about without parental guidance!

A sample of what one class did with an almanacking assignment follows:

CLAY COUNTY ALMANAC

Home Remedies

No Appetite—Losing Weight

Boil 2 cups dogwood bark in 2 cups water. Drink 1/2 cup before breakfast, dinner, and supper.

Blood Builder

Dig sassafras roots in early spring. Wash roots and put in clay pot. Cover with rainwater. Let stand overnight, then boil for 30 minutes. Sweeten with honey or sorghum. Drink as tea four times a day.

Burns

Peel an Irish potato. Scrape meat into pulp. Gather pulp into clean rag; put on burn.

Break off a piece of aloe plant. With the moist broken end, "paint" the burn. Repeat until burning sensation is gone—this method will leave no scar.

Coughing

Mix a tablespoon of honey with a tablespoon of freshly squeezed lemon juice. Take two teaspoons whenever a cough comes on.

Bake three large onions in hot oven for 20 minutes. Wrap onions in an old clean white sock and wear around neck.

■ Trying It Out

Class Almanac

Vicki Lindsay wanted her sixth-graders to see how the oral tradition permits people to pass information down through the generations of families and communities. She felt she could help them gain "a feeling of accomplishment as they contribute a small piece of their world for a class almanac." She started the project by talking with her students about family history. "We talked about certain things that are passed on from generation to generation. We also discussed *The Farmer's Almanac* and things that are contained in it." She passed around a copy of *The Farmer's Almanac* to help students get a sense of what they might include in a class almanac. Students then formed groups, and the groups decided collaboratively for which almanac topics they would be responsible. "I encouraged them to go home and talk to their parents and other family members about things that they could contribute to the almanac," she says. The groups of students had one week to collect and organize their information. Two students volunteered to help type the information on the computer to create the almanac.

Student response to this assignment was very positive. Most students worked well within the group structure. One unexpected benefit was that groups were energized and challenged to contribute even more as other groups shared aloud what they had found each day. Here, for example, are some of the topics and selected items included in Vicki's class almanac:

HOME REMEDIES

1. Cure for hiccups: Have someone jump up behind you and scare you.
2. Cure for a sore throat: Gargle two teaspoons of cold, salty water. Repeat if desired.
3. Cure for a headache: Apply a warm, damp cloth on your forehead until throbbing stops.

BEAUTY TIPS

Tips to give you shinier hair

1. Brush your hair 100 times in the same place.
2. Wash your hair with mayonnaise and raw egg.
3. Rinse your hair with beer.
4. When you are washing your hair, rinse out all the soap and then rinse your hair with vinegar.

For swollen eyelids

1. Put a slice of cucumber over both eyelids until the swelling goes down.
2. Put two spoons in the freezer for 5 minutes. Then take out and put on eyelids.
3. Put calamine tea bags on your eyelids.

FACIAL CARE

1. To tighten pores, mix egg whites and put on face for 10 minutes.
2. For dry skin, mix half of a banana with honey and sour cream. Put it on your face and leave it on for a while. Wipe it off and keep the mixture in the refrigerator.

JUMP ROPE RHYMES

"Lizzie Borden"

Lizzie Borden took an ax and gave her mother 40 whacks

But when she saw what she had done—she gave her father 41.

"Cinderella"

Cinderella dressed in yellow went upstairs to kiss a fellow

Made a mistake and kissed a snake—how many doctors did it take? 1, 2, 3, 4 . . .

"Teddy Bear"

Teddy Bear, Teddy Bear turn around.

Teddy Bear, Teddy Bear touch the ground.

Teddy Bear, Teddy Bear go upstairs.

Teddy Bear, Teddy Bear say your prayers.

Teddy Bear, Teddy Bear turn out the light.

Teddy Bear, Teddy Bear say good night.

Students also collected instructions on how to make a dream catcher and how to make a pretzel wreath. Vicki plans to keep the copy of this class almanac to share with other classes in years to come. The students involved in this almanac project thought it would be good to construct an "author page," listing their names and a brief statement about each person who contributed to the writing.

Vicki recommends that teachers who decide to try the almanacking project seek outside funding so that copies can be made and bound for all students to keep, as well as a copy for the school library. Sandra, another teacher who tried the almanacking project, suggests that a master copy be kept in the teacher's possession, as she had the misfortune of a school staff member's deciding "this is junk to be thrown out" without asking. Vicki also suggests that teachers consider devoting more than a week to the project, and that they rethink group topic assignments. "I would really like to use this activity over a longer period of time; the whole class could concentrate on one topic at a time," she says. She suggests that teachers find several older copies of *The Farmer's Almanac* to use as examples. Additionally, a high potential for process writing in social studies exists with the almanacking project—when teachers plan for the project to take several weeks to complete, editing and rewriting should be an important part of it.

Autographs and Memories

Collect school yearbooks from 30 years ago to the most current year (even better if they are available from the school where you teach!), and have students leaf through them to observe the changes in students' and teachers' dress, hairstyle, fads, names, and so on. Use these questions for guidelines as students peruse the yearbooks, or develop your own:

1. What kinds of clothing did students wear in the 1960s? The 1970s? The 1980s? What was the preferred style of teachers' clothing?
2. How did boys and girls wear their hair in the 1960s? The 1970s? The 1980s? When did hairstyles seem to change most drastically? Did the teachers' hairstyles change or remain about the same? What do you observe about the way women teachers wore their hair? About the way men teachers wore theirs?
3. Look at the uniforms worn by members of various athletic teams over the years. Have they changed? In what way? What do you think was responsible for the changes? Why?
4. What were the names of popular student clubs or organizations (other than sports) in the 1960s? The 1970s? The 1980s? Which organizations remained popular throughout these years? Which are found in some yearbooks, but not in others? Why do you think this is so?
5. Predict what changes may take place in your school's yearbook during the next five years.

■ Trying It Out

Schooldays Autographs
Several teachers shared examples of autographs from their old yearbooks and autograph books in a summer workshop. Some of the more memorable ones include messages both friendly and unfriendly:

I met you as a stranger,
I leave you as a friend.
I hope we meet in Heaven
Where friendship never ends.

Love your friends, love them well,
But to your friends no secrets tell;
For if your friend becomes your foe
Your secrets everyone will know.

Study and work,
Don't be a flop.
Sooner or later
You'll reach the top.

In this book I'll gladly sign
Right upon the dotted line.

I thought, I thought, I thought in vain,
At last I thought I'd write my name.

My house is situated near a lake.
Drop in sometime.

Roses are red,
Violets are blue;
God made me pretty,
But what happened to you?

Remember well and bear in mind
That a faithful friend is hard to find.
And when you find one that is true,
Change not the old one for the new.

Love many, trust few.
Always paddle your own canoe.

Old Sayings

Carol Darling asked her students to interview grandparents or senior citizens for examples of old sayings from their childhood, along with their meanings. The class made a master list, which Carol turned into a matching game.

AN OLD SAYING...

a. _____ He's like a lost ball in
the tall weeds.
b. _____ He's telling a big windy.
c. _____ God won't hoe your taters.
d. _____ If you want to be heard in
the forest, you have to
shake a tree.
e. _____ Like trying to scratch your
ear with your elbow.
f. _____ If hot air was music, she'd be
a brass band.
g. _____ Busy as a bee in a tar bucket.
h. _____ If it were raining soup, she'd
be caught without a spoon.
i. _____ You're making my mad come
a'visiting.
j. _____ He couldn't drive nails in a
snowbank.
k. _____ He jumped into his britches
too far.
l. _____ She feels like a porcupine in a
balloon factory.
m. _____ The old woman in the sky is
plucking geese.
n. _____ He's not broke, just badly bent.
o. _____ He drinks his own bathwater.
p. _____ That's like trying to nail jelly
to the wall.
q. _____ I trust him about as far as I
can throw him.
r. _____ She works like cold molasses.
s. _____ The cow blew bran in her face.
t. _____ I could spell poor with four o's.
u. _____ She's got her "thank you,
ma'am bucket" in her hand.

1. no money
2. believes what he says
3. not handy
4. close by

5. nervous

6. can't get organized

7. get results
8. talks all the time

9. lying

10. won't do your work

11. working hard

12. it's snowing

13. do impossible

14. she's slow
15. hard to do
16. wants a favor

17. wearing shorts

18. unlucky
19. not honest
20. getting angry
21. she has freckles

v. _____ His lantern's lit but nobody's home.

22. has no money

w. _____ He likes to sit and watch the snails rush by.

23. thunder

x. _____ The angels are moving God's piano.

24. slow! doing anything

y. _____ She lives a whoop and a holler away.

25. not paying attention

Using Folktales

Just about as long as there have been folks, there has been folklore. In every part of the world—including your community—there are folktales. Stories preserved through oral tradition teach us about everyday experiences of the common people. Through them, we can learn about the history, geography, sociology, language, music, literature, values, cultural mores, and ethnic heritage of people the world over. With them, we can entertain children, motivate them to learn, and stimulate creative thinking. The interdisciplinary nature of folktales makes them an ideal vehicle for teaching across the curriculum.

Teachers have a great variety of folk tale types from which to choose for use with children. Those which come most readily to mind are animal tales and fables, but epics, myths, legends, tall tales and "just so" stories also lend themselves well to the interdisciplinary format. Recognizable characteristics and examples of each type include:

Animal Tales/Fables: Stories with a moral, in which the protagonists rarely have names but are endowed with human traits (e.g., "The Tortoise and the Hare")

Epics: Long cyclic poems extolling the deeds of human heroes (e.g., "Gilgamesh")

Just-So Stories: Stories intended to explain the "why" of nature and natural phenomena (e.g., Rudyard Kipling's tales)

Legends: Stories based on the alleged deeds of actual historical figures, but not entirely based on fact (e.g., "John Henry" stories)

Myths: Tales embodying the customs, morals, heroes and sometimes religious beliefs of a particular society: Greek, Roman, Norse (e.g., "Pandora's Box").

Tall Tales: Tales of unlikely heroes whose adventures are wildly exaggerated (e.g., "Pecos Bill" stories).

All types of folktales have one basic characteristic in common: They have survived because of the oral tradition. Before written history, people of the world preserved their cultural traditions through storytelling. Settings and details might be altered by individual storytellers, but the essential story structure remained unchanged. The same rhythmic cadence, patterns of repetition, and familiar motifs that contribute to children's enjoyment of folktales today helped to ensure their longevity hundreds of years ago. Folktales have survived because they were meant to be told. Their essential elements continue to speak to the basic human experience, causing children to identify with main characters and internalize the timeless struggles of good and bad, evil and kindness, right and wrong.

Because folktales were meant to be told, the most effective way to introduce the idea of local folklore to your students is to become a "teller of tales." Select a story that you believe is worth telling—one that can be made to come to life in the child's imagination and continue to live vividly in the memory. Learn your story well, reading it several times silently before attempting to read it aloud, then set the book aside and relive the story in your own words. When you are ready to share the tale with children, set the mood for storytelling by asking a thought-provoking question that will enable them to relate the story to their own lives. Then tell the tale, utilizing appropriate gestures, facial expression, voice inflection, and dramatic pauses.

Develop a timely, succinctly expressed conclusion to the tale, then begin follow-up activities immediately, selecting from the following:

THE ORAL TRADITION

Emphasize the oral tradition inherent in folktales by providing children with opportunities to retell the stories they hear. Try these ideas, or create your own:

- Small children can make finger puppets to represent story characters. Encourage them to "tell" the story to one another, using the finger puppets. Let children take their puppets home so that they can share the story with persons outside the classroom. In this way, the tradition of oral history is preserved by even very small children (and who knows—their parents and grandparents may even become inspired!)
- Children in upper primary grades may enjoy a "group retelling" of a folktale. This can be accomplished in several ways, one of which is for the teacher to recall the setting and first line or so of the story and then call on a child at random to continue. The teacher should permit each child to recall only a small portion of the story before calling on another volunteer. As group recall progresses, children will begin to correct one another and/or embellish the tale, emulating the characteristics of oral history. This will provide an opportunity to discuss how and why folktales have changed from culture to culture over the years.
- Older children generally like to tell stories to younger children, so a cooperative arrangement with the kindergarten and first-grade teachers in your school may benefit all students involved. After the children have heard the tale, they should be given the opportunity to retell it for a group of younger children. It may be necessary to use several folktales and extend the assignment over a period of weeks in order to provide opportunities for retelling to all students. Be sure to talk about how the tale changed in the retelling, and why or how this happened.
- Another idea for older students is to have them bring to class tape-recorded versions of favorite childhood tales narrated by their parents or guardians. Over a period of several days, play two or three versions of the same tale and ask children to compare and contrast versions done by people who are modern contemporaries. What factors influence the tellers of tales? Are these factors apparent in the versions they have just heard? Why or why not?

CREATIVE DRAMATICS

Allow children to dramatize the stories they hear. Here are a few suggestions, but feel free to try your own:

Children can...
- Role-play the conflict between main characters in a vignette.
- Pantomime the action of the plot.
- Soliloquize the protagonist's and/or antagonist's feelings.
- Develop a monologue for one or more of the secondary characters to provide a different perspective to the story.
- Dramatize the change of attitude and personality for a character who "learned their lesson."
- Set up a "stage" that reveals only the faces of actors, and have an unseen narrator tell or read the story while the audience sees only the actors' expressions as they hear the story.
- Analyze the predominant cultural values emphasized in a folktale (with help from the teacher), and write a "Greek chorus" into the script of a play. (For example, in the tale "Little Red Riding Hood," a chorus of birds or assorted forest animals could chant at appropriate intervals, "Little Red Riding Hood! Little Red Riding Hood! Always mind your mother!")

■ Act out the story, following the plot exactly—*except* change one incident or one part of the plot about halfway through. How does this affect the rest of the story?

■ Assemble modern substitutions for props and costumes, then act out the story. Does the tale lose something in the translation? Why or why not? What might be the modern translation of such a tale?

■ Create dialogue for a silent character or inanimate object in a folktale.

CREATIVE WRITING

Encourage children to "write it down," putting the story in their own words. Some possibilities include:

■ After reading or telling a folktale, ask children to write a "modern version." You may want to discuss the culture and era from which the tale originated, what similarities and/or differences children can distinguish in their own culture, and how traditions and values have changed since the tale was first told.

■ Also after hearing a folktale, ask children to think about a problem or concern of modern American (or regional America) society, then compose a modern tale that addresses those concerns. Share these with each other and with other classes.

■ Following a tale that attempts to explain the "why" of nature, ask children to consider other aspects of natural phenomenon that an illiterate citizenry might fear. Write a tale "explaining" why things are the way they are.

■ Brainstorm proverbs, morals, and pithy sayings, then have children write a story to illustrate a lesson to be learned.

■ Challenge children to change the ending of a familiar folktale.

■ Divide the class into pairs, assigning one person the role of a folktale character and the other that of newspaper reporter. Have the reporters conduct interviews and write an article about the character. What kinds of information are considered news worthy? Why?

■ Have students reflect on a time when they felt or acted as the character in a folktale did, then have them write about the experience.

■ Offer students the opportunity to design playbills that advertise a movie of the folktale they have heard, or a bookjacket that advertises the book. How would they choose to market the important aspects?

VALUES EDUCATION

Folktales often present issues that can be clarified only through analysis of personal values as they relate to the issue of significance. Children can be made aware of these issues during the study of folktales, and given opportunities to explore their own feelings in relation to moral and ethical questions. Some examples of folktales and related moral issues include:

FOLKTALE	MORAL ISSUE
"The Pied Piper of Hamelin"	What responsibility do we have to abide by written or verbal contracts?
"Hansel and Gretel"	Can we judge people's character by first impressions or the opinions of others?
"The Miller, His Son and Their Donkey"	How much should we be affected by public opinion? At what point should we trust our own judgment?
"Rumpelstiltskin"	What price are we willing to pay for power, wealth, and fame?
"Jack and the Beanstalk"	Does anyone have the right to take the law into his or her own hands?

"Henny Penny"	Should we follow leadership without question?
"The Blind Men and the Elephant"	Does each of us perceive reality differently?
"Beauty and the Beast"	How do we measure beauty?

VOCABULARY DEVELOPMENT

Etymology is the study of the origins of words. Study the origins of unusual words encountered in folktales. African and Black American folktales may contain especially interesting words and word connotations. Some frequently encountered words in other types of folktales include:

rampion: lettuce-like vegetable

bairns: children

sorcerer: magician

rogue: a bad guy

quern: grinder

stile: stairs to climb over a wall

COMPARISON OF SIMILAR TALES

Read or retell local folktales to discover similarities and differences. Try to find out the history behind each tale. Some examples of well-known folktales with inherent similarities include:

"Tom Tit Tot" to "Rumpelstiltskin"

"Mr. Vinegar" to "Gudbrand"

"Cinderella" to "Tattercoats" and "Little Burnt Face"

"Beauty and the Beast" to "East o' the Sun and West o' the Moon"

"Sadko" to "Urashima Taro and the Princess of the Sea"

"Urashima Taro" to "Pandora's Box"

FOODS IN FOLKTALES

Study the cultural origin of and sample foods mentioned in folktales. Where did the food originate? When was it popular? Why was it indigenous to that particular area? Is it still eaten today?

MAP SKILLS

Use world maps to locate the origins and/or travels of folktales; use U.S. maps to locate the "homes" of tall-tale heroes.

CULMINATING ACTIVITY

Following your study of folktales, songs, and customs, arrange to have a Folklore Fair in your community. Perhaps set up displays at the local shopping mall and have children come dressed as folktale characters. At intervals, students and parent volunteers can tell stories, sing songs accompanied by simple musical instruments, put on dramatizations such as plays or puppet shows, and demonstrate the tools and customs of another culture or of a time gone by.

■ Trying It Out

Manners and Responsibility

A team of second- and third-grade teachers—Julie, Jacqui, and Amy—wanted to incorporate folktales from many countries/cultures into their curriculum. They began with the story "Dinner Guests: An African Folktale" (source unknown). To summarize, Turtle was walking through the woods when he felt hungry. He knocked on Spider's (Anansi's) door, who felt obliged to invite Turtle to dinner. Anansi really didn't want to share his food, so he thought up predinnertime rituals such as washing hands, and was able to eat all the dinner while the turtle was occupied with other things. Turtle left Anansi's house thinking, "Anansi says all the right things, but does all the wrong things." Turtle invited Spider to dinner and did exactly to Spider what Spider had done to him. The moral of the story is that even though a person may be saying all of the right things, it is what he or she *does* in the end that really counts.

"Dinner Guests" addresses basic beliefs and values in neighborhoods and communities. Since it is an African folktale, it introduces the effect of cultural values on specific communities. The tale also shows students that certain beliefs or values are not culture specific; the people of many cultures would agree with the moral of this story. The teachers suggest ideas and strategies for using this folktale in the classroom.

Before the Book Is Read.   Start with a bulletin board depicting the setting of the story (see ideas below). This will arouse the children's curiosity. Informal questions and answers about the bulletin board will prepare them for the story. Invite the class to "dinner." Have them bring lunch to the room one day. Afterwards, bring up a discussion about the proper way to act when having a guest or being a guest for dinner. Next, start a discussion about Africa. Talk about stereotypes people might have about African culture. As a class, draw a map of Africa so that all students become acquainted with its geographic location.

Ideas for Bulletin Boards.   Create the setting of the book on the bulletin board. Display the turtle's house as a pond and the spider's house as a grass hut. Display a big African map that can be made of butcher paper and have the students cut out pictures out of magazines of African people and animals. Have them place these pictures on the map and decide where they might live. As a class, put lakes and rivers on the map. Once the map is completed, have the students choose where they think the turtle and spider lived. Highlight the area with a handmade turtle and spider.

The animal and African masks could decorate a bulletin board after being completed in art class. Also display "Swahili" words learned in class in bright colors. The words for *"Hello, Welcome, May I come in,* and *Friend"* especially should be put on the board because these words relate to the folktale. Be sure to hang the spiders and turtles made in art class from the ceiling.

Learning Centers.   Try these suggestions:
   ■ *Dinner Table:* Create a "table" for the entire class by having students learn to set their own place setting. Use this as an art lesson, too. Forks, spoons, knives, plates, and other place-setting items should be made, cut, and pasted onto a placemat made by the students. Take the finished products and set the table! This is a great way to teach students the proper way to set the table.
   ■ *Science Experiment Table:* What sinks and what floats? Fill several tubs with water. Have many different objects for the students to experiment with, such as rocks, flowers, wood, styrofoam, buttons, sponges, and many other items inside and outside.
   ■ *Math Table:* Have a balance on the table. Get a rock that is of comparable size and weight to a turtle and a spider. See how many paperclips (spider) it would take to equal the weight of one rock (turtle). Have the children measure with a ruler the size of a model turtle and spider.
   ■ *Pen-Pal Table:* At this table, have a list of African students that attend an English-speaking school. The students will be able to write to them with the hopes they can become pen-pals. Be sure to include mailing addresses, envelopes, and stamps. The students may bring in their own stationery or use regular paper provided on this table. Emphasize the exchange of culture customs when writing their pals and when sharing about themselves.

■ *Cookbook Corner:* Have large recipe cards on stock and a three-ring binder for the students to write in their favorite recipes. Books on African cooking can be obtained from the library; many students will enjoy skimming through these cookbooks. Encourage them to illustrate their recipe cards. When the cookbook is completed, the pages should be laminated and bound to the binder. The students will be able to enjoy this class cookbook all year.

■ *Story Center:* Give each student individual time to read and look at the story "Dinner Guests" at this center, which could be at a table or on the floor. After reading the story, the student will have the opportunity to rewrite another ending of the story if preferred. This center should be stocked with writing materials and drawing utensils if the student wishes to illustrate the ending. Individual poems reflecting the students' thoughts on the story can be written here, too.

Audiovisual Resources

Cornet Film and Video. (1955). *Animals and their homes.*
> This filmstrip, 11 minutes long, is in color. It includes pictures of animals' homes as they are found near or on water, ground, above ground, and under ground.

Cornet Film and Video (1960). *Animals protect themselves.*
> This 11-minute, color filmstrip presents the principle means by which animals protect themselves through escape, body covering, camouflage, and fighting.

The Greater Cincinnati Television Educational Foundation. (1980). *Animal costume.*
> This 15-minute video includes how colors and patterns help animals to mate, hide from enemies, and sneak up on prey.

The Greater Cincinnati Television Educational Foundation. (1980). *Animal groups, Zoo, Zoo, Zoo.*
> This video shows how animals live together or alone and then come together for common sources of food.

The Greater Cincinnati Television Educational Foundation. (1980). *Do animals talk? Zoo, Zoo, Zoo.*
> This 15-video relates how animals communicate with sounds, visual signals, and smells.

The Greater Cincinnati Television Educational Foundation. (1980). *How animals help each other, Zoo, Zoo, Zoo.*

The Greater Cincinnati Television Educational Foundation. (1980). *How and what animals eat, Zoo, Zoo, Zoo.*

Indiana University Audio Visual Center: (1983) *Living Africa: A village experience.* Bloomington, IN.
> This 35-minute video portrays daily experiences and concerns of people in a small village in West Africa.

National Geographic. (1984). *Spiders.*
> This learning kit goes into depth on the lifestyles of spiders.

Related Readings

Spiders

Climo, S. (1985). *Someone Saw a Spider: Spider Facts and Folktales.* New York: Thomas Y. Crowell.

McDermott, G. (1972). *Anansi the Spider.* New York: Henry Holt.

Oppenheim, J. (1991). *Eency Weency Spider.* New York: Byron Press Visual Publications.

Schnieper, C. (1989). *Amazing Spiders.* Minneapolis: Carolrhoda Books.

Turtles

Ancona, G. (1987). *Turtle Watch.* New York: Macmillan.

Cole, J. (1992). *The Magic School Bus on the Ocean Floor.* New York: Scholastic.

Lambert, D. (1992). *The Children's Animal Atlas.* Brookfield, CT: Millbrook Press.

Africa

Barysh, A. (1991). *The Suitcase Scholar Goes to Kenya.* New York: Lerner.

Feelings, M. (1974). *Jambo Means Hello—Swahili Alphabet Book.* New York: Dial.

Nabwire, C. (1988). *Cooking the African Way.* Minneapolis: Lerner.

Manners and Customs

Anastasio, D. (1988). *Pass the Peas, Please: A Book of Manners.* New York: Warner Juvenile Books.

Breslin, J. (1988). *He Got Hungry and Forgot His Manners*. New York: Ticknor and Fields.

Hazen, B.S. (1974). *Animal Manners*. New York: Golden Press.

Snow, L. (1986). *Children Around the World*. Minneapolis: Dillon.

Local Celebrations

Students learn to recognize another aspect of community folklore when the topic of local festivals or celebrations is brought up. These may be in honor of a local folk hero or an actual historical figure around whom much legend has been built (an example in my community is the Johnny Appleseed Festival), in celebration of ethnic heritage (such as Greek Festival or German Heritage Days), planned around a local geographic anomaly (the Three Rivers Festival in Fort Wayne, Indiana, is one example), or simply reminiscent of the area's beginnings (Settler's Days). Whatever the occasion for celebrating, these festivities are sure to be filled with examples of local, regional, and ethnic folklore. When the folklore of the community is studied, students learn to honor and celebrate diversity at the same time they are exploring their own roots.

■ Trying It Out

Heritage Day

Staff at one local school decided to celebrate the bicentennial by holding a Heritage Day. Letters were sent out ahead of time as a way of involving parents, other family members, and the community at large. Students at particular grade levels were responsible for topical or thematic study of the local area. Teachers were supplied with charts showing how grade-level themes aligned with state and national social studies curriculum guidelines. Files with suggested instructional strategies to enliven the study of the local area were disseminated. On the appointed day, all projects were on display, and all students and teachers dressed in period costumes reminiscent of days gone by. Visitors, parents, students from other schools, local dignitaries, and the media were all present.

Grade-level themes and projects included:

Kindergarten: Family life then and now: Food, clothing, shelter, games, and so on.

First Grade: School life then and now: Students and teachers set up a school museum for visual comparisons of the way school used to be and the way it is now. Several lessons during the week are done the "old" way.

Second Grade: Communication, transportation, and jobs in the community then and now.

Third Grade: Our community: Community booklets made by each student. All students work together to create their community model out of boxes. Pairs of students pick a prominent location or building to depict for use in a large display.

Fourth Grade: State history.

Fifth Grade: The Civil War: Pairs of students choose a project involving Civil War topics to research, present, and display.

Art, music, and physical education teachers also were involved in Heritage Day, as were the cafeteria staff, the media specialist, and all resource teachers. Parents and local craftspersons were invited to set up displays of their own hand-made quilts and quilting, basket weaving, storytelling, candle making, preparing jellies and jams, and baking open-hearth breads. The actual Heritage Day celebration was a big success, and preparing for it was more than half the fun!

Playtime Then and Now

As students research and collect examples of local folklore and family stories, they most likely will encounter more than one adult who admonishes them, "When I was a kid, we didn't have all those expensive toys you kids have now!" or something of the sort. Help them take advantage of these opportunities to explore yet another avenue of local folklore: toys and games of the past and present. Read on to find out how two teachers approached playtime folklore.

Trying It Out

Fun in the Good Old Days

Vicki Lindsay wanted her students to find out what games or pastimes older community citizens had enjoyed as children, to compare these to favorite games and toys enjoyed now, and to understand that games and toys enjoyed may vary according to geographic area and/or culture in which one lives. She used *Soup* (Peck, 1974) to introduce the lesson.

"Read *Soup,*" Vicki suggests, "then discuss how living in the rural 1930s, Soup and Bob didn't have Nintendo, television, or computers. Instead, the boys made games out of common objects around them such as sticks, apples, and a barrel." Students were then instructed to interview an older relative or senior citizen to find out about the games or his or her youth. They had a week to collect their stories and examples of games and toys. Then they shared their findings with their classmates.

"I formed cooperative groups," Vicki notes. "The students shared their findings within their groups, and each group chose one game to teach to the rest of the class."

The students were motivated to study the phenomenon of games and pastimes further, going beyond class requirements and sharing what they had learned during recess. "When I do this again," Vicki reflects, "I'll give them more time to research, and more time to share. I think all the students would have benefitted from hearing what every other student had learned, so next time I'll schedule a 'Back to the Past Day,' when groups can teach their games from the good old days to others. We'll invite grandparents and senior citizens, and interested parents as well, being sure to involve them in the demonstrations. After the game session, we can cool off with homemade ice cream or cold lemonade made from a favorite 'old-time' recipe collected by a student."

While reflecting on the possibilities of this lesson, Vicki considered the variations different cultures might reveal in their choice of leisure pastimes. "This activity will be especially exciting to do with my class next year," she concludes, "because I will have 14 Amish students, all of whom do not have Nintendo, television, or computers. It will be interesting to find out whether my Amish students entertain themselves in the same manner as older Amish in the community, or how the ways these students entertain themselves today differs from the ways their other classmates do."

It's Just Child's Play

Virginia Thorpe introduced her fifth-graders to family history when they read an excerpt from Treva Adams Strait's autobiography entitled "The Storm Cellar" in their basal reader (*Rare as Hen's Teeth*, Heath, pp. 113–132). Students learned about first-person accounts and adults' recollections of their childhoods. Then they listened to "The Good Old Days" by Anna Mary Robertson Moses' recollections from *Grandma Moses: My Life's History* (on audiotape from Silver Burdett, *World of Language, 5th Grade*) as another example of first-person accounts of one's childhood. Virginia's students were especially interested in how children's leisure time was spent 100 years ago. This led to an interest in how their parents and persons of their grandparents' generation spent their leisure time as children, so Virginia asked her students to interview relatives or people from a senior citizens' home about their leisure activities as children. She suggested: "Ask about their leisure-time activities. Did they have a favorite hobby, sport, game? Think about your favorite ways to spend your free time. How do these compare with what you discovered in your interview? How do they contrast? Share your interview orally. Make a poster to illustrate the similarities and differences between children's leisure time activities then and now."

Parents and students alike were enthusiastic about these interviews. Continued student interest in the topic of family history encouraged Virginia to use "A Girl in Old Ohio" (audiotape, *Silver Burdett World of Language*) by Harriet Connor Brown about her mother-in-law's life in the mid-1800s. After listening to the tape, Virginia asked her students to read the text to find out how Maria Brown felt about the changes in her lifetime. What did she look forward to? Which changes were good? Which were not so good? Following this introduction, Virginia's students interviewed their relatives a second time, this time asking questions such as: What did your parents look forward to as they were growing up? How about your grandparents? What do you look forward to? How is this the same as or different from what your parents and/or grandparents looked forward to? Did they realize their dreams? Have you? Why or why not? To share the results of these interviews, students constructed picture time lines and discussed them in class.

Bragging Rights

Use this activity to familiarize students with local heroes and legendary figures, while also helping them appreciate that they do not have to become famous to achieve something of importance. Read the introduction from *People Who Make a Difference* (by Brent Ashabranner, 1989) as a way of introducing biographies and life stories of people who have "made a difference." Have on hand student versions of selected biographies, such as *Florence Griffith Joyner* and *From Rags to Riches* (both by Nathan Aaseng), making certain to depict famous women as well as famous men.

After students are familiar with selected biographies, provide an opportunity to discuss these in class. Ask whether students can think of people in their own lives, or in the local community, who are known for their outstanding contribution in some way. Emphasize that these people need not be famous or wealthy for their contributions to be considered. If prompts are needed, suggest students think in terms of:

An aunt who is thought to be the finest dentist in town

A cousin whose catering is sought by local brides and grooms

A grandparent who grows the best green beans for miles around

Invite students to think of questions they might ask their own special person, and work together to develop interview questionnaires. Assign the development of biographical pocket books for each person interviewed: Fold 9" × 12" pieces of heavy white paper in half, glue the sides together to form a "pocket," and staple several of these pocket pages together at the left margin to create a book. Students place drawings, photos, or copies of relevant documents in the pockets, and write biographical information on the outside. When the pocket books are completed, have students make book covers from colorful construction paper folded and cut to 6" × 9" size. On a day set aside just for that purpose, students "brag" about their special person by sharing the book they have created and, if possible, introducing the celebrity to the class.

Chapter 10

Women's Local History

Women have always been a part of history, but society has not always recognized women's contributions to history as important. A large number of organizations recently have devoted exhibits and publications to women's history: The North Carolina Women Making History exhibit at the North Carolina Museum of History, the National Archives for Black Women's History in Washington, DC, and *Women in the West* (Armitage et al., 1991) are only a few examples. Exploring women's contributions in local history is important, as well.

Teachers not only need to help their students learn about famous and influential women in history, however; we need to encourage students to know more about the changing patterns of the lives of women in their own communities. Howe and Bannan (1995) suggest teachers focus on main themes in U.S. women's history as a way of directing the study of local women's history. Themes such as women's contributions to daily life in times of peace as well as war, sense of place in society during particular eras (such as the early 1900s, the 1920s, the Great Depression, World War II and its aftermath, the 1950s or 1960s), political and social activism, and changes in lifestyle since 1970 each provide a focus for students' research and interviews. A thoughtfully planned oral history project can document the experiences of a representative sample of women in your own local community. Diversity in viewpoints as well as racial, social, religious, and economic backgrounds should be sought as students identify potential informants. Some of my students who have interviewed their own grandmothers or elderly aunts, for example, come to class amazed at what they have learned about someone they thought they had known all their lives.

Government records found in the local courthouse can be useful additions to students' women's history projects. Deeds, wills, military papers, and corporate records for businesses owned by women can be found there. Asking a few questions or notifying court clerks ahead of time about the nature of your students' project can yield access to archives or storage rooms holding records of court proceedings related to women's issues. (Has your county provided relief to poor women, for example, or were women ever arrested for selling liquor?) Clubs, social service agencies, agriculture extension offices (especially those with Home Extension Agents), retired teachers' organizations, women's military organizations, or factories where women worked during WWI or WWII may have or be able to suggest sources for information about local women's history.

For a list of books and organizations that may prove helpful as you and your students consider ways to incorporate women into the curriculum, see the Appendix.

"Excuse Me, Ma'am, I'm Conducting a Survey"

Many women in the community are knowledgeable about women's issues at the local level. Some of them are activists themselves, or know a woman who is. A few senior citizens may even remember when women got the right to vote. One way for your students to find out who these women are is to go door to door, conducting a survey.

Divide the class into small groups. Ask each group to develop three to five questions interviewers should ask local women to find out more about locally famous or influential women. When students come back together in a large group, compile all groups' questions on the board or overhead projector. Have students vote to narrow down the list of questions to the top ten (or five, for primary grades). Make copies of these questions for every student in class.

Before the class begins to canvass the neighborhood, make certain each student has a geographic area to cover. If two students live on the same street, one could interview women on the left side while the other interviews those on the right side. If several students live in the same apartment complex, they can divide up their area by street, building, or floor. In any event, make certain that all students have several opportunities to interview local women.

After interviews have been conducted, students get back into their original groups to compare notes. Each group should be able to come up with several names and events or circumstances relating to local women's history. Come back together in a large group and compile the names from each small group into a master list.

Which women were mentioned by more than one person? Which women on the list were publicly recognized for their work or contributions? Which are known only to local residents? Search newspaper indexes (usually found on CD-ROM at the public library or local university library) and contact local women's groups to find out more on each woman's life. When materials are located, assign a pair of students or a group to research in depth the lives of particular local women. Use one of the ideas mentioned elsewhere in this chapter as a vehicle for the research, and present it to the class or during a school assembly.

Local Women's History in the Making

Several women in the local area may be currently involved with issues that have long-standing attention. When students identify women's activists and interview them about the issues they support, they learn a great deal about "women's history in the making."

Work with students to make a list of women's organizations and active women in the community. (Use the local telephone directory, call the local Women's Bureau, search local newspapers for mentions of area women involved in women's issues, and/or refer to interviews with local women conducted by students.) Count the number of potential contacts, and divide the class into that number of groups. In groups, brainstorm how to best contact and/or approach organizations or local women to obtain needed information. Have students in groups make a list of what information is needed or desired from each organization or person.

After groups contact their identified organization or person, they should determine how to present their information to the class. They may decide to do a skit, role-play a scenario, write and sing a song, compose a poem, create an exhibit complete with docent or narrator, invite a special speaker, show a related video or play a radio broadcast, simulate a television talk-show interview, create a collage with accompanying essay, write or illustrate an advertisement and share it with the class, or other creative product or performance.

■ Trying It Out

"Four Who Dared"

A fourth-grade class in Rensselaer County, New York, worked with college professors and their teacher to research and develop instructional materials about constitutional issues in their community's history. An important aspect of the local history was the struggle for women's rights, both nationally and locally. Students and instructors collaborated to write, star in, develop scenery and props for, and produce a 40-minute play about local women's history they titled "Four Who Dared."

A teacher involved in the project (Jones, 1990) states the project's objectives as:

1. To enable students to understand the meaning of inequality
2. To show how the lives of women and blacks were affected by inequality
3. To illustrate how ideas about changing women's lives differed
4. To relate past inequalities to the present

The students and their instructors also prepared audience materials that augmented the viewing of the original play. These materials were presented to teachers whose students (grades 4–12) would be watching the performance, so that audience members might be informed about specific women's issues, local women represented in the play, and legal or community action taken on these issues from the historic era depicted to the present.

News Brief—Story at Eleven

Simulate a "Meet the Press" program, or (for the more daring) a PBS-type news/discussion group involving a local woman. One student should portray the historic woman, another the host, and three to five other students the reporters or discussants. Do preliminary research on the woman's life and contributions, then help the reporters or discussants prepare several questions each would like to ask the woman on their "show." The host sets the stage, introduces the "famous local woman" and the reporters or discussants, and starts things rolling by giving a very brief overview of her life. Then the questions begin. The student cast as the famous woman must, of course, be very well briefed on "her" life.

As students prepare to participate in the simulated broadcast, assign "Meet the Press" or "The McNeil-Lehrer Hour" or "The McLaughlin Group" as homework. Have students watch the program, take notes on technique rather than content, and write instructions for portraying both the host and the reporter or discussant roles.

Divide students into groups, and assign each group a local woman to research. These groups also will perform together in the "broadcast," so they should begin to decide which group member will assume which role for the show. On the day of the actual "broadcast," videotape students' performance so that they can watch it later—both to admire their own performances and to review facts about the local woman's life.

Local Women's Hall of Fame

Does your community have a Women's Hall of Fame? Has an issue of a newspaper or locally produced magazine featured local women? Is a section of the local history museum devoted to famous local women? If not, here is your students' chance to make a real contribution (and if so, they'll have a fun experience as they learn while creating their own!). Who are/were some of the local women whose lives and contributions influenced the quality of life for other residents? Construct a list (use names obtained from other activities in this chapter, if necessary), and contact the library, the newspaper, and local branches of women's organizations for more names. Have students divide up into groups and begin to research these names in earnest.

Up to this point, students probably have not obtained enough information to write a biography of the locally influential women they have studied, but for the Women's Hall of Fame, biographies are needed. Also, visual representations of each woman included are essential: Look for photos, posters, advertisements showing locally active women, even old newspaper photos, and have these enlarged to poster size. If this is impossible for some or all women on the list, assign one group the job of drawing poster-sized portraits of these women.

Put portraits and other visuals together with biographies of the women chosen, and arrange the entire display in a way that encourages browsing. Suggest that students make copies or secure clippings of articles about the women included, and create a montage or other visual representation of each woman's news coverage as well as her biography. Remind students that other people will see their work when it is finished, so "neatness counts."

The Women's Hall of Fame can be displayed in the hallway of your school, of course, but when students have put this much work into a project that benefits the entire community, a little more exposure is called for. During the early stages of the project, contact the local public library or one of its branches, the local shopping mall, or even a bank, and inquire whether the Local Women's Hall of Fame might be displayed there. Get some media coverage (during March, National Women's History Month, local media will be on the lookout for stories like this), and ask for copies of newspaper or television coverage for all your students.

■ Trying It Out

White House Style

The Lincoln Museum in Fort Wayne, Indiana, featured the country's First Ladies in an exhibit titled "White House Style." Mary Todd Lincoln, Dolley Madison, Martha Washington, Edith Roosevelt, and Hillary Rodham Clinton's lives and times were highlighted, and displays depicted period costumes and women's roles spanning two centuries in the United States. "The role of the First Lady is unique in American politics," a brochure about the exhibit reads. "The constitution assigns no duties to the President's spouse, who is neither elected by the voters nor confirmed by the Senate. On paper, few First Ladies have been granted governmental authority. But in reality, few people have had more opportunity to exercise their political power." Programs and events related to the exhibit included "Grand Presidental Ball and Gala," "First Ladies: Political Role and Public Image," "From Martha to Mamie," "The Finest of Fashions," and "America's First Ladies: Who Were They Really?"

Women's Lives, Then and Now

Encourage students to examine the everyday lives of local women from a national societal perspective, and from testimonials and primary sources at the local level. In the early nineteenth century, the "ideal woman" in the United States was generally believed to be

> *a devoted mother, an usually virtuous person who had to remain aloof from the corruption of politics, a domestic individual who labored most happily and productively within her own home, and a weak-minded, physically inferior being who needs guidance from stronger and wiser people—men.* (Riley, 1986)

Share this sentiment of nineteenth-century womanhood with your students. Challenge them to find examples and instances of everyday life circa 1800–1850 to support or deny this perspective. In the early 1800s, married women's lives did revolve around home, husband, and children, but what details of local women's everyday lives in the era exist to add credence to or to shatter the perspective detailed in the preceding quote? What careers were available to women in the 1800s? Were these careers limited to the helping professions, such as nursing and teaching (see Figure 10.1)?

In the frontier midwest, for example, women's everyday lives included participation in the growing of the family's major food supply, preparing food, spinning cloth from wool or flax fibers, weaving cloth, making soap and preserving food for the winter, sewing the family's clothing, performing household chores, and usually giving birth without the assistance of a medical doctor. In the far-flung cities of the time, women's everyday lives were quite different from their counterparts in the city. Some women who lived in the city could purchase food, fabric, and daily necessities such a soap; these women normally were under the care of a doctor prior to and during the birth of each child. Other women who lived in cities were not financially secure; they might take in sewing, laundry, and/or ironing for other families in order to buy food and other supplies.

As schools and churches were built, women of the early nineteenth century saw these institutions as vehicles for helping those less fortunate than themselves, as well as being places of instruction and worship. Women began to venture outside the home more than they had done in the early days of settlement, when the everyday grind of meeting basic needs demanded their total attention. Churches, for example, provided a social structure whereby women could assist orphans, the sick and elderly, widows, the homeless, and the very poor—for the most part, not even overprotective husbands objected to their wives helping out at the church fund-raiser. Eventually, women's attitudes about and assistance toward those less fortunate than themselves extended to people less well known or less visible in the community and even outside the local area; thus, women became a major force in the movement to abolish slavery.

As more and more women moved in circles outside the home, many people (including some women) insisted that these women were stepping outside their "proper place"—that of caring for home and family. Many debates were featured in the news and popular culture media of the time about whether women had the right to venture outside their "proper place," or whether indeed they had rights at all.

When students have researched and discussed primary sources and books dealing with the lives of local women prior to 1850, pique their curiosity by reading an excerpt or two from a biography of one of the several women who were instrumen-

Figure 10.1 Nurse (circa mid-nineteenth century)

tal in the women's rights movement: Elizabeth Cady Stanton, Susan B. Anthony, Lucy Stone, Lucretia Mott, for example. Ask students whether a woman had the right to purchase property, or inherit land and businesses, or even start her own business in the nineteenth century. They may be surprised to learn that women forfeited all rights to property when they married, and had no right to an income independent from their husbands.

Find out whether a woman's group or dramatics group in your area performs Readers' Theater or will visit in character portraying one of the influential women of the time. Have students work in cooperative groups beforehand to consult their research while developing helpful questions and observations to share with the scheduled visitor. Perhaps students can interview the visitor "in character," as my students once did when a local woman came dressed as Elizabeth Cady Stanton and never stepped out of character. My students learned a great deal about Stanton's life and contributions, as well as about women's issues of the time.

▪ Trying It Out

Time Line of Women's History at the State Level

The Indiana Historical Bureau (1993) prepared this time line of state legislation involving women of the nineteenth century.

SOME ACTS OF THE INDIANA GENERAL ASSEMBLY REGARDING WOMEN

1816	December 11—Statehood
1830	*Godey's Lady's Book* began publication in Philadelphia
1838	February 17—Widows acquire property rights if spouses die without a will
1847	January 23—Protection of married women's property
1847	January 26—Married women may make wills
1847	January 27—Widows allowed $150 of their husbands' effects
1848	February 16—Widows may have personal property of husbands if not valued over $200
1848	Women's rights convention at Seneca Falls, New York
1849	January 12—Widows may have husbands' personal property plus money from the sale of real estate, to bring the total value to $150
1850	Constitutional Convention

The 1850 Constitutional Convention provided opportunities for opponents and supporters of women's rights to be heard. (Published records of this convention provide an interesting sample of opinions from opponents and supporters both—see excerpts below.) Convention members heard 10 resolutions about women's rights—almost one-fourth of all resolutions heard involving human rights.

FROM MEN WHO SUPPORTED WOMEN'S RIGHTS

The legal existence of the woman is suspended during marriage. (p. 464)

The legislation of this country has long enough denied to the wife, the widow, and the orphan, that which justly belongs to them. (p. 1158)

That a woman must be deprived of all her own, and made the merest dependent upon the husband's bounty . . . is a slander upon the sex. (p. 1189)

FROM MEN WHO OPPOSED WOMEN'S RIGHTS

If we establish the principle that the pecuniary interest of women is separate and distinct from that of men, we should establish also their right of representation, and their right of suffrage. (p. 469)

The necessary degree of political knowledge cannot be presumed to exist in women, who, by their domestic duties, are led away from the consideration of the affairs of the State and the affairs of the nation. (p. 469)

You could not glue to her the power which a man has, and which he exercises in the affairs of State and of trade, for if you could, she would then cease to be woman. (pp. 472–473)

Divide students into groups and choose one of the preceding position statements. Examine each statement: What is the point, or message, each tries to make? Are these statements made on the basis of logic, or emotion? What values contribute to each viewpoint? How do the statements and their accompanying values help you understand the lives of the people of the local area 150 years ago?

Sarah Bolton wrote a popular poem of the time called "Paddle Your Own Canoe." The poem was a favorite of women's rights advocates. Read the poem and write a short essay explaining why it was a popular poem.

Interviewing Women Immigrants

While studying family history, some students may realize or be reminded that their ancestors arrived in the United States from another country, as immigrants in the distant or recent past. These students' relatives may be able to provide women immigrants' accounts, diaries, letters, or other memorabilia to aid in the study of women's perceptions of local history. Photographs of women immigrants, accompanied (if possible) by oral history interviews, make exciting primary sources for studying the community from diverse perspectives (see Figure 10.2). Friedensohn and Rubin (1987) recommend strategies and pose questions for studying family or personal photographs of immigrants. Students who have identified immigrant ancestors should:

Figure 10.2 Woman Immigrant from Russia

Photo Information Form

Complete this form and attach it, with a copy of the photograph selected, to your oral history report.

BASIC INFORMATION

Name of person(s) shown _____

Date photograph was taken _____

Location (village, town, state, nation) _____

Reason for photograph (wedding, reunion, etc.) _____

Photographer (name of professional studio, or
 amateur photographer) _____

Owner of photograph _____

SUPPORTING INFORMATION

Date and place of birth/death _____

Age when photograph taken _____

Relationship to other persons in photograph _____

Occupation _____

Social and/or economic standing _____

Date of arrival in U.S. _____

Place of arrival and destination _____

DESCRIPTION/COMMENTS

1. Describe the person in this photograph. (Elaborate on brief answers above.)
2. Are there clues in the photograph that suggest the year or historical period (clothes, furniture, activities, cars, accessories)? Which clues? Explain.
3. Create a time line of the family's immigration history. Where does this photo belong on the time line? Is the women pictured an ancestor of immigrants, an immigrant, or the child/grandchild of immigrants? How is she connected to the migration experience?
4. Are there family stories about the migration process? If so, relate some of these: life in the old country, the trip to America, finding a new home, learning a new language, dealing with being a foreigner in a strange land, experiencing money problems or new work situations, and so on.
5. What can you tell about the social and/or economic background of the woman in the photograph by looking at details in the photo? Is this an accurate estimate of her true social or economic situation? Why or why not?
6. Why did you choose this photo over others available? Why did it interest you? What else would you like to know about the woman or about the photograph?

■ Begin with a family photograph depicting one or more immigrants. Try to explain your own interconnectedness to people of the world as well as those of the local community.

■ Connect a female ancestor in the photograph with your family's immigration history. Was this woman an immigrant, the child of immigrants, or the ancestor of future immigrants? When did the relocation occur?

■ What do you know (or can you find out) about her migration? Tell her tale for the class, being as historically accurate as possible.

"Telling her tale" involves conducting an oral history interview, if the woman or her immediate family members are still living. Consult the section on conducting oral history interviews in the Introduction of this book for vital information on this process. Students who have not identified immigrant ancestors, or those whose ancestors are unavailable for interviews, can conduct oral history interviews with a friend, a friend of a friend, neighbors, or another student. Make certain students include a photographic depiction of the person being interviewed as a part of their report summarizing the person's migration.

A Photo Information Form will help keep students on track as they conduct their interviews and develop subsequent reports. The form should be completed by students and informants to accompany the photograph chosen.

Women Sports Heroes

Have students read the local newspaper for a week or two, consulting the sports section for coverage of women athletes. (Most newspapers will provide a classroom set for free—ask about the Newspapers in Education Program.) As students peruse the sports page, research and discuss whether women have always been as active in sports as men. What types of sports or physical activities were considered "acceptable" for girls and/or women in the United States during their parents' generation? During their grandparents' generation? Seventy years ago? One hundred years ago? Two hundred years ago?

While groups or pairs of students are searching for answers to these questions, have another group interview local residents from a different country or culture to determine what types of sports or physical activities are/were considered "acceptable" or appropriate for girls and women of that culture to undertake. Have the groups compare their results. Have things changed for women so far as sports are concerned in the past 50 years? In the past century? In the past two centuries? How do the sports activities of females in other cultures compare with those of females in the United States? How do students account for these differences?

When students have completed their perusal of the local sports page, have them write a report about local women's involvement in sports. Invite a local woman athlete or woman coach to speak with the class about women's sports issues: Why are there fewer women's professional sports teams than men's sports team? What obstacles do women who want to be professional athletes face that men do not (or may not)? What are the rewards for women who become professional athletes? Amateur athletes? Which Olympic events include women, and which do not? How many Olympic Gold Medals have U.S. women won? Have any local women aspired to Olympic fame? In which sports may women participate locally, and within what structures (i.e., high school basketball at certain schools, swim meets if they belong to the YMCA, etc.)?

"Would You Autograph My Book, Please?"

Are there women in the local community who are published authors? If so, invite one (or more) to speak with the class about the topic of her book or article, writing professionally, and getting published. Perhaps she will read from one of her works.

Chapter 11

Cultures in the Community

Much has been written in the past decade about multicultural education, the need for cultural awareness, and teaching for diversity. Although experts have provided important models for conceptualizing multicultural education, we still have no consensus in the field regarding appropriate aims and content for multicultural/multi-ethnic education, and therefore no identified set of strategies we can rely on to effectively foster cultural awareness in our students' lives.

Materials commonly available for instructional use, such as social studies textbooks, offer little or no help to teachers struggling with the dearth of appropriate cultural education resources. Brophy and Alleman (1996) conducted an exhaustive critique of elementary social studies textbooks and found that "few cross-cultural examples are included in the material on families, neighborhoods, and communities, and the world geography [content] focuses on places more than on cultures" (p. 25). Their findings also report that when social studies textbook content does include information about cultural diversity, the information is "respectful but relatively uninformative."

Clearly, we need to know more about teaching for cultural awareness and understanding. We need information about teacher-tested strategies and resources, and about how these strategies and resources can be used to foster children's understanding of their own and other cultures. Ginejko (1994) says, "cultural awareness means understanding that each of us has a culture that is part of our very being. Together, we all make up the tapestry [of the community]. We each bring threads of cultural values, historical pride, experiences, and aspirations to this fabric" (p. 269). As students and teachers collaborate in their study of the local community, they can begin to understand and respect that cultural differences and similarities are present in all communities to some degree. Appropriately selected and employed resources and strategies can enable all students to develop a consciousness of community cultures that extends beyond their immediate geographic area.

The strategies and resources in this chapter are intended to suggest ways teachers might extend and enrich their cultural education efforts, as well as building students' knowledge base about the concept of community. These strategies and resources fit smoothly into the study of the local community, and draw on its abundant resources to provide students with concrete, real-life examples of diversity and cultural knowledge.

Building a Sense of Community in the Classroom

A study of the community or local history means very little to children who do not comprehend the concept of *community*. Understanding this very basic precept goes a long way toward helping students appreciate the worth and dignity of individuals, the inherent diversity in communities over time, and the value of individual as well as group contributions.

Students' understanding of and appreciation for community can be enhanced by teachers providing regular opportunities for students to behave as a classroom community. Many teachers already do this, perhaps without realizing its import to the study of local roots, through such avenues as community circles, service learning, individual classroom responsibilities, recycling projects, and the like. Lickona (1993) insists that children in classrooms need to *"be* a community—to interact, form relationships, work out problems, grow as a group—and learn firsthand lessons about fair play, cooperation, forgiveness, and respect for the worth and dignity of every individual."

In classrooms where students and teachers work together to create and maintain what Lickona calls a "moral community," three conditions prevail:

1. Students know each other.
2. Students respect, affirm, and care about each other.
3. Students feel membership in—and responsibility to—the group.

Teachers who are committed to developing a classroom community plan activities and experiences that help students get to know each other better and appreciate similarities and differences within the group. These activities will foster and improve the quality of group interaction, encourage caring and respectful communication between and among group members, and engender a feeling of group identity.

In the first part of this chapter, then, suggested ideas and activities will focus on how teachers can assist students at all grade levels in developing an understanding of and appreciation for community as a concept, and for their own roles and responsibilities as citizens of a community. Read on to discover how several teachers have created a sense of community in their classrooms.

■ Trying It Out

Community Circle #1

Mindy Gawthrop's third-graders spend 15 to 20 minutes at least once a week in a community circle group. "The purpose is to build a safe community in the classroom where everyone feels wanted, important, and secure," Mindy states. Community Circles teach students to care about each other, work together cooperatively and effectively, and generally get along with one another. All students in the classroom are involved in the Circle. Using a prop of some kind to pass around often stimulates relevant discussion. "We sit in a circle and pass around a rubber apple as we share," Mindy reflects. Topics discussed in the third-grade class include simple sharing of experiences from the past week, "thinking" topics (one example Mindy gives is sentence completion, such as "Sunny days make me feel . . ."), and actual problem-solving sessions.

The results of her Community Circle efforts have been positive. Mindy shares, "Last year I had a class [where] many students could not get along. [Community Circles] works best with students who are already on the right track with social behavior, but it seems most important to use with groups that aren't on track. I feel students feel safe and display 'community behavior' in the room, but it becomes harder for them in other environments—for example, recess. On the other hand, when my students had trouble waiting in line for lunch, we met and I had them list what the line should look like. They had to agree to what was said, or speak up if they didn't [agree] and tell why. This works much better than my telling them what they did wrong."

Team Building

Tammy Morey's fifth-graders are organized into teams of four to six students. Each team votes on a name and a symbol or sign for its group, which are displayed in a transparent 8" × 11" frame at the front of their group's table or area. Tammy believes the team building idea helps create a sense of community among her students during those important first days of school, and works to maintain that sense all year long. She says, "I have found that the students really encourage each other and help one another to accomplish different tasks. The individuals who at times have a hard time controlling themselves try harder because they are accountable to their group. For example, we have a math mystery problem each week that the group is responsible for solving. As a group they must present their solution to the class. They earn points for helping each other and working hard, which are accumulated toward a class party."

Community Circle #2

Scott Fudge's third-graders have a 15- to 20-minute Community Circle every day. This time is spent in personal sharing, tribe activity (see below), discussion of problems and/or cooperative group behavior, and reflections about the previous day. Since the time also is used for organizing the day, these Community Circles take place first thing in the morning: Scott and the students go over the day's agenda, form new cooperative groups (on occasion) or pair students up to use learning centers, decide whose turn it is to use the pillows or beanbags or cushions at the rear of the room, and review individual and group responsibilities (such as emptying the pencil sharpener, feeding the rabbit or cleaning his cage, and erasing the board).

Classroom discipline is approached in a cooperative way, with students being involved as a community. When a behavior concern is brought up during Community Circle, Scott says, "The students [involved] have to write a sentence on what was done and what could've been done better. All I have to say is they owe me a sentence. They write, and verbalize what is needed [to improve behavior]."

Like Mindy, Scott feels his efforts at establishing and maintaining regular Community Circle experiences have long-term positive benefits for the students. He recalls a time when one student had been absent for six days. "When she came back, the students all cheered" during their Community Circle. "Part of our 'family' had been missing, and was back," he says, smiling.

Tribes

Karen Charters uses a program called "Tribes: Developing Capable People" to inspire a sense of community with her fifth-graders. "The purpose of this program is to help students become capable learners, problem solvers, and community participants," she states. Tribal circles are held at least once each week, more often when needed.

The teacher's role with "Tribes" is that of a facilitator. At the beginning of each circle time, students give compliments to other students and thank those who have helped them since the last meeting. Then, the students take care of any agenda items; these usually include students who are having problems or students who need help solving a problem. "During this phase," Karen notes, "students work out their difficulties or the community offers suggestions or consequences to help solve the problem." Consequences suggested must be relevant, reasonable, and respectful. "Finally," she says, "we usually have a community-building activity or learn a new skill related to building a cohesive community."

Karen, like Mindy and Scott, sees many advantages to the use of structured "circle meetings" in her classroom. She reflects, "Over time, the biggest change [in students' behavior] is students' willingness to solve problems with a win/win solution.

Violence has dropped significantly. I also find students are more tolerant and protective of each other."

Karen continues, "Students remind each other of how we expect members of our community to behave. One example of how this worked was about a young man that is extremely poor, unclean, and usually badly dressed. One of my more popular students insulted him during tribal circle. This is a major taboo. Students in the circle voted to remove the student with insulting behavior from the community, and not allow him to return until he could convince them that other students would be safe in the community. The students set up a list of tasks that the offender needed to accomplish to prove he could be trusted in our community. They were tougher on [him] than any consequence I could have assigned. He learned the rules of our safe community and never breached them again."

Share Time

Julie Funk-Kurtz uses structured sharing time with her preschool class to engender a growing sense of community. Every day, three previously identified children bring in an object from home—anything they want to bring. Each of these three children, in turn, tells the other children in the class about his or her item in a sharing time that lasts 10 to 15 minutes. Julie says, "The class then asks the child three questions. The 'sharer' gets to choose the children who will ask the questions." Children in the class are encouraged to be complimentary rather than critical of the shared description, and to be interested in the actual object shared.

Positive benefits accrue as the preschoolers become accustomed to the sharing format. "Children become more descriptive about what they bring in as the year goes on," Julie reflects. "Children learn what questions are (and what compliments are). They begin to monitor themselves. Children become interested in each other."

Classroom Service Clubs

Terry Snyder's fifth-graders join one of five available classroom clubs at the beginning of each school year. Terry designed the clubs some years ago to encourage his students to develop a sense of community service, but has since realized that these activities also help students develop self-esteem and pride in their school and community environment. Descriptions of the five clubs follow:

Schoolwide Recycling: These volunteers are assigned rooms and teachers in the school building for which they are responsible twice a week. Duties: respectfully enter room, dispense paper, and return wastebasket to room; dump large containers for pick-up by recyclers; complete picture graph to chart the amount of paper recycled per month.

Kindergarten Buddies: Fifth-grade volunteers are matched to students in the kindergarten class (usually there are two fifth-graders per kindergartner "buddy," since there are more fifth-graders). Duties: meet weekly, encourage greeting time, plan and conduct an activity; create bulletin boards; assist during school assemblies; be positive role models.

Nature Club: This extracurricular activity allows students to enjoy nature and outdoor learning experiences at their school. Duties: landscaping projects, grounds maintenance, and nature activities for other classes.

Peer Buddies: This program is connected to students with special needs. Duties: assist designated students at school and on community-based instruction trips as needed. (These volunteers receive specialized training to assist with specific needs.)

Help Wanted: Members take on classroom jobs—those that occur on a regular basis as well as special circumstances. Possibilities: UPS (deliver messages around school); Weather Monitor (read, record data from instruments in Nature Center); Naturalist (feed birds, unlock classroom pet gate, Nature Center chores); Media Tech (operate VCR, library chores); Transit Authority (line leaders); Room Monitor (teacher's assistant); Secretary (paperwork chores); News Reporter (make weekly reports on local, national, and world current events); Pledge (lead students daily in pledge to flag); Mailperson (deliver materials and graded papers, or information from office to students); Science Lab Technician (help teacher prepare science lab experiments); Teller (counts tokens and writes deposit tickets for the classroom banking system).

Family and School Rules

Ask students to think about the rules that exist in their families. Brainstorm a list of possible family rules, or share actual rules and list them on the board. Then ask students to think about why these rules exist: Does a rule that you must finish your homework before watching any television help ensure that entertainment does not interfere with getting an education? Do rules about chores help ensure that no one person does all the work, and that everyone who enjoys living in the home shares in the responsibilities for its upkeep? Do rules about bedtimes or curfews help ensure that growing youngsters get enough sleep and/or rest to stay healthy as they grow?

Invite discussion on who makes the rules in students' families. Do students have a voice in what the rules are and how they are enforced? Point out that the existence of rules usually means a person has rights that are being protected and responsibilities that are being enforced. For example, a rule that states "No kicking allowed" implies that children in the family have a right not to suffer from being kicked, but it also implies that children have a responsibility not to kick another person.

Now ask students to list school rules (or consult the list of school rules posted or published at the school). How do these compare with family rules? Are there similarities? Differences? Where are implications about rights/responsibilities evident in these rules? Discuss the reasons for school rules, who makes them, how students and teachers are held accountable for obeying rules, and what enforcement procedures are used.

Another interesting activity is to compare school rules across cultures, using those listed here or school rules from other countries/cultures:

SCHOOL RULES FROM AROUND THE WORLD

What are "good citizenship rules" in your school or classroom? How might these be different if you lived in another country or culture? Here are some rules children in other countries must obey:

Japan
1. When the teacher enters, rise and bow. Greet the teacher in unison.
2. Come to school prepared with pencils, erasers, pens, paper, and textbooks.
3. Raise your hand to answer questions. Stand before answering.
4. Be quiet during class.
5. Keep to the right in the hall. No running.
6. Help clean the classroom, halls, and yard. Pick up trash, sweep floors and yard, and stack chairs before anyone leaves.

China
1. Cooperate with your classmates. Show group spirit.
2. Respect your teachers and obey them without question.
3. Be courteous at all times. Don't fight.
4. Don't be late. Don't miss school. Listen carefully in class.
5. Join in after-school activities.
6. Protect school property.

Russia
1. Don't embarrass your school or class.
2. Obey your teachers, principal, and parents without asking questions.
3. Come to school on time, clean, neatly dressed, and prepared.
4. Keep your desk clean.

5. Stand when the teacher enters or leaves.

6. Raise your hand to ask or answer a question. Stand straight while reciting.

7. Make notes of all assignments. Show the notes to your parents. Do your homework without help.

Community Rules and Laws

Introduce students to the idea of rules in the community with inexpensive signs purchased at a a hardware or department store (or make your own): No Smoking, Swim at Your Own Risk, Please Don't Walk on the Grass, and so on. Ask if and where students have seen signs such as these. Discuss what each means, and what rights and responsibilities are inherent in each slogan.

Divide into groups. Assign each group a public place in the community; such as library, park, theater, swimming pool, grocery store, shopping mall, restaurant, and the like. Have groups make a list of signs and rules that people must obey at the assigned location. Come back together in a large group and share locations and accompanying lists. Are there similarities? Differences? Why do the differences exist? Do different circumstances sometimes call for different rules? How does the concept of rights/responsibilities come into play here?

To help students understand that *some* rights and responsibilities apply to all people in the United States at all times, share the following summary of basic national rights/responsibilities:

RIGHTS

Freedom of Speech: All people are free to express their opinions.

Freedom of Religion: All people are free to worship as they choose.

Right to Due Process of Law: If someone is arrested, he or she has the right to have his or her side of the situation heard in an open hearing, to a fair and speedy trial, and to be represented by a lawyer.

Freedom of Assembly: People may gather peacefully for any legal reason.

Right to Political Participation: People can vote or run for public office, no matter what their race or religion.

RESPONSIBILITIES

Attend School: People must attend school until they are at least age 16 (in most states).

Obey Laws: Laws help prevent conflicts and allow people to live in peace with one another.

Defend U.S. during War: All adult males must defend the nation against attack; females may choose to do so.

Participate in the Judicial Process: All adults must serve on juries when asked to do so, appear as witnesses in trials, and cooperate with police officials and the courts.

Thinking about Laws

Share with students that laws help provide a civilized structure for their society/community, and give people a process for settling the disputes that do arise as they live and work together. As a matter of fact, people often are heard to say about a situation, "There ought to be a law!" This is one way local laws and regulations come into being: Someone in a particular situation decides "there ought to be a law" to protect and hold others accountable who find themselves in similar situations. Ask students what laws *should* be a part of their local neighborhood or community, then, as a group, establish a "Ten Commandments for _____" (insert local city name) or "Suggested Laws for _____" list. Invite students to write letters to city council members and/or the mayor, explaining the reasoning behind their list and asking that such items receive serious consideration.

What Do You <u>Mean,</u> What Do I Mean?

With this activity, students can come to see the difficulties faced by local lawmakers as they attempt to construct laws that have to be understood and interpreted consistently. Write some tasks (e.g., "Draw a star"; see list below) on separate sheets of paper, then fold the papers and place them in a container. Students divide into pairs, and each student takes a piece of folded paper from the container. Without revealing to the partner what is written on his or her slip of paper, each child writes on a separate piece of paper the directions for completing the task. (The name of the item [e.g., "star"] may not be used in the written instructions.) All students swap the set of written instructions with their partners (still keeping the task written on the folded slip of paper a secret), and attempt to complete their partner's task by following the written instructions. Each child then displays what he or she has drawn, and the partner tells what it was meant to be.

An alternative to this exercise is to place student partners' desks back to back and allow only one partner to draw a slip of folded paper from the container. This partner must give verbal directions to the other student without ever mentioning the relevant word associated with the task (see earlier "star" example above). Partners then turn their desks to face each other. The partner with the folded slip of paper shows the partner who did the drawing what was supposed to have been drawn.

After using either of these alternatives, have students discuss why their drawings do not look like the suggested object. Guide students into a discussion of the difficulty lawmakers face when writing laws that everyone must understand.

SAMPLE TASKS

Draw a house.	Draw a tree.
Draw a clock face.	Draw a star.
Draw a flower.	Draw a rainbow.
Print the word *and* in manuscript.	Draw a triangle.
	Write the number *8*.
Write the word *and* in cursive.	Write your teacher's name.
Draw a rectangle.	Draw a cat.
Draw a square.	Draw a dog.

A Celebration of Cultures

For many decades, the United States was referred to as the "melting pot" of society. It was believed that the customs and traditions brought to this country by immigrants became merged with the existing culture, losing their unique qualities to become a part of the dominant society. A more current perspective of U.S. culture is that of the *salad bowl*. The appetizing image of combined flavors, textures, and colors is a much more accurate metaphor than that of a big pot that reduces all ingredients to an unidentifiable sauce. This change in perspective necessitates a change in educational treatment.

A Cultural Celebration is a strategy for immersing students into in-depth research about a particular culture. Small groups of students research several identified cultures or countries, one culture or country per group. As a culminating event, all groups come together to share their findings in a large group format, providing an opportunity for all students to benefit from the research of others. Use cooperative learning groups, or divide the class in some other way to form groups of four or five students. Each group should select a culture to research, delegate responsibilities for accumulating relevant information, assign tasks for preparing displays, and so on, as indicated below.

When students understand the purposes behind an activity such as a Cultural Celebration, their motivation is enhanced, and levels of group participation increase. The rewards are many, such as:

- Students are immersed in meaningful research.
- Students will appreciate both the diversities and commonalities of various cultures.
- Multicultural awareness will be stimulated.
- Students are involved in interdisciplinary activities related to a single theme.

A mere research report is not sufficient to meet these goals. A good Cultural Celebration takes into account the following:

- All people communicate with one another in a variety of ways.
- All people create stories, music, and crafts that communicate their culture.
- All societies have formal or informal governments and economic systems.
- All societies record people's imaginings of fantastic beings and fanciful themes.
- All people celebrate special times in their lives.

Students' research should take into account these common characteristics of societies, and result in students' understanding how cultures can be similar in nature while reflecting the individuality of their participants.

Using the preceding conceptual framework, students participating in a cultural celebration should be prepared to share their findings with others through the following:

- Research the country or culture in some depth. (Be able to answer classmates' questions.)
- Provide a map of the country in relation to other countries, and a map depicting the country itself.
- Become familiar with the history of the country, its government, and its people.
- Prepare a display of souvenirs, clothing, foods, music, information about traditions (e.g., holidays, family/community celebrations, folklore, etc.), and other items of interest to others who have not studied that country or culture.
- Give a demonstration related to some aspect of the culture studied (e.g., folkdance, tea ceremony, origami, wedding simulation).
- Put together a booklet or brochure identifying key concepts and important information about the country/culture studied for participants to keep as a memento of the experience.

When the groups have identified their cultures and embarked on the research, set a date for the actual celebration. Reserve the gymnasium or cafeteria for setting up displays, and invite other classes, parents, and perhaps the community to participate. Encourage students to plan displays and exhibits early in the term, so materials and resources can be accumulated before the big day. Emphasize that participants should be exposed to multisensory experiences: They should learn about the country or culture through seeing and reading, hearing, touching, smelling, and tasting. In addition, participants should come away from the celebration with a sense of having been temporarily immersed into the cultures represented.

As the celebration begins, each group of students will share brief summaries of their research and explain their displays. Simulations or demonstrations will be given at this time, freeing individual students to circulate around the room, taking advantage of the opportunity to examine others' exhibits. One or two students should remain at each display at all times (students can work in shifts) to answer questions or make explanations for participants. The souvenir booklets/brochures should be prominently displayed and readily available to all students and guests.

When the Cultural Celebration is over, when displays have been dismantled and guests have departed, do not lose the opportunity for additional learning through reflective thinking. Discuss the experience with students. What did they learn? What new knowledge did they gain from the experience? Did they dispel any misconceptions through in-depth study? Has the research of others inspired them to do further research about a particular culture? How would they do things differently next time?

Another question that arises from group experiences such as this is, how will students be evaluated? A sixth-grade teacher who recently tried a Cultural Celebration in her class during a unit on European cultures used a checklist with her students. You may adapt or adjust the checklist to suit your own situations (see pages 173–174).

In conclusion, Cultural Celebrations can help students develop appreciations for and knowledge about cultures other than their own through in-depth research and multisensory experiences. Teachers must set the stage, establish the structure, provide guidance, and encourage the sharing of findings. Students decide on cultures, conduct research, and prepare exhibits. The culminating celebration is topped off with discussion that fosters reflective thinking. And everyone comes away with a better understanding of cultures other than their own.

■ Trying It Out

Although they may not follow precise Cultural Celebration structure, the strategies and activities that follow suggest ways in which teachers in diverse classrooms have attempted to teach about diversity and reduce prejudice through culture study.

Our City's Ethnic Heritage

Pandora Ott's grandmother is a German immigrant. After conducting a taped oral history interview with her grandmother, she wanted to use excerpts to motivate her fourth-grade students to think about the heritage of their local community. "I wanted to make students aware of one aspect of their city's cultural history," she says, "and the discrimination [against resident Germans] which was present at that time. Also I wanted to help students gain an appreciation for the diversities and commonalities between and among classmates."

The lesson began when Pandora had a student locate Germany on the world map. Then she read excerpts from a book about their community prepared by a local historian; these excerpts documented the city's predominantly German heritage. "I used the part of my grandmother's oral history tape in which she spoke of the discrimination she faced when she came to this country," Pandora states. The oral history resource was a stroke of genius. When Pandora explained that the voice they were hearing was that of her own grandmother, who had experienced discrimination after coming to this area, "they all began to talk at once. . . . Their hands went up, asking me if I was from Germany," she remembers, "if I could speak the language, etc. I explained to them that many Germans came here in the early 1900s because of the war in Europe," she says. "Then I focused on the term *discrimination*, and gave them a brief account of some of the discrimination the Germans faced in this country, and why."

Pandora asked students to think about the term *discrimination,* and define it. Some examples were:

"When someone makes fun of you because you are a different color."

"When people act like they are better than you."

"When people make fun of the way you talk."

"When people don't want you around."

"When people are prejustice [sic]."

Following students' discussion of what discrimination means to them, Pandora read Seuss's (1986) *Yertle The Turtle.* "It is about a turtle named Yertle, who believes he is the king of all turtles," she explains. "He piles up all these turtles on top of each other so that he can make a great throne to sit on. Finally, the turtle at the bottom

European Country Report Checklist

Inventory of required and suggested information to be included in each group's report:

I. Important Facts
The following 7 items are required. Each is worth 5 points (35 points total).

_____1. capital

_____2. major cities

_____3. flag

_____4. language

_____5. population and population density

_____6. form of government

_____7. chief products

      a. agriculture
      b. manufacturing
      c. mining

II. Geography
Choose 5 of the following, being sure to include items marked with an asterisk. Each item is worth 5 points (25 points total).

_____1. location in Europe

_____2. map of country

_____3. climate

_____4. terrain

_____5. natural resources

_____6. elevation

_____7. area

III. Culture
Select at least 2 of the following. These are worth 5 points each (10 points total).

_____1. music/dance

_____2. costume/clothing

_____3. food

_____4. customs

_____5. games/recreation

IV. Interesting Facts
Select at least 1 of the following to include in your report (5 points total).

_____1. money

_____2. schools

_____3. architecture

_____4. national anthem

V. Written Report, Oral Presentation, and Display

The report should be at least 2 pages if typed, or 3 pages if handwritten. The written report is worth 15 points, and the oral presentation and display are worth 10 points (25 points total).

Country _____

Group Members _____

_____

_____

_____

Total Points Earned _____

of the stack, named Mack, decides it is not fair to be treated this way." Mack tries to express his feelings of being treated unfairly, but is ignored by Yertle. But Mack has an idea: He burps! The burp knocks Yertle off his throne, where he lands in the mud. The story ends with the sentiment that now all turtles are free, "as maybe all living creatures should be.ms point, Pandora asked students to state the moral of the story. She believes "they were finally truly understanding the meaning of discrimination."

Then, Pandora played an excerpt from her grandmother's oral history tape where the grandmother discusses being "treated as a black person here in this country." This excerpt created an opportunity to expand their discussion from discrimination of Germans locally to discrimination of African Americans in historic and modern times. Grandmother Ott says of local citizens' treatment of herself and other German immigrants in the 1940s, "They felt as if we was not good enough and wanted us to do their dirty work." Pandora admits some concern that African American students in her class would consider her grandmother's comparing her own treatment to that of African Americans insulting, but "I really impressed upon the children that it was wrong for any person to treat another as an inferior, whether they are black or white, from America or another country ... it went really well," she reflects.

Students got into their cooperative groups to brainstorm everyday situations that involve discrimination. Groups role-played their scenarios for the whole class. "I asked them to first demonstrate the discriminatory act, then act out how the situation should have been handled," Pandora states. "The first group acted out a scene in which one girl was making fun of another girl's shoes. The second group did a reenactment of a situation on the playground in which one boy wouldn't let another play kickball because he was not good enough." Other groups chose to demonstrate name calling and racial slurs.

Pandora recalls feeling that she should stop one group's demonstration due to the use of inappropriate language and simulated violence, until she realized students were reenacting an actual event from earlier in the school year. She decided not to stop the role-play, but let it run the planned course. Pandora describes the situation in these words: "A new girl had come to the school and announced she hated 'all blacks and most boys.' During the role-play one girl said, 'I'm new to this school, and I don't like blacks or boys.' The boy in the group called her 'Fatty,' and she called him 'Afro-head.' Then she called him 'skinny' and he called her 'fag.' Another girl in the group told her she was wrong for calling him that name, and he was wrong for agitating her. She explained how they should all be friends, and asked them both to apologize."

Pandora finished the lesson on local heritage and discrimination by reviewing what she had wanted students to learn. Then she told students about the Germanfest celebration that takes place locally every June. She taught them a simple German folkdance called The Chicken, accompanied by German music, and explained that this was one sample of what students might learn if their parents took them to the festival in the summer.

Prejudice Reduction

Tita Gordon teaches in a community where a large number of Amish families send their children to an Amish school. She was concerned that her own junior high school students had developed negative, stereotypic attitudes about their Amish neighbors—especially since recent extracurricular discipline problems were associated with intolerance of Amish ways. Tita decided to teach a five-day unit on the Amish to develop awarenesses of and appreciations for Amish culture.

Tita began her unit by engaging students in a discussion on the Amish, partly to incorporate their knowledge and experience into the unit and partly to gauge the level of misunderstanding. Questions used to guide discussion included: Have you ever heard of the Amish? What have you heard? What do you know about the Amish and their beliefs? Have you ever seen an Amish child? Why don't we have any Amish children in our school?

Then Tita drew students' attention to books like Carolyn Nerer's *Amish People— Plain Living in a Complex World* (McElderry Books, 1976), which had been placed in a reading center for students to peruse during their study of the Amish. The remainder of the lesson was occupied by students' exploration of these books and by their research on the Amish using classroom encyclopedias.

Day 2 of the unit began with a discussion on Amish family life. Tita shared with the students that, of all the Anabaptist sects, only the Old Order Amish have vigorously held to the traditional German customs. She also shared the information that, in an Amish family, each family member has a certain role. "For example," she said, "the mother's role is mainly centered around the house. The girls help their mother cook, clean, and sew. Sons' roles are mainly centered around their father in the field. They rise in the morning with their fathers and work with them all day. The family is very close and very strict." Students consulted books from the reading center and classroom encyclopedias to discover more about Amish family life.

Day 3 covered Amish celebrations: births, baptisms, weddings, funerals, and holidays. Tita reminded her students that most Amish women are mothers within the first year of their marriage, and that babies in Amish families, like most of their families, are born under a doctor's supervision. Unlike the religious beliefs of most students' families, the Amish believe that a person should not be baptized until they have reached their teens. Courtships are kept secret within the two families until two weeks before the wedding, when the engagement is announced. Because marriage is very sacred to the Amish, weddings are very important social events involving everyone in the community and even people from many miles away. The Amish celebrate some holidays important to their beliefs, excluding many commonly recognized holidays such as July 4th and Veteran's Day. Funerals are always held three days after a death, with the body placed in a plain wooden box made by the village carpenter. Students concluded day 3 by role-playing situations in small groups. Each group was given a card with a situation described on it, such as participating in a community building project, planning a weekly menu and related shopping, an Amish courtship, an Amish wedding, and a quilting bee. Students assumed roles and played their parts based on information learned about Amish family roles and traditions.

On the fourth day of the unit, the class used an Amish recipe to make bread, and discussed the ramifications of having to make all food consumed in the home from scratch using such a recipe.

WHITE BREAD

1/2 cup sugar

1/2 cup shortening

Cream and three cups lukewarm water

Dissolve one large cake yeast in 1/2 cup warm water.

Mix 1 1/2 tsp. salt, 1/4 tsp. ginger, 9 cups flour.

Make into loaves, buns, or biscuits.

They continued their discussion by contrasting how the lives of Amish teenagers differ from their own, and concluded by brainstorming a list of ways their lives are the same or similar.

The fifth and final day of the unit was devoted to study of clothing and occupations of the Amish. Important facts included:

■ Amish are required by their beliefs to dress a certain way.
■ Men must grow beards after they marry.
■ Women's dress changes after marriage.
■ Almost all clothing is home-made (with the exception of men's plain blue jeans).
■ Amish have a reputation as hard workers and dependable employees.
■ Most Amish men work in their own businesses as farmers, carpenters, block-layers, or sawmill operators.

Teachers who replicate Tita's unit may wish to find ways other than books to expose their students to the Amish way of life, such as a video, filmstrip, audio recording, or even a visit to an Amish farm. Tita also suggests that soap making can be easily substituted for the bread making activity.

Freedom Quilt

Scott Fudge wanted to broaden his third-graders' study of communities by introducing the lives of slaves living on pre–Civil War plantations. "Since our school and community is all white," he says, "I wanted to introduce a part of the African American history and its relation to our study of communities. I wanted to focus on the community the slaves lived in on the plantation and I wanted the students to have an idea of what life was like for the African Americans on these plantations, and why they wanted to escape to the North." Scott gathered the students on the reading circle carpet, and read *Sweet Clara and the Freedom Quilt* to them. The story focuses on a young slave girl on a plantation, and the older female slave in the "big house" who teaches her to sew and quilt. "While Clara sewed, she heard about slaves trying to escape on the Underground Railroad," Scott explained to the attentive students, "and she used her newfound sewing talents to create a quilt." The quilt's design was based on descriptions of the geography and local landmarks Clara heard about as visitors to the "big house" talked about those who had escaped. She wants the quilt to be a "map" that others can use to escape to freedom. Eventually, Clara herself used the directions shown on the Freedom Quilt to escape, leaving it behind to help others.

"After reading the story," Scott says, "we discussed what it meant to be a slave." Students tried to draw comparisons between Clara's life as a slave and the students' lives, brainstorming such examples as cleaning your room, taking out the trash, doing work for brother/sister, washing the dishes, and so on. "That was all they had to base their ideas on," Scott reflects. "I began to explain to the students what it meant to be a slave in the United States back in the 1800s. I focused on the long hours and hard work, separate living quarters, and the beatings. The students were very shocked at what I described," he notes. "They could not believe that people would treat other people in that manner."

To bring closure to the literature-based lesson, Scott's students wrote in their journals a response to these questions: Imagine you are a slave in the mid-1800s. How do you feel? How do you feel about slavery versus freedom? Would you try to escape? What would you do to escape?

"I would have liked for the students to learn more about the hardships imposed upon the slaves," Scott says. As he plans to teach the lesson with a future class, he suggests that teachers wishing to replicate this lesson consider having one of their cooperative groups designated "Slaves of the Day." "They would have to pass out the papers, carry books for others, be at the end of the line, not talk unless called on, etc.

Here are some other questions I need to think about before teaching this lesson again,"
he adds. "How do you talk about cultural diversity in your classroom when the students do not have experiences to connect it with? What would be some suggestions
to teach about different communities that have culturally diverse undertones (different
from students' community)? What would be some age-appropriate life experiences the
students could be involved with to learn more about cultural diversity?"

Likenesses and Differences

Tracey Malcolm-Myers wanted students in her primarily white, upper-middle income
level neighborhood to learn about the similarities between and among cultures.
"Even though people from other cultures may pray to a different god, or speak
another language, or dress differently," she says, "all cultures have certain characteristics that are similar. One of these characteristics happens to be that most cultures
share stories."

Tracey played a tape of the African folktale "Anansi's Narrow Waist" while showing her first-graders the book's illustrations. They talked about the story, then she
read the Native American folktale "Why Turkeys Have Red Eyes." (Both were available in a teachers' anthology that accompanied her social studies series.) At this time,
students divided into groups of three. Tracey gave each group a set of cards on
which were written the following possible writing topics:

Write a tale explaining why zebras have stripes.

Write a tale explaining why elephants have long trunks.

Write a tale explaining why bees buzz.

Write a tale explaining why lightning bugs glow.

"I thought I needed to supply the cards because it would be too difficult for first-
graders to come up with their own topic," she reflects, "however, I had two groups
ask if they could write about why cats chase mice and why bees sting."

A very teachable moment occurred when Tracey was playing the tape of
"Anansi's Narrow Waist," read by Mr. Mustapha. (Tracey had selected this tape to use
after hearing the narrator speak at a teachers' workshop.) "The children became very
interested in the tape's narrator. I found myself explaining that, as a child, Mr. Mustapha lived in a mud house. He and his family had to grow their own food, and not
every child got a chance to go to school. But because Mr. Mustapha was a hard
worker and enjoyed school so much, he was allowed to go to school. I told them that
he worked so hard that they even let him come to America to go to college, and is
now a teacher." Tracey was somewhat amused when one first-grader asked whether
she had gone to Africa to talk with Mr. Mustapha in order to find out all this information! Another teachable moment occurred when, after sharing the two folktales
with her students, Tracey asked if the tales were true. This question led to a lively
discussion about how to tell fiction from nonfiction, or tales from factual accounts.
"The children decided that, in fiction stories like the two tales read in class, animals
can talk and act like people," she recalls.

As groups of students worked on producing their own folktales, Tracey circulated around the room, assisting. "I . . . asked them if Africa has the only culture that
tells stories. That way, I could prepare them for the final question: Do people in all
countries share stories?"

After the groups' stories were finished, Tracey typed them on the classroom
computer, printed them out, and shared the printed versions with each group. Then
group members were able to compare and contrast their stories with those of other
groups. After students illustrated their finished stories, they were bound into a book,
and a a copy was left in the school library for students in other classes to read. "I
hope this lesson will help them grow with an understanding that people are people,
regardless of skin color—an issue they do not deal with in their neighborhoods
often," Tracey concludes.

Culture Kits

Help your students expand their awareness of and appreciation for cultures by creating your own Culture Kit. A Culture Kit is a portable, self-contained "museum-in-a-box" used by students as they learn about the people and society of another country. Properly designed, this learning can lead to greater understandings and appreciations for the diversity of culture in their own classroom or community. The kit contains attractively displayed materials and well-designed activities stored in a durable decorated container. Each Culture Kit is designed so students can learn independently or in pairs, and at their own pace.

Culture includes "all of the human-made components in a society and their symbolic meanings, such as tools, language, values and institutions" (Banks & Clegg, 1985, p. 205). Your Culture Kit will include examples of and details about the "human-made components" of a particular society. In keeping with the "salad bowl" analogy of multicultural education, the emphasis of the Culture Kit is on *similarities among and between* cultures.

Students will gain an understanding of characteristics shared by all cultures if you focus on the following five concepts as you develop the Culture Kit:

1. *All people communicate with one another in a variety of ways.* Oral language is the most obvious form of communication. The use of media (letters, books, newspapers, print resources of all kinds) and technology (radio, television, telegraph, electronic mail, and even drums) in a culture should be considered, also.
2. *All people create stories, music, and crafts that communicate their culture.* Legends, fairytales, folktales, songs, ballads, symphonies, operas, paintings, sculpture, artistic designs on commonly used items—all are ways the peoples of various cultures communicate their history and values to each other.
3. *All societies have formal or informal governments and economic systems.* Democracies, autocracies, parliaments, monarchies, or dictatorships—all cultures adhere to some form of leadership. In addition, all cultures over time invented and/or maintained a preferred form of payment for goods and services.
4. *All societies record people's imaginings of fantastic beings and fanciful themes.* Whether it be mythology, formal or informal religious teachings, or the Loch Ness Monster, another characteristic shared by all cultures is a belief in the supernatural.
5. *All people celebrate special times in their lives.* Societies the world over celebrate or commemorate births and birthdays, marriages, deaths, and life passages (such as bar mitzvahs).

In order to facilitate students' awareness of geographic, social, and political aspects of the country being studied, you should include several examples of the following kinds of materials and activities in your Culture Kit. (It helps if you have traveled to the country being studied, but many teachers have developed Culture Kits for countries they have never visited.) You will also need to develop (and keep current!) an Item Inventory, listing all items and activities contained in the kit. Experience shows that this inventory is best stored taped to the lid of the kit container. Instruct students to "take inventory" each time they use the Culture Kit by matching the items contained with those listed on the Item Inventory.

A MAP OF THE COUNTRY OR AREA

If you belong to American Automobile Association (AAA), this part is easy—just ask for a map from your local representative. Another simple way to obtain a map of the country is to consult *Maps on File*. As a last resort, make an enlarged copy of the map from a recent encyclopedia.

MAPS DEPICTING LARGER GEOGRAPHIC CONTEXT

If the Culture Kit is on the country of France, for example, include a map showing France in the larger context of Europe.

TRAVEL BROCHURES

Pick up brochures at your local travel agency. If you have enough lead time, write to the country's travel bureau or tourist department and request a packet of materials. Collect two copies of brochures with attractive photographs depicting the countryside and/or people; one copy can then be cut up to decorate the Culture Kit container or nearby bulletin board. Factual information contained in these brochures (or in a consumer travel book about the country, such as those available from your local AAA) can be used in the activities you develop. Although books are too bulky to store in the kit, you'll want to collect informational, children's, and picture books to supplement the items in your kit.

MISCELLANEOUS INFORMATION

Most information about the country's flag, motto, sons, monuments, and so on is readily available in *Culture-Grams* (probably in your local library) or in a recent encyclopedia. Patriotic songs and folksongs may be found in sing-along collections.

POSTCARDS

Postcards may come from your personal collection or from family members and friends. I have found appropriate postcards by rummaging through boxes at flea markets and antique stores. The best way to make sure you have postcards to use in future Culture Kits is to ask everybody you know to send you postcards when they travel. Explain how you plan to use them in your classroom, and people who have never make a practice of sending postcards will start doing it!

EXAMPLES OF MONEY

As with postcards, foreign money is easiest to get if you have your own private collection. If foreign currency is difficult to acquire, ask acquaintances at the local ethnic grocery or restaurant for their help (do shop there or eat there to thank them for their trouble). When all else fails, create your own facsimiles.

SOUVENIRS OF ALL KINDS

Take care that souvenirs do not depict the people or their customs in a stereotypic way. With that said, such examples as fabric, rugs, vases, carvings, dishes or eating utensils, books, clothing, and musical recordings are wonderful additions to the Culture Kit. I purchased a placemat in Kenya that features popular recipes using indigenous ingredients.

TRAVEL DIARIES AND/OR TRIP ITINERARIES

Travel diaries can be special features of a Culture Kit, because they give students a "you are there" feeling about the country being studied. Laminate handwritten pages to protect this primary source from the wear and tear of heavy use.

EXHIBITS OF DAY-TO-DAY LIFE

It is easy to save these interesting items while traveling *if you're thinking about it*. Most people automatically throw candy wrappers, magazines, menus, and so on away, but for teachers who want to create Culture Kits, they are a veritable gold mine! Any small souvenir with words printed in the native language will apeal to children. When I attended a conference in The Netherlands a few years ago, we endured a six-hour channel crossing on a ferry. Hundreds of passengers consumed incredible amounts of chips, candy bars, English biscuits, and soda—and whenever an opportunity presented itself, I introduced myself as a teacher who "wants your trash to use in my classroom." In addition, when we dined in a restaurant where paper menus were protected by plastic covers, I asked if I might pay for a copy "to use in my classroom back in the States." (I was never allowed to pay.)

NEWSPAPERS

Even if you have only one (or even part of one) newspaper, it will be a valuable addition to your Culture Kit. Advertisements, classifieds, front-page headlines, and comics all give students a feel for the culture being studied. It is especially useful to include a copy of the local newspaper dated the same day as the cultural newspaper. Students can compare and contrast what was considered news for that day, and compare reporters' coverage of the same world events.

PHOTOGRAPHS

Again, use your own collection, or that of a family member or friend. The fact that these are real snapshots taken by someone they or their teacher knows goes a long way toward making the experience real for your students. Slides make a good photographic addition, too, if you have access to a slide projector (or are handy with HyperStudio and a scanner). I once found a picture book about England at a used book sale—complete with a set of slides attached. Although the book was somewhat dated, the slides were beautiful photographic depictions of major landmarks. They were an impressive addition to my Culture Kit, and only cost about a dollar.

ACTIVITY CARDS FOR STUDENTS

This is where the real work comes in. So far, you have been cumulating and organizing; now you need to help students make sense of what they are seeing. Develop math activities related to demographics, money, and menus; develop social studies and language activities related to newspapers, diaries, photographs, souvenirs, and language-rich "discards" such as candy wrappers. Use your creativity, or draw from the examples of teacher-created Culture Kits that follow.

I recommend that you store your Culture Kits in a heavy-duty plastic tub with a tight-fitting lid (Rubbermaid has several good models). You will also find that you will need to "move up" to a larger container, since the kit keeps growing. Start out with a bigger, sturdier container than you think you will need. Pique students' curiosity by decorating the container with pictures and words to represent the culture being studied in a constructive, nonstereotypical way. Find a place of honor for the Culture Kit, such as its own table or center space, and encourage students to explore!

■ Trying It Out

Germany

Regina developed her Culture Kit on Germany. Some map-related activities from her Kit used with fourth-graders include:

MAPPING RESOURCES

Purpose: To integrate skills needed to read a resource map to find basic information about German resources

Instructions: Each country has products that are produced or grown inside its boundaries. These are called *resources.* Find the enclosed resource map of Germany. Using the key, list three resources from Hamburg, Berlin, and one city of your choice.

LET'S PLAY HIDE AND SEEK!

Purpose: To reinforce basic map reading skills and general knowledge of Europe

Instructions: Many countries make up the continent we call Europe. On the enclosed map, find Germany. On your paper, write the names of two countries neighboring Germany on the west. Write the names of two countries neighboring Germany on the east.

East Africa

Rhonda developed a Culture Kit on East Africa, using souvenirs and materials saved by her father when he was stationed there in the military. She added maps and children's books to update the collection, then designed activities for children to use as they explored items in the kit, such as these:

MUSICAL INSTRUMENTS

Look at the handmade drum, maraca, and shaker. Write down your observations: Based on what you know about woods and other materials native to East Africa, what are these instruments made of? Compare these materials to those used to make similar musical instruments in the United States.

Handle the instruments gently. Make some soft music. Compare the sounds you create with the music you like to listen to. How is it the same? How is it different?

EAST AFRICAN ART

Look at the burlap picture. Write down what you think the two women in the picture are doing. What does the picture tell you about the people of Zaire? How do the women of Zaire carry their babies? What are they using to support the babies as they carry them? How does this compare with the ways Americans carry their babies?

Look at the East African doll. How is the doll like American dolls? How is it different? Why do you think the doll has a basket on her head? Would you like to carry a basket on your head and your baby on your back? Why or why not?

Look at the creche (Christmas nativity scene). Do you notice similarities in this nativity scene, compared to those you may be familiar with? Do you notice differences? List the similarities and differences on your paper. Why do you think the differences exist?

Greece

Teresa developed a Culture Kit on Greece to use with students in grade 5 and above. Some activities she suggests include:

Compare the Greek flag with the U.S. flag. Look up the meaning of the Greek flag in the book *This Is Greece*. How does the meaning of the Greek flag compare to the meanings of the stars and stripes in the U.S. flag?

Observe Greek coins and paper money. Compare to U.S. coins and paper money. Estimate the U.S. value of the Greek drachma. Check your guess by consulting one of the travel books. How many drachmas would you need to see a $4.00 movie matinee?

Compare the Greek Coca-Cola can with the U.S. Coca-Cola can. Notice trademark, volume, and ingredients. Try to translate ingredients on the Greek can (with the help of the Greek/English dictionary). Convert the volume listed on the Greek can to ounces.

Examine the six Greek children's books. View the pictures and try to decide what the story is about. (Hint: One of the books is the Greek version of Cinderella; another is the Greek version of Snow White.) How are these stories similar to the fairytales you know about? How are they different? How do you account for the similarities and differences?

Israel

Debby's Culture Kit is on Israel. She includes examples of Hebrew culture with related activities, such as:

HEBREW ALPHABET

Look at the yellow stickers on the lid of the Culture Kit box. These are the letters of the Hebrew alphabet. Write down on a piece of paper how many letters there are in the Hebrew alphabet. How many letters are there in the English alphabet? Which language has more letters?

Find the yellow stickers on the lid of the Culture Kit box and the Aleph-bet ruler. Get a partner. Have your partner take the ruler and say a Hebrew letter. Try to find the letter on the lid of the Culture Kit, and match it with the one on the ruler.

Write your name using the Hebrew alphabet.

DREIDEL

Find the Dreidel spinner and game instructions. You will need two other people to play the game with you. First, read about how the game is played in Israel and America during the Jewish holiday of Hanukkah. Then, follow the instructions and learn to play the game. The person who wins gets to keep the candy!

Thailand

Kim uses materials collected from her travels in Thailand in her Culture Kit. When I visited her third-grade classroom, the room was decorated like a Thai restaurant, with desks pushed together to form "tables for four" complete with paper cloths. Each pair of students was supplied with an authentic Thai menu and English translations. Kim played Thai music softly on her tape player, and walked into the classroom dressed in a Thai silk costume and Thai shoes. She welcomed her students using Thai words, then translated them. Then she turned to the chalkboard and wrote:

Appetizer

Entree

Salad

Dessert

Beverage

She instructed the students to read the menus and select one food item from each category for their "order." She circulated around the room as a waitress and "took" their orders as the music continued to play. Then she brought in a tray of Thai finger food for students to sample. With this introduction, Kim's students couldn't wait to explore her Thai Culture Kit!

Oral History Interviews for Studying Cultural Diversity

Oral history interviews with people of cultures other than one's own can yield much valuable information for classroom study and help students make new friends in the process. Identifying and interviewing recent or first-generation immigrants in the community is an excellent way for students to study cultural diversity within the community setting.

First, students need to be well-versed in the oral history procedure (see the Introduction of this book for information about and strategies for conducting oral history projects). Then, informants need to be identified and invited to participate in the project. As a way of identifying enough informants for the entire class to participate, contact local ethnic and/or religious groups, such as the Jewish Federation, Greek Orthodox Church, or United Hispanic Students. (I once identified a number of immigrants and refugees by contacting the local branch of Catholic Charities, an organization that assists political refugees and potential immigrants through translators and financial help.) After an initial telephone call, mail a letter reiterating details about the class project and asking for volunteers. Depending on the organizational structure, volunteers may either contact a staff member of the organization, or they may elect to write or telephone the school. Another way to make certain all students in the class participate in these interviews is to pair students with a single informant.

Decide on a theme for the students' interviews, then work in cooperative groups to develop interview questionnaires (making certain to use open-ended questions to get the most detailed responses). A list of potential themes for studying ethnic culture through immigrant oral history interviews follows these instructions.

After interviews have been conducted, students should work with the computer lab teacher to transcribe their interviews. Transcriptions can be brought back to the classroom, where, over a period of one to two weeks, students edit the question/answer format into a story or report focusing on the selected theme. These then are shared with other class members, whose interviews focused on the same or other themes. Comparisons among and between countries and cultures will result.

**SUGGESTED THEMES AND SUBTHEMES FOR IMMIGRANT
ORAL HISTORY INTERVIEWS**

Apple Dumplings (Holiday Celebrations)

Looking at food and its role in holidays

Grouping students by interest or priority in holiday/traditions

How do traditions come to be in families/groups/countries?

Looking at generational differences, and intensity of desire to pass on traditions

Comparing across countries of similar foods, roles of children, gift giving, decorations, family roles, religion's role

Can you have holidays without others?

Adapting during holidays when you are away from your culture

Examining the role family plays in setting the tone for holidays

Who promotes certain holidays (i.e., patriotic), and why?

Arranged Marriages (Dating and Marriage Customs)

Discussion of how marriages are arranged

Places the informants are from; time period discussed

Traditions and rituals within and among countries

Contrasting dating and marriage customs

Economics

Religion

Amount of input children have in spousal selection (for themselves)

Dating customs

Marriage ceremonies

Values desired in a potential spouse, and to make preferences known

Issues of respect and obedience to parents

Family Life

The Joy Luck Club (movie—excellent example of two cultures that collide)

Students' interviews of mothers and/or fathers to find common threads to bridge the "generational gaps" for diverse cultures

■ Trying It Out

Arranged Marriages and Potato Dumplings

I worked with a group of students as they conducted interviews with recent immigrants. We used the themes "Arranged Marriages" and "Potato Dumplings" from the preceding list. Excerpts from the interviews follow:

ARRANGED MARRIAGES (DATING CUSTOMS)

Vel (India)

We have tried to maintain marriage customs. Even though our son is 25, you'd be surprised that he doesn't date. He feels, "Dad, when I decide to get married, you can help me." Parents help, guide their children, not necessarily just for dating, but then deciding to get married. That is the tradition back home.

So that's the kind of value system still intact in a kid who is 25 years old—[who has] grown up in this country for the past 23 years. He still maintains the [old country] values. There are a lot of Indian communities living here who have daughters who . . . as long as [his mother and I] found the family, the background, and the girl [acceptable] . . . we would agree to a marriage. But [we also] talk about the possibility of finding the right girl back home in India. We still have some time—he is only 25. Normally, 26 is the age boys get married . . . girls, 22.

Juanita (Mexico)

If you want to go somewhere, like to the mall, you have to take your brother with you. Girls don't date until they are seventeen years old. It just seems the parents' attitudes and parents' mentality have a lot to do with it. . . . Life is really focused on the family.

POTATO DUMPLINGS (HOLIDAY TRADITIONS)

Gertrude (Germany)

If I make a meal for Christmas, I cook usually different. Not Thanksgiving. Thanksgiving I make the traditional American dinner because it's an American holiday. So I make turkey and stuffing, but for Christmas I either make ducks, geese, because that's what I was used to from over there. So I do cook different.

And potato dumplings—I have to have potato dumplings! They're a round ball. If you've been to Munich, they only have them in the southern part of Germany. They don't even make them up north. They're raw potatoes . . . mixed together and stewed. Oh, they're so good when you put pork roast gravy over it. I tell you, I could just eat and eat!

Sigrid (Germany)

Christmas in Germany was . . . I never got any presents. I didn't know you were supposed to get presents for Christmas! When we went Christmas Eve to church, there would be a tree that just appeared. It was all decorated with cookies. And it was always just a little table model type Christmas tree. We sang songs, and read the Bible, and it was . . . I always felt very warm. I suppose it was very boring, but I always had a very warm good feeling about it.

Christmas morning when I woke up, we always had like a plate, a big plate of fruit, nuts, and maybe a chocolate bar . . . not very much, but that was Christmas. Then we went to church and everybody was happy. We didn't beg and beg for days and days and we didn't shop for days and days. And my whole town was that way. So the Christmas was . . . more Christlike.

Martha (Germany)

[For Thanksgiving] they have a meal, and then take a lot of stuff in to church (whatever you got in the garden). They take it in to church in baskets and set it around the altar. Then the Father or minister or whoever blesses it, and then after the sermon, they take this to the poor people, the elderly, and the shut-ins.

Phung Hang (Vietnam)

I was born in Vietnam, but our grandparents are originally from China. So we celebrate all our holidays, and we also celebrate at Christmas time. And at Christmas time, or the Thanksgiving, I try to do like everybody does—in American way.

The way that we celebrate the Chinese New Year is just like in the old times. The people worked all year 'round, and it comes to the New Year's—that's a time for like a harvest. And people would take time off and we would not do anything—just kind of relax . . . a time of the year to relax.

And the New Year for us is like starting from the beginning—so all the things that you did from the past year, or anything wrong, or people not get along . . . January first is the day that we started again with a new improvement. The Chinese New Year is the only time that a kid gets dressed in new clothes. We got more food and everything is right— it is the best time of the year. And everything started again—the kid had to promise the parent that "I'm going to do good the rest of the year" . . . the resolution. Everything in the past is forgiven; everything that is wrong, just forget about it. People forgive each other. And even, like, if you have debt, you tried to pay it off at the end of the year. At the beginning of the year you start again fresh.

Angelique (Germany)

At Christmas time I will have a real Christmas tree with real candles, and usually I invite my good friends. It is kind of a treat for them, because it's very dangerous [lit candles]. So I guess that's why I never gave up that tradition. The German houses don't burn that easily because it's stone, the floors are stones. So it's not that dangerous [there] really. I like the smell of the Christmas tree so I keep doing that.

Annie (Austria)

During holidays, especially Easter time, we crack eggs and that is kind of a custom or tradition that we have always done. You hardboil the eggs, then you tap them to see who has the strongest egg. It's kind of silly, but you go around the table and see who has the strongest egg. It's fun and we're still doing that.

Communicating with Communities around the World

Current technology makes it possible for children to "reach out and touch someone" in another country just by using the Internet. If your school is fortunate enough to have a televised link via computer to a site that can hook your class computer up to school computers in other countries, students have even more opportunity to learn about the communities of the world. Help your students explore what it means to be a member of a community outside the United States by exchanging e-mail with students in other countries. (These pen pal-type links can be found by searching the Education topic area of the Internet.)

■ Trying It Out

Letters from Africa

Students at Village Elementary School became e-mail pen pals with students in South African schools. This pen pal arrangement was part of a year-long study of South Africa, and included televised links between two classes. Students exchanged e-mail messages with one another weekly, and made many cross-cultural connections. Excerpts from this e-mail project demonstrate the kinds of information exchanged:

Subj: Keypals? Yes!!
Date: Wed, Oct 9, 1996
From: [Sea Point Primary] Cape Town

I received your e-mail via our Schools' Network, and I am in the process of setting up a mini project with my grade 5 class.

I would love you to be one of the groups helping me. My pupils will ask questions which need simple answers, and we shall be doing a class project with maps and graphs and things, so we need you to simply answer our questions.

I already have schools from Canada, England, Australia, and Argentina, so this should be fun.

We are REAL beginners, so there won't be anything fancy!

We also have one computer in our media centre connected to the Internet, but 16 others in a special computer room. Next January and February, I would be very happy to assist you with your Southern African project.

Regards
Ingrid Johannesson (Grade 5 Teacher, Sea Point Primary, Cape Town)

Subj: From Jeff and Jessica
Date: Thu, Oct 24, 1996
From: [Village Elementary, USA]

Dear South Africa,
My name is Jeffrey. I am a fifth grader at Village Elementry. What is the name of your school? How is it down in Africa? Do you have lots of elephants in South Africa?

Dear Friends,
Hi, my name is Jessica. I am a fourth grader at Village Elementary. My teacher is Mrs. R. She just had her baby, and his name is Jordan. Do you e-mail to other countries? This is our first time. Please write us back.

P.S. We think this is cool.

Subj: Re: From Jeff and Jessica
Date: Fri, Oct 25, 1996
From: [Cape Town school; several replies]

Hi, my name is Elia. I live in Cape Town, SA. Our schools' name is SACS; it is the oldest school in southern Africa I am a sixth grader. We have elephants but they are all kept in nature reserves & zoos. Did you know that the whole of the UK can fit into one of our nature reserves?

My name is Matthew and sorry to disappoint you, but there are no elephants living in Cape Town.
    Our school is SACS Junior which is at Cape Town, the bottom of Cape Town.
    This is a very hot country, we get more or less 4 seasons.

Dear Jeff, my name is Ross. I am a 6th grader at S.A.C.S. Junior. Well all I have to say about the weather is that first it's COLD and then HOT so we more or less have all 4 seasons.
    About the elephants, they are all in our Game Reaserves. We mostly have dogs, cats, and birds.

Dear Jessica, my name is Ross. My school's name is S.A.C.S. My teacher's name is Mr. Gilmour.
    About e-mailing to other countries: No we don't. This is probably the first time we've e-mailed out of the school grounds.
    Well, that's my story. Please write back.

P.S. I THINK THIS IS RAD. BYE BYE.

    Hi my name is Riyaaz. The name of my school is S.A.C.S. It stands for South African College School. Sorry we don't have any elephants here in South Africa. Where is Elementary Village?
    We live in a civilize society and not in tents or huts. I'm in the 6th grade.

Hi, my name is James, I'm a sixth grader at (S.A.C.S.) South African College School. I would like to know where your school is. All of our elephants are further up country.

P.S. Please write back!

Hi. I'm Peter. No, we don't have elephents here in Newlands, but we have dogs and cats.
    Write back and tell me where Village Elementry is or I will have to send you a virus.

Patrick and Matthew B. seem to have tired of the usual response to the elephant question given by their classmates. These e-mail responses show their sense of humor:

Hi
My name is Patrick I am in standard 4 (6th grade). Our school is in the most southern part of Africa. Yes we do have elephants. We are very scared of them because they run around in our streets and guess what—there are lions in our gardens. Our school is normal. Our schools' name is S.A.C.S.

Hi
My name is Matthew B, I am in standard 4 (6th grade) at S.A.C.S. (South African College School). It is nice in South Africa, it rains quite a lot in the winter months. Yesterday a stampede ran through our house (HA! HA!).

Subj: Nov. 5, 1996
Date: Tue, Nov 5, 1996
From: [Village Elementary, USA]

Hi Matthew, my name is Erik
I live in Fort Wayne, Indiana. It is located in the United States of America. Village Elementary is located on the street of Werling. I am 11 years old. I am in the 5th grade. Our principal is named Mr. H. He is nice and tall. I like sports. Do you know where lions or others animals are at? What are your favorite movies? I like Twister. Our country is getting cold here. If you could go to anywhere in the United States where would you go? How does it feel to live in South Africa? Is it fun? How long do you stay in school? Is your time and day different?

Your friend,
Erik

Part

III

Using Books to Teach about Family and Local History

This section provides ideas and activities for teaching about family history using particular children's trade books. It also contains an annotated bibliography of children's trade books related to family, local, and oral history topics. These books are recommended by classroom teachers and/or university professors experienced with integrating children's books with the curriculum.

The reasons for using children's books to teach about or expand on historical topics are many. Researchers criticize social studies textbook content, saying it does not tell the full story or give voices to underrepresented groups. Quality children's books selected by mindful teachers for their capacity to extend or enrich topical study serve to enliven social studies textbook content. Many educators are recognizing the value of interdisciplinary and thematic instruction; reading, writing, and subject-matter content are easily integrated through the use of children's trade books. Topics covered in or related to the book being read, book chapters, and sometimes even entire books lend themselves well to cooperative group learning activities.

Using Picture Books across Grade Levels

When the words *picture book* are mentioned, images of toddlers on parents' knees, bedtime stories, and preschool classrooms spring to mind. Picture books actually have many uses in the classroom, and well-prepared picture books have been used successfully even with students in high school settings.

Picture books can help young children better understand the passage of time, and when picture books tell the life stories of individuals from the perspective of a young child, students' identification with the story's narrator increases learning even more (Harms & Lettow, 1997). Life stories told in picture books can offer information about the past, help students draw comparisons between stories and what is happening in their own families, and present appropriate models for students to emulate as they struggle to develop their own identities.

Although picture books have long been associated with preschoolers and teachers of very young children, they can be valuable resources for learning in intermediate and middle grades, as well. Books featuring pictures or well-done illustrations often present information about people and their actions, serve to bolster students' language usage, and help children develop habits of mind needed to comprehend historical knowledge (Levstik, 1991). For older readers, picture books can add depth to specific topics of study. Burleigh's (1991) *Flight,* for example, expands on the facts surrounding Charles Lindbergh's first solo flight across the Atlantic by describing the actual dangers Lindbergh faced during this flight, and the fears he must have felt.

Sensitive or difficult topics can be introduced or expanded upon through the use of appropriate picture books. Post–Civil War treatment of African Americans can be enhanced through biographies such as Towle's (1993) *The Real McCoy: The Life of an African-American Inventor.* In this book, Elijah McCoy, whose parents were runaway slaves, was born in Canada and educated in Scotland during the American Civil War. He finds, however, that his racial heritage hinders him from getting a job worthy of his education. Eventually, McCoy uses his ingenuity to invent the automatic oil cup for locomotives, providing an alternate perspective to outdated textbook treatments of post–Civil War African American stereotypes. Hopkinson's (1993) *Sweet Clara and the Freedom Quilt* turns a tale from African American oral tradition into a picture book detailing how slaves created quilts to use as maps when planning Underground Railroad escapes.

Farris and Fuhler (1994) suggest books to help students learn about how the environment has changed over time. Many of these books are appropriate resources for stimulating students' thinking about how the local community and surrounding areas have changed over the years. Cherry's (1992) *A River Ran Wild: An Environmental History* chronicles the New England Nashua River Valley's existence from 1400 to 1990, showing how human intervention can do severe damage to the natural environment, thus endangering future life in the area. The author compares the Native American's philosophy toward nature and environmental preservation with that of many English settlers who arrived in the 1600s. Native Americans relied on the land and respected its resources, while English colonists cleared the land for farming. A thoughtfully done border of tools and artifacts from the periods depicted surrounds the text in *A River Ran Wild,* encouraging discussion and further research about everyday objects used during these eras. A slightly different perspective of human intervention on the environment is communicated in Brown's (1991) *The World that Jack Built.* In the cadence of the familiar children's rhyme "The House that Jack Built," the author begins with an image of a verdant green valley unaffected by progress, gradually shifting to a nearby valley with no inhabitants. Neither people nor animals can live in this lifeless valley due to unchecked pollution from the factory "that Jack built."

Picture books that encourage insights into various cultures include Yee's (1991) *Roses Sing on New Snow,* Dooley's (1991) *Everybody Cooks Rice,* and Heide and Gilliland's (1990) *The Day of Ahmed's Secret.* In *Roses Sing on New Snow,* the hardships faced by Chinese immigrants in early twentieth-century America are depicted. Another important feature of this book is its treatment of the very current domination of females by males in Chinese culture. Maylin does all the cooking in her father's restaurant, but he proudly tells all customers and visitors that his sons are the cooks. When the governor of South China comes to town, Maylin's brothers are asked to cook a favorite dish in the governor's presence, and Maylin eventually receives credit for her contribution to the family business. A little girl searching the community for her brother discovers families everywhere preparing rice in *Everybody Cooks Rice.*

The interesting twist to this tale is that while everybody prepares rice, each family prepares it differently according to their cultural background. In *The Day of Ahmed's Secret,* while Ahmed wanders the busy city of Cairo holding his secret close to his heart, the reader sees the city from Ahmed's perspective and gains a sense of every-day life in another part of the world.

My Great-Aunt Arizona (Houston, 1992) and *Miss Rumphius* (Cooney, 1982) both offer life stories told by the main character's great-niece. Great-Aunt Arizona was born and reared in the Blue Ridge Mountains. She taught in the same one-room school she had attended as a child, and remained on the mountain for the rest of her life—all the while dreaming of faraway places she and generations of schoolchildren might visit. Miss Rumphius, on the other hand, lives on the coast and grows up want-ing to travel as her uncle did. She satisfies her wish to make the world a more beau-tiful place by traveling throughout the countryside, planting lupine wherever she goes. A young girl in *This Quiet Lady* (Zolotow, 1992) tells the story of her mother's life up to the point when she became a mother through a series of family photo-graphs.

Picture books such as Garland's (1993) *The Lotus Seed* and Say's (1993) *Grand-father's Journey* can help young children learn about families from other cultures as children like themselves tell these stories. In *The Lotus Seed,* a grandmother's migra-tion to the United States from Vietnam, and her experiences growing up in Vietnam, are told by her granddaughter. And a young boy narrates the tale of his grandfather's trip from Japan to the United States as an immigrant on a ship, with many details about the grandfather's early life in Japan in *Grandfather's Journey.* These two books also deal with setting and achieving goals, a theme found in Johnston's (1988) *Pages of Music* and Franklin's (1992) *The Old, Old Man and the Very Little Boy.* The story of Paolo, who grew up to become a professional musician and orchestra leader after being inspired by shepherds playing their pipes, is told in *Pages of Music* to illustrate the point that this famous musician kept his goal of returning to his child-hood home to bring music to the shepherds and other people there. In an African vil-lage, a little boy sits and listens intently to an elderly man tell his stories in *The Old, Old Man and the Very Little Boy.* "Were you ever young?" the little boy wonders. "Inside this old, old man lives a very little boy," the elderly man replies. When the little boy grows old, he remembers the old man's reply, and realizes a life goal never to stop feeling young.

Other picture book stories focus on the way a goal can become a driving force in one's life. Values such as hard work, dedication, persistence, and imagination help main characters realize their life-long dreams. Shefelman's (1992) *The Peddler's Dream* tells the story of a young Lebanese man who decides to seek his fortune in the United States and then bring over his bride. Azar endures many difficulties as he tries to make enough money as a traveling peddler to open his own store, but even-tually is successful. Weller's (1992) *Matthew Wheelock's Wall* tells the story of a man who works very hard to clear a stony field and ends up building a strong rock wall from the stones without using any mortar. DePaola's (1988) *The Art Lesson* focuses on a young boy who knows he wants to be an artist before he even starts to school. Even though the formal educational bureaucracy seems to conspire to keep young Tommy from realizing his goal, he goes on to become an artist-illustrator (and the author of *The Art Lesson).* And in Cooney's (1992) *Hattie and the Wild Waves,* a young girl also dreams of becoming an artist. Even though in Hattie's society young women of upper-middle-class status do not aspire to such goals, Hattie overcomes social pressures and focuses instead on her dream.

Chapter 12

Suggested Activities for Using Children's Books

All books are listed alphabetically by author.

Bunting, Eve. (1990). *The Wall.* New York: Clarion Books.

A boy and his father go on a long trip to visit the Vietnam Veterans' Memorial in Washington, D.C., and find the name of the boy's grandfather, who was killed in the Vietnam conflict.

Introducing the Book

Show students a plaque or trophy commemorating something. Ask: What is this? What does it stand for? Help students understand that such small objects are meant to honor or recognize a person for something. Then lead them to consider what a memorial for thousands upon thousands of people might look like.

As the Book Is Being Read

Find Washington, D.C., on a map. Discuss what is meant by "our nation's capital." Ask: Why do you think the memorial wall was built here?

The boy in the story says, "The wall is black and shiny as a mirror. In it I can see Dad and me." Ask students to speculate about what materials were used to make the wall. Look at the illustration of the wall. Ask students to estimate how high or tall they think it is. Ask: Why do you think many visitors leave flags beside the wall after their visit?

After the Book Is Read

Together with students, find Vietnam on a world map or globe. Ask: What continent is Vietnam a part of? The Vietnam military action was considered a "conflict," not a war. Discuss the differences in the terms. Do some research to find out why a war was never declared.

Invite a Vietnam veteran to visit the class (see the Introduction of this book for special hints on Interviewing a Guest). Research the topic beforehand, and have small groups develop several questions related to a subtopic of the research for interviewing the guest.

Practice letter-writing skills as students write letters to patients in a veterans' hospital. Encourage students to be sincere and respectful in their questions and statements in the letters. Another idea is to have students design posters depicting sources of patriotic pride. After they write short essays to accompany the posters, display these in the hallway.

Extend the discussion engendered by *The Wall* by reading or providing the following books on the topic:

Ashabranner, Brent. (1988). *Always to Remember*. New York: Dodd, Mead.

Ezell, Edward Clinton. (1987). *Reflections on the Wall*. Harrisburg: Stackpole Books.

Green, Carl R., & Sanford, William R. (1991). *The Vietnam War Soldier at Con Thien*. Mankato: Capstone Press.

Katiakis, Michael. (1988). *The Vietnam Veterans Memorial*. New York: Crown Publishers.

Flourney, Valerie. (1985). *The Patchwork Quilt*. New York: Dial Books.

The Patchwork Quilt tells the story of how a family works together to create a quilt. Tanya's grandmother collects and stitches together fabric swatches cut from the old clothing of each family member: from Tanya's Halloween costume, Mam's Christmas dress, Papa's workshirt, and brother Jim's corduroy pants. After Grandma falls ill, Tanya and her mother work together on the quilt, and discover that Grandma is not represented by a fabric swatch. Tanya cuts several squares from one of Grandma's old quilts to represent her grandmother. Grandma gets well, finishes the quilt, and dedicates it to Tanya.

Introducing the Book

Bring in a quilt from home to show the students. Let them examine it and touch it. If possible, spread the quilt on the floor and invite students to sit on it as you read the story. Another suggestion is to brainstorm a list of things class members like to do with their grandparents.

As the Book Is Being Read

Provide some old clothes for cutting up and a square paper "pattern." As the story is being read, allow one or two children to cut out squares from the clothing, using the pattern. Pause during the reading and ask: How does it make you feel to cut out these squares? How would you feel if this were your shirt (or dress, or pants)? How do you think Tanya felt when she and her mother cut squares of their clothes? How did Grandma feel? How did each of these people feel when the quilt was finished?

In the story, Tanya's family points out the many different colors represented by squares in the quilt. Have students identify and name the different colors in the quilt you bring to class. Also, give each student a square of paper (roughly the size of a quilt square). Ask them to write a sentence about their own grandmothers and illustrate. Put all squares together with colorful yarn to make a paper patchwork quilt.

After the Book Is Read

Send home a note to parents asking for squares of old clothing that once belonged to their child (send the paper pattern for reference). When students return fabric swatches to school, let them work together to make the top of a quilt. If possible, have someone in the neighborhood finish the quilt from materials the school provides or, if students are old enough, have a community member demonstrate the basics of quilting and let the students do the work.

An alternative to the classroom quilt idea is a "classroom family collage." Ask students to bring swatches from their old clothes (send home a note), but when these are brought to class, have students cut the clothes or swatches into various-sized pieces. Supply each student with a piece of colored construction paper, and have students glue their fabric swatches onto the construction paper in a collage fashion. Label the collages with students' last names, and have the student who created the collage "sign" it (in artistic fashion). Display these on the bulletin board or in the hallway before sending them home. You may wish to ask students to write descriptions of clothing items represented by each swatch, and tell something of its history and the history of its wearer (time lines are good accompanying details for such descriptions). Alternatively, have students imagine they are an article of clothing and write a creative piece personifying the clothing as they use actual historical data.

Another possibility is to use swatches from students' old clothes to create a "family coat of arms" (several teacher resource books contain information about the coat of arms idea). Important items to include on a family coat of arms are the state bird or flower of their birth state, their last name and its meaning (if known), and country or countries ancestors migrated from.

For very young children, a family handprint tree may be a good alternative to a classroom quilt or family coat of arms. Supply varied colors of construction paper for children to take home and to collect the handprints of each family member. (Do a demonstration in class by having children trace their own handprints on the paper or an aide trace their hands, after which they cut these out.) Tell them to get handprints for every family member who lives with them or nearby. Students bring these back to school (show them how to protect the newly cut out handprints by placing them between the pages of a book), and glue them in collage fashion on a larger piece of paper or poster board. Label the collage with the family's last name, as in the preceding collage description, and have children "sign" the collage.

Discuss ways family memories or histories can be preserved other than making a quilt. Make a list of ideas brainstormed on the board or overhead projector. Ask students to find out how their own families preserve or honor their history. Share these orally in class (have students bring examples from home, if parents will permit). This is also a good opportunity to have students create a family tree (see Chapter 1 for a description of how to do this).

Put on a Grandparent's Day celebration. (Many teachers recommend this take place in September, early in the school year, so that grandparents become aware of opportunities for volunteering at the school and contributing their expertise to class projects.) See the description in Chapter 1 of how to conduct a Grandparent's Day.

Garaway, Margaret Kahn. (1989). *Ashkii and His Grandfather.* Tucson: Treasure Chest Publications.

This is a story about a little Native American boy who, when he turned age 6, went sheepherding with his grandfather. Ashkii learns many traditions and, with the help of his grandfather, kindles his own special talents.

Introducing the Book

Ask: Do you like to spend time with your grandparents? What do you do when you are with your grandparents? What is a tradition? What do you know about Navajo Indians?

As the Book Is Being Read

Talk about family traditions. Invite students to talk about their relationships with their grandparents or other older adults. Do students know whether their grandparents (or other older adult) is especially good at a particular craft or skill? Find out what the children know about sheep and sheepherding. Discuss *heritage* and its importance to families and communities with students.

After the Book Is Read

Take drawing materials outside, and invite students to sketch what they see. Repeat this on the next day, comparing drawings to determine how students, like Ashkii, improve with practice. Invite students to share other artwork or handicrafts with the class. Talk about vacations or family trips, and what students have learned on these trips.

Garza, Carman Lomas. (1990). *Family Pictures: Cuadros de Familia.* San Francisco: Children's Book Press.

Paintings related to the author's childhood, growing up as a Mexican American in Texas, are the focus of this book. Each painting deals with family traditions and customs commemorated by Garza's family. Bilingual text.

Introducing the Book

Talk about family traditions. Brainstorm some common traditions or customs, then speculate on whether how one celebrates an occasion might depend on how one's family has celebrated it. Find out what children know about Mexico, about Texas, about migration.

As the Book Is Being Read

In Readers' Theater fashion, portray individual scenes from the book as you recite the text from memory (or tape it beforehand, or have another person read the text while you portray the scenes). Simulate the cake walk mentioned in the book. Discuss different ways of doing things (such as celebrating birthdays), and prejudices that sometimes arise when families have different outlooks.

After the Book Is Read

Find out more about Mexico and Mexican American families. Invite a parent or other community member to speak on how festivities are celebrated in his or her Mexican American family. Have students investigate their own family's traditions, share these with classmates, and look for similarities as well as differences. Discuss how knowing about the ways other people celebrate special days and occasions enriches our lives and our learning.

Good, Merle. (1993). *Reuben and the Fire.* Intercourse, PA: Good Books.

An Amish boy and his five sisters witness the burning of a neighbor's barn and, in the Amish tradition, participate in the community interaction involved in the barn-raising that follows.

Introducing the Book

Bring an Amish doll and a Barbie (or similar) doll to class. Ask: How are the dolls different? How are they the same? Why do you think one doll has no facial features? What do you know about the Amish? Do you do chores at home? Which chores? Who is responsible for which chores in your home? Do you think these chores are hard work? Ask students to listen for Reuben's chores in the story, and compare them with the chores they do at home.

As the Book Is Being Read

Have some students listen for ways the Amish culture is different from their own, and another group listen for ways the Amish culture is similar to theirs. Ask them to write down the similarities/differences noted.

After the Book Is Read

Discuss items on the similarities/differences lists. Ask: How is your life like Reuben's? How is it different? Talk about Reuben's chores. Ask: How are these different from your chores? How much work is involved in the chores you do, compared to Reuben's chores? Why does Reuben have so much work to do?

Brainstorm all the things "uniquely Amish" that the students can recall from the book. Using this list, have them pretend they live in an Amish community, and write a short story about an everyday event. What kinds of problems would they have? What kinds of holidays do they celebrate? What do they do for fun? Which chores must they complete in an average day?

If possible, bring an Amish girl doll and an Amish boy doll to class. Have small groups of students write a skit or puppet play depicting an exchange between a boy and girl in an Amish community. Use the dolls to share these plays with the class.

Extend research on the Amish with these books:

Ammon, Richard. (1989). *Growing Up Amish.* New York: Athenum.

Bial, Raymond. (1993). *Amish Home.* Boston: Houghton Mifflin.

Faber, Doris. (1991). *The Amish.* New York: Doubleday Books.

Hesse, Karen (1993). *Poppy's Chair.* New York: Macmillan.

A young girl named Leah is learning to cope with her grandfather's death by spending time with her grandmother, trying not to remember painful memories. She learns that remembering the good times she and Poppy shared is not so bad after all.

Introducing the Book

Ask: Have any of you had a grandparent who died? How did it feel? Why do people respond this way to death?

As the Book Is Being Read

Engage students in a discussion about how Leah might be feeling during various parts of the book.

After the Book Is Read

Talk about how Leah learned to deal with the pain and sadness she felt after her grandfather's death. Ask students to recall happy memories they have shared with an elderly person. Invite the school counselor to speak with your students about death and dying.

Howard, Elizabeth Fitzgerald. (1991). *Aunt Flossie's Hats (and Crab Cakes Later).* New York: Clarion Books.

Two sisters, Sarah and Susan, visit their great-great-aunt Flossie on Sunday afternoons. They look forward to trying on Aunt Flossie's large collection of hats, and hearing the special story behind each one before they go out for crab cakes as a treat. Aunt Flossie shares the story of the Baltimore fire.

Introducing the Book

Wear a hat to school. If possible, bring in a collection of hats and have the class vote on their favorite as you model them. Wear the favorite one as the book is read. Have students make hats out of sheets of newspaper (use the familiar paper boat model for this). They can decorate the hats with colored markers and feathers or ribbons made from colored construction paper, and wear them as the book is being read.

As the Book Is Being Read

Have a "hat parade" with students wearing the hats they have made, to recall the parade in the book. Each student must tell the story behind his or her hat (be creative!). Talk about parades and celebrations. Why were the people of Baltimore having a parade on the day of the fire? Locate Baltimore on a national map, then on a state map.

Invite a firefighter to speak to the class, demonstrating fire safety. Ask the firefighter to talk about how fires were fought many years ago as compared to now. Discuss whether any memorable or tragic event that involved the whole town has ever happened locally. What was it? Who remembers it? Invite one of these people in to be interviewed by the class (see information on Interviewing a Guest in the Introduction of this book). Try to find newspaper accounts about the event to help students develop questions to ask during the interview.

After the Book Is Read

Send home a letter inviting parents to send an object to school that recalls a family memory. State in the letter that each child must be prepared to tell the object's story, and how it is important to the family and/or community. Videotape these stories over a period of several days, if possible (see the activity called Family Storytelling Festival for ideas on how to do this).

Igus, Toymoi. (1992). *When I Was Little*. East Orange, NJ: Just Us Books.

Noel goes to the country to visit his Grandpa Will. They go fishing, and Grandpa Will shares stories with Noel of how the local area has changed over time.

Introducing the Book

Ask students to recall a happy time they shared with their grandparent or other older relative. Have them draw a picture illustrating this memory, and share their drawings and stories with the class.

As the Book Is Being Read

Some scenes in the book are in color, and some are in black and white. Ask students to watch for these changes. What does this mean? (Black and white scenes depict Grandpa Will's memories of how the area once looked.) Invite the children to predict whether the next scene will be in color or in black and white before the page is turned. At one point, Grandpa Will talks about sucking on chips of ice to stay cool. If the day is warm, prepare some ice to pass around for children to suck on as this part of the book is being shared.

After the Book Is Read

Invite an older person to speak to the class about how things have changed in the neighborhood or community over the years. Prepare the guest ahead of time to speak about topics similar to Grandpa Will's: landscapes, entertainment, transportation, and so on. This is also an excellent opportunity to host a Grandparent's Day (see Chapter 1).

Study the history of automobiles, especially how they have changed over the years. Look at photos or models of Model A cars, the particular auto Grandpa Will mentions in the book.

Bring an old washboard to class, and an old phonograph similar to the one Grandpa Will recalls, or invite a guest to demonstrate how these things were used. Have students write a story about what life was like for Grandpa Will and his friends, incorporating concepts such as the washboard and phonograph. If possible, allow children to scrub some dishtowels or socks on the washboard with a pan of water underneath.

Train students in the oral history technique (see Oral History the Introduction of this book for details). Then ask them to interview a grandparent (their own, if possible) about life when he or she was a child and how things have changed. Concentrate especially on how things have changed in the local area.

King, Margaree Mitchell. (1993). *Uncle Jed's Barbershop*. New York: Simon & Schuster.

Uncle Jed was Sarah Jean's most favorite relative. He traveled all around the county during the 1930s, cutting people's hair, but when he came to visit, he would always share his dream of opening up a barbershop. Many hardships prevent this, but finally Uncle Jed opens his own shop late in life.

Introducing the Book

Bring in enough shaving cream for all students to experiment with fingerpainting (it cleans up easily from desks or tables). After the clean up, tell children they must listen carefully for the place where Uncle Jed uses shaving cream in the story.

As the Book Is Being Read

Locate the southern states on a U.S. map. Have the students name each state, and notice its location in relation to its nearest neighbors. The author is from Mississippi; have students locate Mississippi on their own desk maps (if available).

Uncle Jed loses his savings and cannot open his long-dreamed-of barbershop. When Earnest Walters comes by the house to tell Uncle Jed this, stop and ask students whether they have ever saved for something and had to spend the money for something else. Has this ever happened to their family? How did they feel? How did family members feel? How do they think Uncle Jed felt?

Some places in the book allude to treatment due to racial differences. Ask students to listen for parts of the book when someone is not being treated right. Who is being mistreated? Who is doing the mistreating? Why? How do they think this feels? Have they ever felt this way?

After the Book Is Read

Uncle Jed lost his savings during the Great Depression. Study the Depression and its affect on local citizens. The effects of segregation on Sarah Jean's family are also discussed in the book. Talk about the history of integration. Discuss how it must feel to be treated differently because of one's color. Play the "Blue Eyes/Brown Eyes" game to help students understand what it means to be treated differently because of one's eye color, and talk about how this experience translates to skin color.

Invite a local barber to class to talk about how barbershops and barbering have changed and stayed the same over the years.

Waddell, Martin. (1990). *My Great Grandpa.* New York: G. P. Putnam's Sons.

This books tells the story of a day in the lives of a little girl and her great-grandpa, whom she pushes in his wheelchair through the small town in which they live. They visit neighbors, the house where great-Grandpa used to live, the grocery store, and the park. Great-Grandpa may be weak in some ways, but he has personal strengths, too. The story captures a day in a very special relationship.

Introducing the Book

Talk with children about their relationships with their grandparents. Discuss the word *great-grandparent,* and the fact that it means "the parent of one's grandparent." Send home a letter asking that students be allowed to bring a photo or snapshot of their grandparents or great-grandparents (if these are living) to school for a bulletin board display. Invite grandparents and great-grandparents to lunch with the students, and to visit the classroom afterward. Have their photos displayed on the bulletin board when they arrive.

As the Book Is Being Read

If grandparents are present during the planned visit, prepare one person beforehand to read the book aloud to the class, and let children sit with their grandparents as the story is read.

Discuss how people's bodies function less well as they age, especially if proper diet and exercise is not observed. Brainstorm ways to prevent some of the difficulties of aging (such as regular exercise, eating healthy food, continuing to exercise one's brain, visiting the doctor regularly, etc.).

After the Book Is Read

Help students make finger puppets depicting extended family members. Work in small groups to write short skits or plays about living in extended families, and present these to the whole class.

Plan a field trip to a residential retirement or nursing home (see hints on Planning Effective Field Trips in Chapter 8). Spend several days preparing for this visit, perhaps with each student making a gift or planning a special treat (such as singing a song with or reading with an elderly person at the home).

To extend this topic, make use of the following related books:

Alexander, Martha G. (1969). *The Story Grandmother Told.* New York: Dial Press.

Baker, Jeannie. (1978). *Grandmother.* London: A. Duetsch.

Brooks, Ron. (1978). *Timothy and Gramps.* New York: Bradbury Press.

Goldman, Susan. (1980). *Grandpa and Me Together.* Chicago: Whitman.

Hutchins, Pat. (1978). *Happy Birthday, Sam.* New York: Greenwillow.

McPhail, David M. (1979). *Grandfather's Cake*. New York: Scribner.

Pomerantz, Charlotte. (1982). *Buffy and Albert*. New York: Greenwillow.

Winter, Jeanette. (1988). *Follow the Drinking Gourd*. New York: Dragonfly Books.

In pre–Civil War South, a sailor named Peg Leg Joe did what he could to help free the slaves. Joe would get a job at a plantation, and at night he would teach the slaves a very special song—a song that could lead them to freedom. Important treatment is given to the topic of the Underground Railroad.

Introducing the Book

Brainstorm types of transportation routes (paths, trails, roads, ocean crossing, airways, railroads, etc.). What do all these things have in common? Tell students *Follow the Drinking Gourd* is about something called the Underground Railroad, which was not a railroad at all but a special way of getting from slavery to freedom. Ask them to listen for hints in the story about the Underground Railroad.

Before students enter the classroom, hang pictures or mobiles representing constellations around the room (or, if available, turn out the lights and use a constellation stencil with a flashlight to simulate stars on the ceiling). Ask: Do any of these constellations look like a drinking gourd? What might that phrase mean? (Discuss connections between *dipper* and *drinking gourd*.) Invite students to listen closely to the story to understand about the Drinking Gourd, and its significance to slaves of the nineteenth century.

Read excerpts from explanatory notes in the book to prepare the children for unfamiliar phrases or words. Display a map of the United States and, during the story, trace the route the slave family travels toward freedom.

As the Book Is Being Read

Discuss Peg Leg Joe's willingness to help people he had never met before. Ask: Why might someone take on a mission such as this one? Have you or a member of your family ever helped anyone you had never met? Why? How did it make you feel?

Point out the illustration of James on the auction block. How would it feel to stand on an auction block, being sold? Talk about James's feelings of humiliation, and the meaning of the word *humiliation*. Ask students to think about how it felt to be a slave about to be sold at auction, and how it felt to be a buyer. How do you think each person felt toward the other? How did it feel to be a slave who could be bought or sold, and made to work for someone without pay? How did it feel to be able to purchase a human being? Do you think this is right? (Explain that many people at the time thought it was not right, and wanted to do something about it. Peg Leg Joe is one.)

If possible, bring a hollowed-out gourd to class and demonstrate how it may have been used to dip and drink water long ago. Compare the shape of the drinking gourd to the constellation in the story.

After the Book Is Read

Research information about the Underground Railroad. Divide the class into groups for this, and assign each group a subtopic: influential people, routes and locations, stories of slaves who escaped, and (if relevant) local people/places involved in the Underground Railroad.

Extend the topic with these books, or use them as research resources:

Ferris, Jeri. (1988). *Go Free or Die*. Minneapolis: Carolrhoda.

Ferris, Jeri. (1988). *Walking to Freedom*. Minneapolis: Carolrhoda.

Hopkinson, Deborah. (1993). *Sweet Clara and the Freedom Quilt*. New York: Knopf.

Ringgold, Faith. (1992). *Aunt Harriet's Underground Railroad in the Sky*. New York: Crown.

Yarbrough, Camile. (1979). *Cornrows*. New York: Coward-McMann.

This story delves into Mike and Shirley's recent family history in the United States, then deals with their family's roots in Africa. Mama and great-Grandmaw start to tell how cornrowed hair figures into their family tree, and stories of family history result.

Introducing the Book

Show examples of braided hairstyles originating in Africa (such as cornrows) through pictures, photos, or real-life models to provide a frame of reference for the title of the book.

As the Book Is Being Read

Note African countries mentioned by Mama and great-Grandmaw in the book, and look for these on the globe or world map as they occur. Shirley nicknamed her little brother "Me Too." Ask students whether they or their brothers or sisters have nicknames. What are they? Who gave them these names? Where do the names come from, or what do they mean?

Mama and great-Grandmaw remember times in Alabama when the family lived there. Have a student give a brief report on the state of Alabama, noting Civil Rights activities that took place there.

After the Book Is Read

Plan a field trip to a museum featuring African or African American exhibits (see section on Planning Effective Field Trips in this book). Plan a "togetherness" luncheon or snack. Invite family members, especially elder ones, to attend and bring a dish representing their family's history. Have visitors bring old family photographs or albums to share. For inspiration, consult or read aloud Thompson's (1989) *Let's Celebrate Kwanzaa: An Activity Book for Young Readers* (Gumbs and Thomas Publishers).

Chapter 13

Annotated Bibliography of Children's Books on Family History

Children's books related to or written about family history provide students with opportunities to learn about and consider the importance of their personal and family histories, and to extend and transfer that learning to the broader context of local, state, national, and world history. Books dealing with family history topics also offer students the chance to discuss, think, and write about such family issues as immigration, cultural traditions, ethnic customs, religious practices, divorce, aging and dying, sibling rivalry, and family conflict while beginning to see how the family as a small social unit reflects the needs and behaviors of society at large.

Family history books serve as motivation for conducting research and collecting stories about one's own family and families represented in the community. Some family history books may be used as models while students write their own "family history books" or create family memory albums. Other types of family history books offer valuable information and documentation about the local community and its history not found elsewhere. A person or organization in your town may have undertaken an oral history project in the recent past and donated the transcribed interviews (usually in bound book form) to the local public library. I found a set of these volumes prepared by the state Home Demonstration Club (affiliated with the Department of Agriculture, as is 4-H Club); housewives from all areas of the state had been interviewed about everyday life, providing a treasure-trove of information and idea sparkers for interview topics.

I have chosen not to classify the books listed in this chapter by grade level. This decision was made after more than two years of reading, sharing, and talking about these books with practicing teachers. They, more than any source I read on the subject, taught me that when writers place limits on teachers' use of children's books by indicating grade levels, many valuable books originally intended for primary levels are not used by teachers at intermediate or middle levels. These books, they believe (and have shown me), can be used effectively with older students to introduce topics, motivate discussion, provide illustrations, and stimulate further research. For this reason, all books are listed in a simple alphabetical format, by author.

Ackerman, Karen. (1988). *Song and Dance Man.* New York: Alfred A. Knopf.
    This Caldecott winner is a fondly told account of visits to grandfather's house, where he and the grandchildren would often sneak off to the attic to recall his days as a former vaudeville performer.
Alexandra, Martha. (1971). *Nobody Asked Me If I Wanted a Baby Sister.* New York: Dial.
    A little boy is jealous of his new baby sister.
Alexander, Martha. (1969). *The Story That Grandmother Told.* New York: Dial.
    Gramma tells Lisa's favorite story about a real cat and a green cat-shaped balloon.
Bahr, Mary. (1992). *The Memory Box.* New York: Albert Whitman.
    Zach describes how he and Gramps fill an old box with special photos, medals, souvenirs, and letters to recall their life together. The story is made especially poignant because Gramps has just been diagnosed with Alzheimer's disease.
Bartone, Elisa. (1993). *Peppe the Lamplighter.* New York: Lothrop, Lee and Shepard Books.
    Peppe, the son of Italian immigrants in turn-of-the-century New York, must find work to support his young brothers and sisters while his father is ill. Ted Lewin's richly colored illustrations emphasize the warmth and drama of this immigrant family story.
Beil, Karen Magnuson. (1992). *Grandma According to Me.* Chicago: Doubleday.
    A young girl shows her grandma how much she loves her by telling what she likes about her.
Borack, Barbara. (1967). *Grandpa.* New York: Harper.
    A pleasant and simple tale about the wholesome fun a little girl has with her grandfather.
Bunting, Eve. (1988). *How Many Days to America?* Boston: Houghton Mifflin.
    Caribbean island refugees brave a dangerous boat trip to come to America, where they have a special reason to celebrate Thanksgiving.
Carlson, N. (1988). *I Like Me!* New York: Viking Press.
    A book to encourage children's positive self-esteem while thinking and learning about themselves and the world around them.
Caseley, Judith. (1986). *My Sister Celia.* New York: Greenwillow Books.
    Emma's grown-up sister Celia always saves her Saturdays just for Emma. Then one day, Celia brings Ben home to meet their parents. Will their relationship still be special? Celia, Ben, their new baby, and Emma start their own family traditions.
Cooney, Barbara. (1982). *Miss Rumphius.* New York: Viking.
    A young girl tells the story of her great-aunt, who dreamed of traveling the world while listening to her uncle's tales of places far away. The great aunt had a goal of her own: to make the world a more beautiful place. As an adult, wherever she traveled, she planted lupine to make this dream come true.
Cooney, Barbara. (1988). *Island Boy.* New York: Viking.
    Four generations of family gather on great-grandfather's island farm.
Cooney, Barbara. (1990). *Hattie and the Wild Waves.* New York: Viking.
    As a girl of a upper-middle-class family in the nineteenth century, Hattie's dream of becoming an artist seems unreachable. Neither her society nor her family support Hattie's goal, but the voices she hears in the ocean waves seem to say that someday she will draw beautiful pictures.
Crews, Donald. (1991). *Bigmama's.* Minneapolis: Greenwillow Books.
    Nothing is ever different at Bigmama's when the family goes there for their summer vacation—nothing except the family stories, that is!
Crofford, Emily. (1981). *A Matter of Pride.* Minneapolis: Carolrhoda Books.
    The story of two very different families and their ways of coping with the Depression is told through the eyes of Meg, the daughter in one of the families. Evocative of daily life in 1930s America.
DePaola, Tomie. (1989). *The Art Lesson.* New York: Putman.
    Tommy knew he wanted to be an artist before he even started school, but a succession of school-related events make it seem as though this will never come to pass. Finally, Tommy does fulfill his goal, becomes a well-known illustrator and author, and publishes a book called *The Art Lesson.*
Drucker, Malka, & Halperin, Michael. (1993). *Jacob's Rescue: A Holocaust Story.* New York: Bantam Books.
    Jacob Gutgeld recalls the terrifying years of his childhood in Poland when a Polish couple hid him and other Jewish children from German Nazis. The book is based on a true story

and is told from the perspective of a father recounting important family history to his young daughter.

Flagg, Fannie. (1987). *Fried Green Tomatoes at the Whistle Stop Cafe.* New York: McGraw Hill.
A novel that spawned a major motion picture (try to rent the videotape after reading the book), this book captured the American public's imagination and renewed our interest in oral history. Use with older students due to disturbing elements involving accidental deaths.

Flournoy, Valerie. (1985). *The Patchwork Quilt.* New York: Dial.
Sometimes family heirlooms have sentimental value, even if their monetary value is very little. Wonderful book to stimulate thinking about family artifacts or heirlooms.

Franklin, Kristine L. (1992). *The Old, Old Man and the Very Little Boy.* New York: Atheneum.
In an African village, a very old man tells the stories of the village to a very young boy. The boy asks, "Were you ever little?" The old man replies, "Inside this old, old man lives a very little boy." Good to suggest the passing of time and continuity of family.

Friedman, Ina R. (1984). *How My Parents Learned to Eat.* Boston: Houghton Mifflin.
A little girl tells the story of her parents' courtship—her father the American sailor, and her mother the Japanese schoolgirl. Each learns something of the other's culture and ways of doing things.

Garland, Sherry. (1993). *The Lotus Seed.* San Diego: Harcourt Brace Jovanovich.
A young girl tells the story of her grandmother's life in Vietnam, where she once plucked a lotus from the Imperial Garden and carried its seed with her for good luck for the rest of her life. Grandmother later migrated to the United States.

Godden, Rumer. (1992). *Great-Grandfather's House.* New York: Greenwillow.
Beloved novelist Godden turns her attention to children's literature in this story about a young girl who reluctantly spends time with her great-grandfather at his home in Japan. Godden tells the story through the eyes of a child; the reader runs the same gamut of emotions as reluctance turns to respect for family heritage.

Griffith, Helen V. (1986). *Georgia Music.* New York: Greenwillow Books.
A little girl always looks forward to visits with her grandfather during the summer months, especially the music they make together. Their visits are strained and unhappy after Grandfather moves into a nursing home, until the little girl finds a way to "bring back the music." Beautifully illustrated with James Stevenson's trademark watercolor/pen and ink drawings.

Helmering, Doris Wild. (1981). *I Have Two Families.* New York: Abingdon Press.
Patty tells how it feels to have "two families" now that mommy and daddy are divorced.

Hoban, Russell. (1960). *Baby Sister for Frances.* New York: Harper.
One of the classic Frances the Badger series.

Hoguet, Susan R. (1983). *I Opened My Grandmother's Trunk.* New York: Dutton Children's Books.
A humorous book about a child who opens her grandmother's trunk and takes out ridiculous and impossibly large objects. Good lead-in for lessons on artifacts and memorabilia.

Hoobler, Dorothy, & Hoobler, Thomas. (1992). *The Trail on Which They Wept: The Story of a Cherokee Girl.* Morristown, NJ: Silver Burdett.
The story of "The Trail of Tears," told through the eyes of a young Cherokee girl whose family must leave their land and join other Cherokees on their long journey to a new home. Sensitively illustrated by S. S. Burrus, who is of Cherokee heritage.

Houston, Gloria. (1992). *My Great-Aunt Arizona.* New York: HarperCollins.
A girl tells the story of her great-aunt, who grew up in the Blue Ridge Mountains, became a teacher at the one-room school she attended as a child, and dreams of faraway places she and the students could someday see.

Howard, Elizabeth Fitzgerald. (1991). *Aunt Flossie's Hats (and Crab Cakes Later).* New York: Clarion Books.
Sarah and Susan always visit Aunt Flossie on Sunday afternoons—it's a family tradition. They especially enjoy trying on Aunt Flossie's old hats, for each one has a story. One Sunday when Aunt Flossie recalls a hat story involving Sarah, Susan, and their parents, the girls join in the storytelling. Particularly useful for motivating first- through sixth-grade students to recall and/or ask their own parents about stories involving family traditions.

Igus, Toymoi. (1992). *When I Was Little.* Orange, NJ: Just Us Books.
Noel loves to go fishing with his Grandpa Will in the summer, and he especially loves it when Grandpa begins to tell what it was like when he was little. Charming look at a special moment between an African-American grandfather and his small grandson; useful for triggering pleasant family memories at any grade level.

Johnson, Angela. (1989). *Tell Me A Story, Mama.* New York: Orchard Books.

A girl and her mother remember the girl's favorite stories passed down through generations of family members.

Johnson, Angela. (1990). *When I Am Old with You.* New York: Orchard Books.

While talking with her grandfather, a little girl imagines the things they will be able to do together when she "grows old."

Johnston, Tony. (1988). *Pages of Music.* New York: Putnam.

The story of Paola, who was inspired to become a musician after hearing the shepherd's pipes on the island where he lived as a child. Paola became a famous musician and orchestra leader, then returned to his island to keep a promise to give a concert for the people there.

Kimmelman, Leslie. (1990). *Me And Nana.* New York: Harper & Row.

Natalie's grandma isn't a "grandma" type person at all. Her visits are always exciting, and she and Natalie can always think of something new to do or try. Excellent book for encouraging very young children to talk about their families.

Knight, M. (1993). *Who Belongs Here? An American Story.* Gardiner, ME: Tilbury House.

A children's history book about immigration to the United States.

Kraus, Joanna Halpert. (1992). *Tall Boy's Journey.* Minneapolis: Carolrhoda.

Kim Moo Yong, a small Korean boy who has been orphaned, is adopted by an American couple whom he has never seen. The reader is treated to vivid, emotional descriptions of Kim Moo Yong's many adjustments in his new homeland, powerfully told by a woman who herself adopted an orphaned Korean child.

Levinson, Riki. (1985). *Watch the Stars Come Out.* New York: E. P. Dutton, 1985.

A story of a grandmother's migration to America on a big boat, told in the family oral tradition.

Levinson, Riki. (1986). *I Go with My Family to Grandma's.* New York: E. P. Dutton.

At the beginning of the twentieth century, five cousins, each with their own families, go to visit grandmother's house in a borough of New York City.

McCloskey, Robert. (1952). *One Morning in Maine.* New York: Viking Press.

Sal loses her first tooth, and her family takes a vacation.

Mayer, Mercer. (1991). *Just Grandpa And Me.* A Golden Book.

Little Critter goes on an adventure with grandpa. (See also *Just Grandma and Me, Just My Little Brother and Me,* and *Just Me and My Mom*).

Miles, Miska. (1971). *Annie and the Old One.* New York: Little, Brown.

A little girl must come to grips with her beloved grandmother's impending death.

Morimoto, Junko. (1992). *My Hiroshima.* New York: Viking Press.

The author's happy childhood in Hiroshima was abruptly and tragically halted on August 6, 1945, when her world was destroyed by an atomic bomb explosion.

Morris, Ann. (1990). *Loving.* New York: Lothrop, Lee & Shepard.

Family members in many countries and cultures around the world are depicted doing things that show love and concern for one another.

O'Connor, Karen. (1992). *Dan Thuy's New Life in America.* Minneapolis: Lerner Publications.

Photo essay of 13-year-old Dan Thuy Huynh's family's migration to the United States from Vietnam. Wonderful example of a culminative product based on an oral history interview.

Paek, Min. (1988). *Aekyung's Dream.* San Francisco: Children's Book Press.

A recent Korean immigrant learns about her new, baffling culture.

Parish, Peggy. (1988). *Amelia Bedelia's Family Album.* Minneapolis: Greenwillow Books.

Part of the classic Amelia Bedelia series; Amelia shows off her family album and tells about each family member portrayed in her usually haphazardly humorous fashion.

Peck, Robert Newton. (1974). *Soup.* New York: Knopf.

Join Soup and friends as they make toys from "found" objects and play games to pass the time in 1930s Depression-era America.

Pellegrini, Nina. (1991). *Families Are Different.* New York: Holiday House.

An adopted Korean girl discovers that she is not the only one who is "different" when she learns about her classmates' different family types.

Polacco, Patricia. (1991). *Some Birthday!* New York: Simon & Schuster.

Instead of the traditional cake and party, Daddy suggests the family celebrate little Patricia's birthday by going to Clay Pit Bottoms—home of the notorious Clay Pit Bottoms monster! Use to help children remember special or unusual celebrations from their own family history.

Root, Phyllis, & Marron, Carol A. (1983). *Gretchen's Grandma.* Chicago: Raintree Publishers.

When her grandmother comes from Germany for a visit, Gretchen discovers they can understand each other despite their language differences.

Rylant, Cynthia. (1985). *The Relatives Came.* New York: Bradbury Press.
One summer a large group of relatives comes to visit, causing happy chaos.

Say, Allen. (1993). *Grandfather's Journey.* Boston: Houghton Mifflin.
A boy tells the story of his grandfather's life in Japan and later journey on a ship across the ocean to make his home in the United States.

Schefelman, Janice Jordan. (1992). *A Peddler's Dream.* Boston: Houghton Mifflin.
A young Lebanese man comes to the United States to realize his dream of owning his own store, and undergoes many obstacles and hardships as a traveling peddler while earning his living. He sends for his bride to join him, and eventually sees his dream come true.

Smith, Robert Kimmel. (1984). *The War with Grandpa.* New York: Dell.
Peter, a fifth-grader, is writing a "true story" for his English class. He decides to write about the time when his depressed grandfather moved in with his family and uses Peter's room as his own. Peter has waited a long time to get a room of his own, and even though he loves Grandpa, gets very unhappy about the new living arrangements. The battles ensue.

Stanek, Muriel. (1989). *I Speak English for My Mom.* Chicago: Addison Wesley.
In the Mexican American Gomez family, daughter Lupe must translate for her mother (who speaks only Spanish) until Mom decides to learn English a get a better job.

Tews, Susan. (1993). *Nettie's Gift.* New York: Clarion Books.
Going to Grandma Nettie's house is one of Sarah's favorite things to do. She and Grandma Nettie love to walk in the nearby woods, when her grandmother tells her what it was like when she was growing up. Soft, luminous illustrations by Elizabeth Sayles draw the reader into the story in a dreamy fashion.

Toll, Nelly S. (1993). *Behind the Secret Window.* New York: Dial Books.
Subtitled "A Memoir of a Hidden Childhood during World War Two," this riveting account reminiscent of Anne Frank's Diary plunges older children into everyday events of family life under extreme circumstances. Illustrated with 29 of the author's own paintings.

Uchida, Yoshiko. (1978). *Journey Home.* New York: Aladdin Books.
After being released from a U.S. detention camp, a Japanese American family returns to California to find a new home and try to build a new life.

Undry, Janice. (1970). *Mary Jo's Grandmother.* New York: Whitman.
When Grandma is injured in a fall, Mary Jo walks two miles to get help during her Christmas visit.

van Leeuwen, Jean. (1992). *Going West.* New York: Dial, 1992.
From their home in the East to the new land in the West, we follow the adventures and hardships of a family's cross-country trip by prairie schooner.

Vigna, Judith. (1983). *Daddy's New Baby.* New York: Whitman.
A little girl is jealous of her new half-sister until she gets to help take care of her.

Vigna, Judith. (1984). *Grandma without Me.* New York: Whitman.
Family tradition is shattered when a little boy's parents divorce and they no longer go to Grandma's for Thanksgiving dinner. Grandma helps keep them close by starting a family scrapbook.

Viorst, Judith. (1972). *Alexander and the Terrible, Horrible, No Good, Very Bad Day.* New York: Atheneum.
From the time Alexander gets up in morning until he goes to bed that night, everything goes wrong with his day.

Walh, Jan. (1972). *Grandma Told Me.* New York: Little, Brown.
Grandma's imagination takes her and her small grandson on an exciting adventure.

Weller, Frances Ward. (1992). *Matthew Wheelock's Wall.* New York: Macmillan.
Jerusha Wheelock's great-great-grandpa built a stone wall around his fields more than 100 years ago. Its enduring quality, and the stories that surround it, provide a sense of continuity for his family even now.

Williams, Vera B. (1982). *A Chair for My Mother.* Minneapolis: Greenwillow Books.
After all their furniture is lost in a fire, a little girl, her waitress mother, and her grandmother save their pennies to buy a comfortable armchair so her mother can rest her feet at the end of the day.

Yolen, Jane. (1988). *Devil's Arithmetic.* New York: Viking Press.
Hannah resents her Jewish heritage until time travel takes her to a small Jewish village in Poland during the Nazi occupation.

Ziefert, Harriet. (1986). *A New Coat for Anna.* New York: Knopf.

In post–World War II Europe, Anna's mother barters with a sheep farmer, a spinner, a weaver, and a tailor to get a new coat for her daughter.

Zolotow, Charlotte. (1971). *A Father Like That.* New York: Harper.

After his parents separate, a little boy wishes for a father.

Zolotow, Charlotte. (1972). *William's Doll.* New York: Harper.

Should a little boy have a doll? William thinks so. Explore this and similar family dilemmas with your students.

Zolotow, Charlotte. (1992). *This Quiet Lady.* New York: Greenwillow.

A young girl looks at a collection of family photographs and tells the story of her mother's life, up until the time she became a mother.

Chapter 14

Annotated Bibliography of Children's Books on Local and Community History

Reading, talking about, writing about, and expanding upon books that deal with topics related to communities and community issues helps students make sense of their world. Learning that neighborhoods and communities have many characteristics in common enables children to broaden their understanding of interdependence, cultural and ethnic diversity, ecology, human/geographic interactions, economic development, and the roles of institutions. They learn about the passage of time, and the connections between events and people's perceptions of time passing. They develop deeper understandings of humans' responsibility toward each other and their environment.

Check with your local public library to find out whether books about local history are available. Those books written by local authors are especially valuable—you may be able to arrange for the authors or their descendants to speak to your class. Books containing photographs of your town or community "as it was then" are helpful for comparing and contrasting "then" and "now." In addition, consider the following books (listed alphabetically by author):

Adoff, Arnold. (1970). *Malcolm X*. New York: HarperCollins.
   A chronicle of the life of Malcolm X, from his troubled younger years to his emergence as a respected leader in African American issues.
Allen, Thomas B. (1989). *On Granddaddy's Farm*. New York: Knopf.
   Nostalgic account of the author's summers on a farm in Tennessee.
Ancona, George. (1989). *The American Family Farm*. San Diego: Harcourt Brace Jovanovich.
   Photo essay depicting the everyday lives of three farming families in different parts of the United States.
Baylor, Byrd. (1982). *The Best Town in the World*. New York: Charles Scribner's Sons.
   A father tells his young son all about the town where he grew up.
Belton, Sandra. (1993). *From Miss Ida's Porch*. New York: Four Winds Press.

As the day draws to a close in an African American community, young and old alike gather on Miss Ida's front porch to hear the stories of times gone by. What was it like to live here 50 years ago? How have things changed—both in the neighborhood and all around?

Blos, Joan W. (1987). *Old Henry*. New York: William Morrow.

Old Henry, a senior citizen, moves into a dilapidated house in an upscale neighborhood, and likes the house just the way it is. This thought-provoking story deals with the dignity of individuals within a community setting.

Brown, R. (1991). *The World That Jack Built*. New York: Dutton.

A lovely green valley is contrasted with its neighboring valley, uninhabited by people or animals due to unending pollution caused by "the factory that Jack built." The text is patterned after the children's rhyme "The House That Jack Built"; useful for considering changes in the local environment over time.

Bunting, Eve. (1990). *The Wall*. New York: Clarion Books.

A boy and his father visit the Vietnam Veterans' Memorial in Washington, D.C. Good introduction to researching local residents' involvement in military action.

Byers, Betsy. (1991). *The Seven Treasure Hunts*. New York: HarperCollins.

Good resource for motivating map making.

Cauley, Lorinda B. (1984). *The Town Mouse and the Country Mouse*. New York: G. P. Putnam's Sons.

A retelling of the classic children's story.

Cherry, Lynne. (1992). *A River Ran Wild: An Environmental History*. San Diego: Gulliver Green/Harcourt Brace Jovanovich.

A depiction of the changes in a New England river valley from 1400 to 1990, this book deals with how human philosophies of land treatment and interdependence influence land use. Excellent examples of Native American versus English colonist philosophies.

Cleary, Beverly. (1988). *Ramona and Her Father*. Santa Barbara, CA: Cornerstone Books (large print).

An older neighbor teaches Ramona and Beezus "how things used to be."

Cohen, Carol Lee. (1988). *Mud Pony*. Chicago: Scholastic.

A Native American story of how a poor boy becomes a powerful leader. Mother Earth turns the boy's mud pony into a real one, but when the pony turns back into mud, he must find strength within himself rather than rely on others.

Dorros, Arthur. (1991). *Abuela*. New York: E. P. Dutton.

A young girl's fantasy of flying over New York City with her grandmother, looking at the many city sites below, can serve as an introduction to aerial photographs of the local area for young children.

Dorros, Arthur. (1991). *Follow the Water from Brook to Ocean*. New York: HarperCollins.

Explanation of how water flows from small springs or brooks to rivers, over waterfalls, and eventually into the ocean.

Dragonwagon, Crescent. (1990). *Home Place*. New York: Macmillan.

While hiking in the woods, a family finds traces of a long-ago existence and begins to wonder about the family who lived there.

Ellis, Sarah. (1989). *Next-Door Neighbors*. New York: Macmillan.

Twelve-year-old Peggy moves to Canada, where she quickly learns to appreciate how neighbors in a community depend on each other.

Fleming, Virginia. (1993). *Be Good to Eddie Lee*. New York: Philomel Books.

Christy thinks Eddie Lee, a boy with Down syndrome, is just a pest until he shares his special nature discoveries with her on a trip to the woods.

Freeman, Dorothy, & Macmillan, Dianne. (1989). *My Best Friend Mee-yung Kim*. Englewood Cliffs, NJ: Nulian Messner.

A young Korean immigrant teaches her teacher and classmates about her culture, and learns from them as well.

Fox, Paula. (1991). *Monkey Island*. New York: Bantam Doubleday Dell.

An 11-year-old New Yorker is abandoned by his mother and must learn to fend for himself in a hostile city. He is befriended by two homeless elderly men, who help him learn to cope. May inspire research on plight of the homeless in the local area.

Geras, Adile. (1990). *My Grandmother's Stories: A Collection of Jewish Folk Tales*. New York: Knopf.

This collection celebrates the values and experiences of Jewish community members, while introducing or expanding children's knowledge about and understanding of a religious/ethnic group. "Saving the Pennies," for example, teaches the importance of cooperation and responsibility.

Good, Merle. (1993). *Reuben and the Fire*. Intercourse, PA: Good Books.

Details the excitement and fellowship involved in an Amish barnraising.

Gray, Nigel. (1989). *Country Far Away*. New York: Franklin Watts.

The similarities between two boys' lives (one in a rural African village, the other in a modern western hemisphere setting) are revealed through parallel illustrations.

Greenfield, Eloise, & Little, Lessie J. (1989). *Childtimes*. New York: HarperCollins.

Three generations of African American women reminisce about their childhoods.

Hale, Lucretia. (1989). *The Lady Who Put Salt in Her Coffee*. New York: Harcourt Brace Jovanovich.

Originally published in 1867 as part of the "Peterkin Papers" (humorous chronicle of Victorian family life and children's classic), this adaptation by Amy Schwartz charmingly tells the legend of Mrs. Peterkin's struggle to get the "salty" out of her coffee.

Heide, Florence P., & Gilliland, Judith H. (1990). *The Day of Ahmed's Secret*. New York: Lothrop, Lee, & Shepard.

As Ahmed hurries through the bustling city of Cairo, hugging his secret close to his heart, the reader is treated to his perspective of the town. Good lead-in to studying and describing the local community or city from the perspective of one who lives there.

Heide, Florence P., & Gilliland, Judith. (1992). *Sami and the Time of Troubles*. Boston: Houghton Mifflin.

Story of a young boy's optimism and family survival set in war-torn Lebanon.

Hendershot, Judith. (1987). *In Coal Country*. New York: Knopf.

Set in Ohio in the 1930s, a child describes what it is like to grow up in a coal-mining community.

Hiscock, Bruce. (1991). *The Big Tree*. New York: Aladdin Books.

The story of the life of a tree from 1775 to the present, telling about changes in the environment and neighborhood over the years. Excellent way to introduce the topic of "how our community's geography has changed over time."

Hopkinson, Deborah. (1993). *Sweet Clara and the Freedom Quilt*. New York: Knopf.

Clara, a young slave girl growing up on a southern plantation, makes a quilt map to lead local slaves on their Underground Railroad journey. The story is based on African American oral tradition.

Keegan, Marcia. (1991). *Pueblo Boy: Growing Up in Two Worlds*. New York: E. P. Dutton.

A preadolescent Native American boy lives in a very modern world while learning about his ancient heritage.

Lasky, Kathryn. (1983). *Sugaring Time*. New York: Macmillan.

Photo essay about a maple sugar farm in Vermont.

Leedy, Loreen. (1991). *The Great Trash Bash*. New York: Holiday House.

In the town of Beaston, the animals work together to find better ways of trash control.

Levine, Ellen. (1989). *I Hate English*. New York: Scholastic.

An immigrant from Hong Kong learns English with assistance from members of her new community.

Lomas Garza, Carmen. (1990). *Family Pictures (Cuadros de Familia)*. San Francisco: Children's Book Press.

In bilingual text with lovely illustrations, the author describes her childhood growing up in a Hispanic community in southwestern United States.

Lord, Bette Bao. (1984). *In the Year of the Boar and Jackie Robinson*. New York: HarperCollins.

A Chinese girl comes to Brooklyn in 1947, and begins to like her new home when she discovers baseball.

Lyon, George Ella. (1990). *Come a Tide*. New York: Orchard Books.

Members of a community help one another survive a spring flood.

MacLachlan, Patricia. (1991). *Three Names*. Charlotte Zolotow Book.

Great-grandfather reminisces about his years as a student in a one-room schoolhouse on the prairie. Great introduction to the study of old country schools in the local area.

Mason, Miriam E. (1991). *Hominy and His Blunt-Nosed Arrow*. New York: Macmillian.

Native American story that accurately portrays the lives of Miami Woodland Indians in the midwest. Look for similar books approved for instructional use by Native American tribes in your local area.

McDonald, Megan. (1991). *The Potato Man*. New York: Orchard Press.

> On the couch with his two attentive grandchildren, Grandpa recalls the Potato Man. "Abba-no-potata-man" the one-eyed Potato Man used to chant as he came down the street in his horse-drawn wagon. "Tell us another one!" insist the children. (See *The Great Pumpkin Switch* also by McDonald.)

McDonald, Megan. (1992). *The Great Pumpkin Switch*. New York: Orchard Press.

> Grandpa tells his grandchildren how he once broke his sister's prize pumpkin, and how the Potato Man sold him an even bigger pumpkin to replace it.

McGovern, Ann. (1965). *"Wanted Dead or Alive": The True Story of Harriet Tubman*. New York: R. R. Bowker.

> Detail's Harriet Tubman's fight for freedom, and her work with the Underground Railroad (Permabound editions still available).

Mitchell, Margaree King. (1993). *Uncle Jed's Barbershop*. New York: Simon & Schuster Books for Young Readers.

> Sensitive description of the treatment of African Americans living in a southern town about the time of the Great Depression. Deals with segregation, sharecropping, African American culture.

Mochizuki, Ken. (1992). *Baseball Saved Us*. New York: Lee & Low Books.

> Shorty, a Japanese American, describes his family's life in a Japanese internment camp during World War II. The people in the camp learned that their pulling together as a community was vital to the survival of their sanity and safety.

Polacco, Patricia. (1990). *Just Plain Fancy*. New York: Bantam Books.

> Naomi and her family live in an Amish community, where Naomi's story of an abandoned egg found near the road is woven throughout with examples of "the plain life" of traditional Amish. Especially good for use in communities with Amish populations.

Polacco, Patricia. (1992). *Mrs. Katz and Tush*. New York: Dell.

> This story of a neighborhood represents the ethnic diversity present in daily lives. Larnel, an African American boy, learns of Poland and stories of the Jewish culture as he helps Mrs. Katz with her kitten Tush.

Provensen, Martin, & Provensen, Alice. (1984). *Town and Country*. New York: Crown Publishers.

> Everyday life in the big city and everyday life on the farm are described and accompanied by beautiful illustrations.

Ringgold, Faith. (1992). *Aunt Harriet's Underground Railroad in the Sky*. New York: Crown Publishers.

> In this dramatic story of fact and fantasy, Cassie and her brother fly among the stars and meet Harriet Tubman, who shows them how their ancestors survived slavery and escaped through the Underground Railroad. Good to use to explore the community's or region's involvement in Underground Railroad activities.

Rylant, Cynthia. (1982). *When I Was Young in the Mountains*. New York: Dutton.

> Tells the story of a woman's childhood spent in the Appalachian Mountains. Use when exploring childhood days with local citizens, change over time in the local community, or family stories.

Schwartz, David M. (1991). *Supergrandpa*. New York: Lothrop, Lee & Shepard.

> Gustav Hakansson defied tradition and nonbelievers when he rode his bicycle over 1,000 miles in the 1951 Sverige-Loppet, the longest bicycle race in the history of Sweden. The fact that he was 66 years old at the time just seemed irrelevant. This local legend is still very much alive in the hearts and minds of the people of Sweden. Great book to introduce students of any age to the idea of local legends.

Spier, Peter. (1988). *People*. Chicago: Doubleday.

> Photographs and illustrations of people from all over the world, with descriptions of everyday life practices and belief systems.

Terkel, Studs. (1986). *Hard Times: An Oral History of the Great Depression*. New York: Pantheon Books.

> Reknown oral historian Studs Terkel takes us into the hearts and minds of survivors of the Depression as they recall their own experiences and reflect on modern interpretations of this era in American history. Especially good for older audiences.

Towle, W. (1993). *The Real McCoy: The Life of an African-American Inventor*. New York: Scholastic.

Biography of Elijah McCoy, born to runaway slaves in Canada and educated in Scotland during the American Civil War, but unable to find a job befitting his education because of his racial background. McCoy eventually becomes a famous inventor, having designed the automatic oil cup for locomotives which earned the name "the real McCoy" from train workers.

Van Allsburg, Chris. (1990). *Just A Dream*. New York: Houghton Mifflin.

In this environmental fantasy, a young boy dreams of a troubled earth. He awakens with a different attitude about conserving the environment.

Yee, P. (1991). *Roses Sing on New Snow*. New York: Macmillan.

Maylin's family migrates from China to America in the early twentieth century and opens a family-operated restaurant. Details mistreatment of early Chinese in the United States, as well as mistreatment of women and girls by men in Chinese culture.

Chapter 15

Children's Books and Cooperative Learning

Cooperative group work, when properly used, builds interpersonal bonds and engenders a sense of interdependency in the classroom. When cooperative groups are functioning well, the classroom becomes a community in a very real sense, and students' understanding of themselves as a part of a living community is enhanced. Many of the books listed in Part III lend themselves to cooperative group activities. The suggestions offered here are intended only as an instructional hors d'oeuvre—to whet your appetite for constructing your own book-related cooperative learning experiences. All books are listed alphabetically by author.

Fleischman, Sid. (1992). *Jim Ugly.* New York: Dell.
> In the 1800s, a father, his adolescent son, and their dog "Jim Ugly" get involved in mysterious circumstances in the Old West. Good complement to *Sarah Plain and Tall.*

Divide the class into groups of 3 or 4 people. The objective is to produce a newspaper using a page layout computer program. The newspaper should include:

2 advertisements

3 articles

1 weather summary

Price of the newspaper

Title of the newspaper

Names of reporters

To prepare students to write the articles, have them interview students who pose as characters from the book. (Ideas include "Tell our readers what it is like to be an actor"; "Tell our readers the father's version of the diamond theft"; or "Tell our readers about your heroic dog Jim Ugly".) To prepare for the weather summary, learn about the geography of the area, seasonal changes in arid regions, and common weather patterns. To prepare for the advertisements, have students research products that would have been popular in the 1800s.

Harness, Cheryl (1992). *Three Young Pilgrims*. New York: Macmillan.
Experience the journey on the Mayflower to America, and the early days in the new colony, through the eyes of three young pilgrims.

After reading the book, divide the class into five groups. One group is in charge of food, one of living quarters, one of traveling arrangements, one of exploration, and one of potential hardships. Make assignments to fit each group:

◼ *Food Group:* Determine the amount of space available on the *Mayflower*, the type of storage available, what kinds of food the Pilgrims would want to take with them, and how this food will be preserved and prepared during the trip.

◼ *Living Quarters Group:* Determine the amount of space available on the *Mayflower* for living quarters, how many people will travel on which ships, which families will travel together and which apart (and how decisions will be made about who travels where), storage space for supplies needed when they reach their destination, and what amount of supplies each family and/or person will be allowed to take with them.

◼ *Traveling Arrangements Group:* Determine the chosen route to the New World, where ships will land, and the time needed to make the journey.

◼ *Exploration Group:* Explore the new land and determine where to build; set up temporary living quarters while homes are being built; return to the ships and bring their family and friends to the temporary quarters.

◼ *Hardships Group:* Investigate the hardships the Pilgrims faced and make a list of these. Include items dealing with food, living space, sailing/travel, and dangers in the new colony.

Have groups keep records or journals of their findings, and present them to the class as a whole once research is completed.

Lowery, Lois. (1993). *The Giver*. New York: Houghton Mifflin.
The Giver brings the future to the present—a society where all are equal and life is perfect. A boy questions this "perfect" world.

Lead the class in a discussion comparing and contrasting their community with the one presented in the book. Divide the class into groups of 4 or 5 students. Each group must designate a recorder (takes notes), a respecter (makes certain all have a chance to contribute), and a materials gatherer (collects and returns needed supplies). Make the following assignments, to be completed within groups:

I. Create a community where people can live and work and go to school. Develop and write the bylaws for your community.

Determine:

Family Units: Comprised of which members? Determined by natural selection, traditional methods, or arranged? If arranged, by whom? Function of the family unit? Roles of various members in unit? Who determines role(s)?

Occupations: Diversity? Does everyone work outside the home? What occupations are available? Selection by free choice, or assigned? If assigned, by whom?

Location: Where is the community located? What about the location determined settlement in the past? What about the location is important in the present? What will be important in the future? What are the other physical characteristics of the community? Weather? Terrain? Name?

Education: Schools? If there are no schools, what do children do? How do they learn? If schools exist, what ages are schooled? Who determined this? Who are the teachers? How are they selected? What are teachers like? How is graduation determined? What subjects are taught? Which extracurricular activities are permitted?

Governing Body: Democratic, monarchy, or committee governed? How are leaders selected? What is the judicial system like? What happens when people break the laws? Who decides the consequences?

II. Make a model of the community, and draw a map illustrating it. Label the major areas in the community. Give a title to the model, and list the designers on your label.

Materials:

Clay	Glue	sticks/twigs
Rocks	Plaster	grass/sand/dirt/leaves
Rope/wire	Fabric	Wood
Craft Sticks	Paint	Cardboard Boxes

III. Write a story about your community on the computer. Include illustrations and the map of the community. Identify:

Main character	Plot
Supporting characters	Resolution
Conflict	Ending
Theme of story	

IV. Share your community with the class. Show the model while reading, acting, singing, or storytelling about your community.

Ray, Delia (1990). *A Nation Torn.* Lodester Books.
> Introduces the concept of Underground Railroad, and deals with the important role Harriet Tubman played. In 19 trips south to free slaves, Tubman was never captured and never lost a slave entrusted to her care.

Have students design a route that the Underground Railroad could use while trying to free someone from slavery. The route can start at your school and can run two to three miles north. Choose a stopping point. Remember—slave catchers are everywhere! How will you get the people entrusted to your care safely through the three miles to freedom? How will you plan stops to rest and eat? Work as a group to create a map that shows your route and plans.

Spinelli, J. (1990). *Maniac Magee.* Little, Brown.
> This story resembles a parable in which an orphaned, homeless boy encounters racism and battles ignorance.

After reading Chapters 19 and 20, in which Maniac Magee challenges "the Knot," talk about problem solving and its importance in our everyday lives. In groups, ask students to consider this problem (from *Problem Parade* by Dale Seymour):

> There are four football players standing in a line. In the order they are standing, they are wearing jerseys numbered 32, 11, 25, and 88. The players' names (in alphabetical order) are: Abe, Bob, Cal, and Dom. Based on the following clues, can you determine which player wears which jersey?
> 1. Abe wears a jersey # divisible by 8.
> 2. Bob wears an odd # jersey.
> 3. Cal likes rock music.
> 4. Dom is standing next to Abe.
> 5. Abe is shorter than Dom.
> 6. Bob is taller than Dom.
> 7. Cal is shorter than anyone.
> (answer: #32—Cal; #11—Bob; #25—Dom; #88—Abe)

Let each group relate how they arrived at their answers. Then have children design their own problems for classmates to solve.

Taylor, Mildred D. (1990). *Mississippi Bridge.* New York: Bantam Skyland Books.
> This book focuses on a racially motivated tragedy that happened in Mississippi in the 1930s, with segregation as the main topic.

Before reading the book, divide the class into two groups, based on some feature that is beyond students' control. For example, those with last names beginning with

A to L; those with birthdays in January, March, July, September, and November; those wearing blue today; and so on. One group is to be discriminated against, while the other group is allowed privileges.

Have the group being discriminated against wear armbands or other physical symbol so that it is easy to tell which group an individual student falls into. "Discriminate" on the following criteria, or make up your own:

Sit in the back of the room.

Line up for activities last.

Use the restroom farthest away from the classroom.

Use the least convenient drinking fountain.

Sit separately from the rest of the class and the teacher at lunch.

After lunch (or at the midpoint of the day), switch the treatment. The group who was "favored" during the first half of the day becomes the "discriminated against" group, and vice versa.

Now read the book. Break the two original groups into smaller (three or four people) groups. Have them discuss how they felt being treated as they were; how they felt when the roles were reversed. Ask groups of students to list areas where discrimination is seen or felt today and what they can do to eliminate it. Close with a large group discussion.

(Due to the sensitive nature of this activity, it may be wise to let parents and administrators know what is going to happen beforehand, and what objectives you hope to accomplish.)

Appendix: Resources, Organizations, and Contacts

Contact for information about membership and/or curriculum resources.

Professional Organizations

American Bar Association
Youth Education Publications
ABA Division for Public Education
541 North Fairbanks Court
Chicago, IL 60611-3314
http://scratch.abanet.org/publiced/home.html

Center for Civic Education
5146 Douglas Fir Road
Calabasas, CA 91302-1467
http://www.civiced.org

Educators for Social Responsibility
23 Garden Street
Cambridge, MA 02138
http://www.benjerry.cm/esr/about-esr.html

ERIC Clearinghouse for Social Studies/Social Science Education
Indiana University
2805 East Tenth Street, Suite 120
Bloomington, IN 47408-2698
http://www.indiana.edu/~ssdc/eric_chess.html

National Center for History in the Schools
UCLA, Dept. of History
405 Hilgard Avenue
Los Angeles, CA 90095-1473
http:www.sscnet.ucla.edu/nchs

National Council on Economic Education
1140 Avenue of the Americas
New York, NY 10036-5803
http://www.ncee.org

National Council for Geographic Education
Indiana University of Pennsylvania
16A Leonard Hall
Indiana, PA 15705
http://www.ncge.org

National Council for History Education
26915 Westwood Road, Suite B-2
Westlake, OH 44145-4656
http://www.history.org/nche

National Council for the Social Studies
3501 Newark Street, N.W.
Washington, DC 20016-3100
http://www.ncss.org/online

National Geographic Society
1145 17th Street, N.W.
Washington,DC 20036-4688
http://www.nationalgeographic.com/main.html

Social Studies Educational Consortium
P.O. Box 21270
Boulder, CO 80308-4270

Family History and Genealogy Web Sites

My Geneology and Family History (Hatfield, Alley, & Graham)
http://www.itoday.com/david/chat.html

Puerto Rican / Hispanic Genealogical Society
http://linkdirect.com/hispsoc/rguest.htm

Geneaology (Genealogists, Family History, Family Roots, Family Trees, Geneology, Geneologists)
http://info.rutgers.edu/Directories/Outside_Rolodex/Card
card_id_77 307.shtml

Karen's Family History
http://www.cvc.net/cvcmem/Karfree/family.html

Researching Your Irish Family History
http://www-medlib.med.utah.edu/navigator/projects/winter97/klind sey.htm

Digging Up Bones—Appalachian Geneology
http://www.netscope.net/~gkcruey/melung.htm

Sources for Old-Time Radio Recordings

CATALOGS

A-1 Record Finders
P.O. Box 10518
Glendale, CA 91209-3518
http://www.aonerecordfinders.com

Rare Records
P.O. Box 10518
Glendale, CA 91209-3518

RTS Music Gazette
3700 S. Plaza Drive, Bldg. F, Ste. 211
Santa Ana, CA 92704-7434

Nostalgia Lane
33 Portman Road
New Rochelle, NY 10801-2104

INFORMATION

Radio Dial
Radio Historical Society of America
P.O. Box 190
Cloquet, MN 55720-0190

Indiana Recording Club
1729 E. 77th Street
Indianapolis, IN 46240-2820

PERIODICALS

Good Old Days
Nostalgia
Liberty

BOOKS

Buxton, Frank, & Owen, Bill. (1966). *Radio's Golden Age: The Programs and the Personalities.* New York: Easton Valley Press.
Buxton, Frank, & Owen, Bill. (1972). *The Big Broadcast 1920–1950.* New York: The Viking Press.
Dunning, John. (1976). *Tune in Yesterday: The Ultimate Encyclopedia of Old-time Radio 1925–1976.* Englewood Cliffs, NJ: Prentice Hall.
Hackett, Walter (1973). *Radio Plays for Young People.* Boston: Plays, Inc.
Pitts, Michael. (1976). *Radio Soundtracks: A Reference Guide.* Lanham, MD: Scarecrow Press.
Poteet, G. Howard. (1975). *Published Radio, Television, and Film Scripts: A Bibliography.* New York: Whitson Publishing.
Terrace, Vincent. (1981). *Radio's Golden Years: The Encyclopedia of Radio Programs 1930–1960.* San Diego: A. S. Barnes.
Wylie, Max. (1939). *Best Broadcasts of 1930–39.* New York: Whittlesey House (scripts and commentary).

LIBRARIES AND COLLECTIONS

Broadcast Pioneers Library
1771 N. Street, NW
Washington, DC 20036
202/223-0088
    A history of broadcasting research library containing tapes, scripts, periodicals, books, and photographs.

Chicago Museum of Broadcasting
800 South Wells Street
Chicago, IL 60607-4529
312/987-1516
    Radio archives includes tapes from 1920 to 1960; patrons may listen to recordings or rerecordings.

Foothill Electronic Museum
Foothill College
12345 El Monte Road
Los Altos, CA 94022
415/960-4600
    Museum with exhibits emphasizing the early years of radio.

Friends of Old Time Radio
c/o Jay Hickerson
P.O. Box 4321
Hamden, CT 06514-0321
203/248-1887
http://old-time.com/hickers.html
    An informal organization of radio buffs.

Museum of Broadcasting
One East 53rd Street
New York, NY 10023
212/752-4699
    The nation's principal repository of modern audiovisual history, containing some 10,000 radio broadcasts.

Society to Preserve and Encourage Radio Drama, Variety, and Comedy (SPERDVAC)
P.O. Box 1587
Hollywood, CA 90078-1587
213/947-9800
    This organization has assembled one of the best-maintained radio archives in the world. Tapes are available on loan to members (annual membership fee).

Women's History Resources

Ash, M. (1989). *The Story of the Women's Movement*. Chicago: Childrens Press.
Evans, S. (1989). *Born for Liberty: A History of Women in America*. New York: The Free Press.
Friedensohn, D., & Rubin, B. (Eds.). (1984). *Generations of Women: In Search of Female Forebears*. Jersey City: Jersey City State College.
Gurko, M. (1974). *The Ladies of Seneca Falls: The Birth of the Women's Rights Movement*. New York: Macmillan.
Hymowitz, C., & Weissman, M. (1978). *A History of Women in America*. New York: Bantam Books.
Kerber, L., Kessler-Harris, A., & Sklar, K. (Eds.). (1995). *U.S. History as Women's History*. Chapel Hill, NC: University of North Carolina Press.

Myres, S. L. (1982). *Westering Women and the Frontier Experience, 1800–1915.* Albuquerque: University of New Mexico Press.

Warren, R. (1975). *A Pictorial History of Women in America.* New York: Crown Publishers.

White, D. (1985). *Aren't I a Woman? Female Slaves in the Plantation South.* New York: W. W. Norton.

Woloch, N. (1984). *Women and the American Experience.* New York: Knopf.

WEB SITES FOR WOMEN'S HISTORY

Prominent Women Buried at Arlington National Cemetery
http://www.mdw.army.mil/fs-P16.htm

Students Write about Women They Admire
http://collegian.ksu.edu/issues/v099b/sp/n118
/cam-essay-Tegtmeier.html

Prominent Women
http://www.rust.net/~cbledsoe/resource/promwom.htm

Women's History Project—Introduction
http://www.ozemail.com.au/~mghslib/projects/stwh00.html

ORGANIZATIONS THAT OFFER WOMEN'S HISTORY PUBLICATIONS FOR ELEMENTARY STUDENTS

HerStory for Futures Unlimited
2123 Marineview Drive
San Leandro, CA 94577-6324
510/483-4246
http://library.usask.ca/herstory/index.html

National Women's History Project
7738 Bell Road
Windson, CA 95492-8518
707/838-6000
http://www.nwhp.org

Women in the World Curriculum Resource Project
1030 Spruce Street
Berkeley, CA 94707-2628
510/524-0304

References

Armitage, S. (Ed.). (1991). *Women in the west: A guide to manuscript sources.* New York: Garland.

Banks, J. A., & Clegg, A. A. (1985). *Teaching strategies for the social studies.* White Plains, NY: Longman, p. 205.

Barton, K. (1994). *Historical understanding among elementary children.* Unpublished doctoral dissertation, The University of Kentucky.

Baum, W. K. (1975). Oral history. *Looking At* (September): 1–2. Boulder, CO: ERIC Clearinghouse for Social Studies/Social Science Education.

Berliner, D. (1985, May). The field trip: Frill or essential? *Instructor, 94* (9): 14–15.

Braun, J., & Sabin, K. (1986, Nov./Dec.). The class reunion: Celebrating elementary heritage. *The Social Studies,* 77 (3): 257–260.

Brooks, J., & Brooks, M. (1993). *In search of understanding: The case for constructivist classrooms.* Alexandria, VA: Association for Supervision and Curriculum Development.

Brophy, J., & Alleman, J. (1996). *Powerful social studies for elementary students.* Fort Worth, TX: Harcourt Brace, p. 25.

Bucher, Katherine T., & Fravel, Mark. (1991, Jan./Feb.). Local history comes alive with postcards. *Social Studies and the Young Learner,* 3 (3): 18–20.

Campbell, D. E. (1996). *Choosing democracy.* Englewood Cliffs, NJ: Prentice Hall.

Diaz, S., Moll, L., & Mehan, H. (1986). Socio-cultural resources in educating other people's children. In *Beyond language: Social and cultural factors in schooling language-minority children.* Los Angeles: California State Dept. of Education and California State University.

Elkind, D. (1981). *The hurried child: Growing up too fast, too soon.* Reading, MA: Addison Wesley.

Farris, P. J., & Fuhler, C. J. (1994, Feb.). Developing social studies concepts through picture books. *The Reading Teacher, 47* (5): 380–387.

Field, S., Labbo, L., Wilhelm, R., & Garrett, A. (1996, March). To touch, to feel, to see: Artifact inquiry in the social studies classroom. *Social Education, 60* (3): 141–143.

Finkelstein, J., & Nielsen, L. (1985, May/June). Celebrating a centennial—An approach to teaching historical concepts to young children. *The Social Studies, 76* (3): 100–102.

Friedensohn, D., & Rubin, B. R. (1987, Sept./Oct.). Count these women in: Immigration history through photographs and oral interviews. *Social Studies, 78* (5): 217–220.

Ginejko, M. L. (1994). Social studies, bilingualism, respect, and understanding: Making the connections. In P. J. Farris & S. M. Cooper (Eds.), *Elementary social studies: A whole language approach.* Madison, WI: Brown & Benchmark, pp. 267–280.

Giroux, H. (1983). *Theory and resistance in education: A pedagogy for the opposition.* New York: Bergin and Garvey.

Harms, J. L., & Lettow, L. J. (1997, April/May). Life stories in children's books. *Social Education, 61* (4): 205–206.

Hennings, D. G., Hennings, G., & Banich, S. F. (1989). *Today's elementary social studies* (2nd ed.). New York: Harper & Row.

Howe, B. J., & Bannan, H. M. (1995, March/April). Women's history, local history, and public history. *History News, 50* (2): 7–11.

Indiana Department of Education. (no date). *Indiana Grandparent Week activity booklet.* Indianapolis: Office of School Assistance.

Indiana Historical Bureau. (1989, September). *The Indiana Junior Historian: 7,* 13.

Indiana Historical Bureau. (1992, November). *The Indiana Junior Historian,* pp. 2–5.

Indiana Historical Bureau. (1993, March). *The Indiana Junior Historian,* pp. 2–3.

Joint Committee for Geographic Education. (1984). *Guidelines for geographic education.* Washington, DC.

Jones, R. (1990). *Four who dared: Women who made history in Rensselaer County.* Troy, NY: Russell Sage College, ED346004.

Jorgensen, K. L. (1993). *History workshop: Reconstructing the past with elementary students.* Portsmouth, NH: Heinemann.

Kennedy, Toni. (1995). Once upon a time and place: Stories of the family. In M. Burke-Hengen & T. Gillespie (Eds.), *Building community: Social studies in the middle school years.* Portsmouth, NH: Heinemann.

Kirman, J. (1995, Jan.). Teaching about local history using customized photographs. *Social Education, 59* (1): 11–13.

Leigh, A. T., & Reynolds, T. O. (1997). Little windows to the past. *Social Education, 61* (1): 45–47.

Leon, Warren. (1980, Nov./Dec.). Preparing a primary source package on your community's history. *Social Education,* pp. 612–617.

Levstik, L. (1991, Sept.). Literary content. *Education Digest, 57* (1): 41.

Levstik, L., & Barton, K. (1997). *Doing history.* Mahwah, NJ: Lawrence Erlbaum.

Lickona, T. (1993, Sept.). Creating a moral community in the classroom. *Instructor,* pp. 69–72.

Martinello, M., & Cook, G. (1994). *Interdisciplinary inquiry in teaching and learning.* New York: Macmillan.

McAdoo, H. P. (1993). *Family ethnicity.* San Francisco, CA: Sage.

McCarty, D. (1994, Nov./Dec.). Kids writing for kids. *Teaching Pre K–8, 25* (3): 67–69.

Miculka, Linda. (1997, Jan./Feb.). Photographs slide into the classroom. *Social Studies and the Young Learner, 9* (3): 8–10.

Miranda, Wilma. (1983, Spring). Using community resources in the classroom. *Educational Horizons,* pp. 137–140.

Moulton, L., & Tevis, C. (1991, March/April). Making history come alive: Using historical photos in the classroom. *Social Studies and the Young Learner, 3* (4): 13–15.

Murphey, Carol E. (1991, Jan./Feb.). Using the five themes of geography to explore a school site. *Journal of Geography, 90* (1): 17–21.

National Council for the Social Studies. (1994). *Expectations of excellence: Curriculum standards for social studies.* Washington, DC: National Task Force for Standards in Social Studies, Bulletin #89.

Oldfather, P. (1994). *Motivation in the culturally sensitive classroom.* Research Report. College Park, MD: National Reading Research Center.

Olsen, M. W., & Gee, T. (1989/May). Discovering roots: An oral history project achieves many middle school objectives. *Middle School Journal,* pp. 29–31.

Perkins, D. (1994). Learning your way around thinking. *Educational Leadership, 51* (7): 86–87.

Poplin, M. (1991). *The two restructuring movements: Which shall it be? Transformative or reductive.* Unpublished manuscript.

Rickards, M. (1988). *Collecting printed ephemera.* Oxford, England: Oxford University Press.

Riley, G. (1986). *Inventing the American woman: A perspective on women's history, Vol. 1, 1607–1877.* Arlington Heights, IL: Harlan Davidson.

Schroeder, J. (1996). Sailing the seven seas: Using the tools of historians and researchers. In Short et al. (Eds.), *Learning together through inquiry.* York, ME: Stenhouse Pub., pp. 51–72.

Sears, A., & Bidlake, G. (1991, July/Aug.). The senior citizens' tea: A connecting point for oral history in the elementary school. *The Social Studies, 82* (4): 133–135.

Simons, E. R. (1990). *Student worlds, student words: Teaching writing through folklore.* Portsmouth, NH: Boynton/Cook, p. 1.

Social Science Consortium. (1988). *Global issues in the elementary classroom.* Boulder, CO: Author.

Southern, W. T. (1993). Simulations. *Prufrock Journal,* p. 28.

Swanson, C. (1985). Folklore genres. In B. Belanus (Ed.), *Folklore in the classroom.* Indianapolis: Indiana Historical Bureau, pp. 5–10.

Turner, T. N. (1989a, Jan./Feb.). Interactional drama—Where the long ago and far away meet the here and now. *The Social Studies, 80* (1): 30–33.

Turner, T. N. (1989b, May/June). Putting time in a bottle—Or a box! *The Social Studies,* pp. 124–125.

Turner, T. N. (1994). *Elementary social studies.* Boston: Allyn and Bacon.

Turner, T. N., & Hickey, M. G. (1991, March/April). Using radio tapes to teach about the past. *Social Studies and the Young Learner, 3* (4): 6–8.

Welton, D. A., & Mallan, J. T. (1992). *Children and their world* (4th ed). Boston: Houghton Mifflin, p. 326.

Subject and Author — Index

Children's Book Index